MW01613593

Birthed Through the Fire
From Separation and Divorce
to Newness in God

Steven R. Kirk

xulon
PRESS

Copyright © 2011 by Steven R. Kirk

Birthed Through the Fire
by Steven R. Kirk

Printed in the United States of America

ISBN 9781613790915

All rights reserved solely by the author. The author guarantees all contents are original and do not infringe upon the legal rights of any other person or work. No part of this book may be reproduced in any form without the permission of the author. The views expressed in this book are not necessarily those of the publisher.

Unless otherwise noted, all Scripture quotations are taken from the HOLY BIBLE, NEW INTERNATIONAL VERSION®. Copyright © 1973, 1978, 1984, 2011 by Biblica, Inc. Used by permission. All rights reserved worldwide.

www.xulonpress.com

Contents

Acknowledgments

I would like to thank my wonderful daughter, Kayla Kirk, who encouraged me to write this book. She is truly a blessing to me and has helped me in so many ways. I am proud of the relationship we have developed throughout her life and, most importantly, in the past twenty-two months.

I would also like to acknowledge several people who had a profound influence on my life. First are my parents, Bill and Janet Kirk, who are such a blessing to me. In raising me, they formed the man I have become, and through their great role modeling, I learned how to be a productive member in society.

Ed Bettinger went through the fire of divorce and shared many great insights and thoughts with me. He helped me to understand the process of divorce and to embrace the reality that there is life after it takes place.

Also, Pastor Doug Vagle of the Waters Church and therapist Joanne spent hundreds of hours with me to prepare me for the future.

Last of all, I would like to acknowledge Judy Vos, a woman I admired from afar for over three years because of her walk with Jesus Christ and her very strong Christian faith. She became a friend who helped me in the days and months after the destruction of divorce, and now she is my wonderful wife that I pray with, attend church with, and do Bible studies with. We have become a couple walking daily with God as our center.

Introduction

This is a book about my journey that began one fateful day in September as I watched my wife leave after twenty-six years of marriage. During my journey, I found many books written about the pain of divorce. However, these were written totally from a woman's point of view, and I wanted to share the pain of divorce from a man's point of view in order to help other men. In my study, I was shocked to find that many women who were leaving their husbands were saying the same thing my wife Lynn had said to me: "I love you, but not in the way that a wife loves a husband."

But I am getting a little ahead of myself here. The relationship between Lynn and me started many, many years ago in a small town in Wisconsin. She was five years old when I first saw her, and I was eight. Throughout our early years, we had no attraction to each other. In our early teen years, I even teased her with various names, but the one that always stuck in both our heads was "Bucky Beaver." This name hurt her to the core, and sad to say, it framed the way she saw herself for years to come.

Lynn and I had very little contact with each other for the next few years, until I was a senior in high school and she was a sophomore. Looking at her with new eyes, I remarked to a friend, "I guess I shouldn't have called her names—she's beautiful!"

It was another year before we ran into each other again, and taken with her beauty, I wanted to date her. My sister Kim asked Lynn if she would go out with me, and much to my surprise, she said yes. I waited a few weeks, until finally Lynn asked Kim, "Is your brother ever going to ask me out?" Well, I did, and we hit it off right away. We started dating seriously, and after seven months, I asked her to marry me. She said yes, and we began to plan our marriage as a twenty-one-year-old and seventeen-year-old couple.

Two months later, an old girlfriend asked to get together with me for a drink, and I accepted her offer. I called Lynn to inform her of my plans, but she was devastated and hung up on me. Within minutes her father arrived at my parents' house and confronted me, saying, "If you don't love my daughter, then tell her that and break off the engagement." Heeding his advice, I went to Lynn's house and told her I wasn't ready for marriage. That night I broke off the engagement and launched a thirty-six-hour drinking binge.

Over the course of the next two years, Lynn and I would date for a while, but then I would get nervous and break off the relationship. One early morning, Lynn came home and found a girl in my driveway. Lynn and her family lived across the street from my parents where I was living at the time, and confronted me about it. Afraid, confused, and regretful, I talked with her for a while, and then, in an attempt to keep her in my life, I asked her again to marry me. She said yes again that morning, and we once again started dating seriously.

A few months later, I realized my life was going in the wrong direction. A girlfriend, sex, drinking, drugs, and working many hours of overtime to gather material possessions were not giving me the fulfillment I needed in life. At this same time, a colleague asked if I wanted to go to church with him, and I said yes—shocking as it was to me! That day in church, I realized I needed to change my selfish, self-centered, and uncaring ways about people, especially Lynn. I asked Jesus Christ to come into my life and to forgive me of my sins. That morning I asked Him to be my personal Savior and the master of my life.

Many things changed that morning for me, and I found new compassion for Lynn, my parents, and other people. Within two weeks of my decision to follow Christ, Lynn also decided to accept Christ as her personal Savior. We also agreed as a couple not to have sex again until our wedding day, which was set for July 9, 1983—more than seven months away.

Lynn and I began attending church, serving Christ, and learning His ways. And true to our promise, we did live purely for those months preceding our wedding day. At this time, I was twenty-three, and Lynn was nineteen years old. After we married, we went off on a weeklong honeymoon. During that time, one event we tried was golf, which Lynn was not very good at. I pushed her hard to keep up and work harder, but my harshness only caused her to break down and cry.

Over the next twenty-six years, we lived for Christ the best we could, experiencing highs and lows as we moved around the country and as I climbed through the ranks of the organization where I worked for almost twenty-seven years. Another major stress in our relationship was the very difficult time we had with having a child. Lynn had six miscarriages before we finally had our wonderful daughter Kayla, and then she one more afterwards.

Years later I was fired from my job but found another one six hundred miles from our home and friends. Our daughter soon graduated from high school and started college fifteen hundred miles from our home. That was late August 2008.

In early September 2008, I began to realize something was wrong in my marriage, and Lynn and I began having deep conversations about the future. In the third week of September, a colleague's father passed away, and I attended the out-of-town funeral. That week I realized how short life is and recognized my need to draw closer to Lynn. With a new focus on God and each other, I was convinced our future could be better than ever.

I returned home with a newfound love for Lynn, and we enjoyed a wonderful dinner and evening together on September 26. I spoke every word that Lynn had wanted and needed to hear throughout the years but that I had been too afraid to say. We went home and enjoyed each other's company for a while longer until finally going to bed. About 3:00 a.m., I woke up, and Lynn was moving about the bedroom. I asked her what was wrong, and she said the dog needed to go out. I left it at that and went back to sleep, but deep inside I knew better. Something was terribly wrong.

On the morning of September 27, Lynn and I awoke, enjoyed each other's company, and had breakfast before I went off to play golf for the day. We kissed and hugged in the garage as my ride arrived. The last thing we both said that morning was "I love you." Twelve hours later, I arrived home and noticed Lynn's clothes in her car. As I opened the door to our house, Lynn was running down the stairs with a suitcase in her hand and a shocked look on her face. That day was the last day Lynn and I would live in our home as husband and wife.

From the very start, this book was written with a sad heart. I have chronicled some of the hurt within this introduction, and I will expand upon it as each chapter unfolds. I have shared my thoughts as recorded in my journal (italicized entries) and added commentary to paint a picture as best I could of what happened. Make no mistake, I do not believe in divorce and would tell anyone, "What God has put together, let no man rip apart." I was a part of something that God calls special, but it failed because I was a part of it, as was Lynn.

My story does, however, end on a high note, and you will see the wonderful hand of God in my relationship with Him and with my wife Judy. Though my daughter Kayla suggested that I expand my audience by omitting my many mentions of God, I could not do that, because without Him I would not be the man He wants me to be: a loving, caring, forgiving, sharing son, friend, husband, and, most importantly, man of God.

For those of you men who do not know the Lord but are going through the fire of separation and divorce, I urge you to start your journey with Him. Lean on Him and trust in Him, and the anchor of Jesus Christ will hold you steady and make you a better man and person. For all you women going through the fire, the same holds true for you too. When and if your September 27 comes, be prepared for the fire that awaits.

And now, let my story begin, and may it never end!

Chapter 1

The Birthing Process Begins

"In this you greatly rejoice, though now for a little while you may have had to suffer grief in all kinds of trials. These have come so that your faith—of greater worth than gold, which perishes even though refined by fire—may be proved genuine and may result in praise glory and honor when Jesus Christ is revealed."
1 Peter 1:6–7

The Last Two Months Together

Life can take you by surprise. It's easy to fall into a rut and continue until something suddenly wakes you up. That's what happened to me shortly after my twenty-fifth wedding anniversary on September 27, 2008.

I started noticing something seemed off when my wife Lynn scheduled a book-club meeting at our home on the night of our twenty-fifth anniversary. When I mentioned the fact that it was our anniversary, Lynn simply said she had forgotten and then followed it up with "Should I change the date?"

"No, we can celebrate it on the weekend," I answered, disappointed, but willing to accommodate her plans.

My daughter Kayla and I went out to dinner that evening, and the next day Lynn happily commented that the meeting had been the best book-club meeting ever. That day I also received my anniversary card, and it stated, "You have been a good provider. Love,

Lynn." Little did I know that I would hear those words for many months to come and would grow to hate them.

A few months earlier, in May of 2008, I had sensed a great need to walk by faith in God. Little by little, I had allowed the things of the world entrance into my life, and I felt a need for accountability to walk after God. I knew I wasn't right with God, and that made things not right with Lynn. Although I cried out for God's glory to be manifested in my life, I kept repeating the same sins over and over again, day after day.

In late July, I wrote in my journal: *"To have purpose and passion for the things of heaven is my desire. I seek You this day to release my calling and my destiny. Open my mind and heart for the calling, and prepare my way."*

Just a little later, in early August, I recorded: *"I am going through life with little purpose and direction when it comes to Your kingdom. I know You have called me and set me apart to be about Your work. I am confused, unfocused, and at times not sensitive to Your Spirit and direction. Guide me, direct me, let me hear Your voice loud and clear over the noise that is in the world. Bless the work of my hands, and bless Lynn and Kayla with all that is good and right in Your kingdom."*

The very next day, I started to sense changes taking place and recorded my thoughts: *"Times are changing, people are changing, and the future is unclear. Where do I go from here, and what do I do? I need Your guidance and direction. I start the day headed in the right direction, only to find myself in a place I choose not to be. Forgive me of my sins. Cleanse me, wash me, renew me, and let me walk in Your fullness."*

I continued seeking God, and in the middle of August, I wrote: *"Bring the blessings, Lord, in a mighty way. Bless Lynn in her schoolwork, and bless Kayla in her job, at school, and in her upcoming time in Florida. Bless the work of my hands in my job, in playing golf, and, most importantly, in helping others succeed in life. I want to be a role model, caregiver, and life bringer in this land."*

"May the words of my mouth and the meditation of my heart be pleasing in your sight, O L ORD, my Rock and my Redeemer."—Psalm 19:14

The day before Kayla was to leave for school in Florida, the last day that Lynn, Kayla, and I would ever share the same house, I penned: *"I must work hard every day and do the best I can, and then good things will happen for me. Open the doors, swing wide Your gates, and let Your mercy fall on my soul. Pour out Your wisdom, and may it seep into my mind so that I walk in Your ways."*

Lynn, Kayla, and I traveled to Florida, and the trip started out wonderfully. We went to Busch Gardens and enjoyed a great day at the park, followed by a fantastic dinner. The next day we went to Orlando and spent the day at SeaWorld, another wonderful family day. But then, like an omen, a hurricane moved through the area. The storm clouds rolled in, not only in the natural realm but also in the spiritual and relational realms, and it rained for the remainder of our visit.

We had checked into a condo that was a forty-five-minute drive from the University of Central Florida, where Kayla would be attending school. Kayla had decided to rush at several different sororities, so that meant traveling back and forth several times throughout the day and evening. But then something strange happened. The rains came, and I felt as though I was losing my mind. I couldn't bear to be in the car, so Lynn readily agreed to drive Kayla back and forth, never complaining about the task. Wanting to be alone, I neglected my daily devotions and started sinning. My selfish behaviors emerged from hiding, as did the sins of my flesh. I just wanted to be alone and enjoy drinking and spending time on the Internet. I had a vague sense that my relationship with my wife was falling apart and that something or someone was in the midst of the crumbling.

To this point, I had checked Lynn's cell phone only once before in our marriage. The first time had been a month earlier when my suspicions were aroused because the cell-phone bill had come to the house and been paid. That was the only bill Lynn had paid, and all the paperwork associated with it had disappeared. Also, every time I drove past our carrier's place of business, I had a strong sense that something was wrong, that the phone was an issue and partly responsible for my unsettled feeling.

So, alone in the room, I checked Lynn's phone for the second time in our marriage but found nothing out of the ordinary. I concluded that everything must be my issue. For some reason, I just couldn't get on track. Maybe the pressure of seeing Kayla leave was overwhelming to both Lynn and me and was the source of whatever was going on in our lives.

The trip ended with Lynn and me crying with Kayla in her dorm room and then walking around Orlando and going to a movie before traveling home to Minnesota. When we arrived home, I knew changes had to take place in my life and in my relationship with Lynn. The first journal event I wrote in late August stated: *"Kayla is now off to school, making new friends, starting the second chapter of her life. God, protect her from all harm. Give her a double portion of Your Spirit, and guide her in right thinking and action. Do the same with Lynn and me. You are the protector and guide of our lives. You are my friend, counselor, and guide. Protect me, and guide me into Your righteousness."*

"Steve, I Just Snapped and Don't Feel Anything"

In early September, Lynn and I went for a long walk. I still felt something was wrong between us, although we were going to church together, sleeping together, eating together, and taking walks together. Something was wrong, and I sensed it.

While on the walk, I asked her point-blank, "Lynn, what is wrong?"

She turned to me and answered, "Steve, I snapped. I don't feel anything anymore."

Shocked by her words, I knew we had to change going forward. For Lynn to say that meant something deep within her was not right, and I bore part of the responsibility for the word *snapped*. From that moment on, I started spending more time with Lynn, encouraging her in her schoolwork, helping around the house more, sharing at the dinner table, and doing whatever else I could.

Throughout that summer, as the day grew closer for Kayla's departure for college, I had also realized that I was experiencing a deep pain of separation, loneliness, and confusion. And that hurt me, Lynn, and even Kayla. I felt like my world was in a tailspin and feared I was not fulfilling my responsibilities.

On September 3, I wrote the following: *"It's a new day. Should I be content to be average, a C player in life? Do C players really succeed more than people who put it all out there? Are they happier in life? Can I scale back and become content as an average person getting average results? I look for the answers from You, Lord God."*

By September 15, more concerns over Lynn and her behavior arose when I prayed, and I recorded my musings: *"Change is in the air, and it is not good, I can tell. Something is not right in Lynn's and my relationship. A stranger has entered, filling our heads with confusion and doubt. Come forth, Lord God, and bring clarity to these times. Pull back the spirit of confusion, doubt, pain, and unforgiveness. Let this be a time of restoration, peace, love, total forgiveness, and unity."*

The very next day I wrote some more: *"Lord, I still feel the pulling away and lack of relationship. Is there someone else? Is there a change between Lynn and other people? Does she have a relationship with another man? Reveal the darkness and the hidden life, and make it clear and in plain sight. If there is nothing, break the darkness and mistrust I feel at this time. What happened to the total peace and comfort I had at one time in my life? Bring that feeling back now and in the future. Flow through me, Holy Spirit, and guide my steps and my life."*

My nagging doubts and fears did not relent, and on September 24, as I was preparing to attend a colleague's father's funeral without Lynn, I wrote the following in my journal: *"Lynn, if I die on this trip today or tomorrow, I want you and Kayla to know I love you and care for both of you—my wife, partner, and best friend for over twenty-five years, and my wonderful daughter that I am so proud of! Change the world for the better, both of you, and do not forget to serve God each day of your life. Don't change your plans to finish college and to pursue your desire for a job. Find good men who will treat you better than I did, if you can. Have fun, live life to the fullest, and serve God. I will see you on the other side with a smile, a hug, and kisses. I love you and always have."*

Arriving home on September 26, I wrote: *"I made it back from the Upper Peninsula! Happy days, I think, are ahead—or maybe not. It is up to Your hand, God, and my listening and walking after Your Word. May I clean up my life, read Your Word, and do well in the days ahead."*

Viewing Life Through the Eyes of Death

I think funerals help change us because we take inventory of who we are, what we have become, and, most importantly, how we treat other people. Returning home from the funeral, I realized how much I loved Lynn but how little I had shared that sentiment or expressed it in my actions. I journaled my feelings, but I seldom shared them aloud with Lynn, though I knew she had always wanted that in our marriage. During the trip, I made a commitment that once I returned home, things would be different.

I called Lynn on September 25 and asked if she wanted to go out to a very nice restaurant on the twenty-sixth. She said yes and made reservations for 6:30 p.m. That day I took a nap as I waited for Lynn to get home. When she got in, I asked her out of the blue to run the Verizon bill detail report so I could see the activity. A while later she came upstairs with a high-level report that I thanked her for. As we looked at each other, we both knew something was wrong, but we said nothing and made ready for the evening.

That evening Lynn looked wonderful, and we went to dinner and enjoyed the food and conversation. I told her things I thought she had always wanted to hear: that I loved her, couldn't live without her, and she meant the world to me. We had a wonderful time at the restaurant. After we got home, we listened to music and enjoyed some wine and conversation until Lynn said she was ready to go to bed. We enjoyed our entire evening together.

At 3:00 a.m., I heard Lynn moving around the house, but before I could get out of bed to check on her, she came back into the room. I asked what was going on, and she said, "The dog needed to go out." I felt there was more to it than that, but since it was 3:00 a.m., I said nothing and went back to sleep.

My Darkest Days: September 27 Through October 5

The morning of the twenty-seventh, Lynn and I ate breakfast together before I went golfing for the day. A friend of mind was picking me up, and Lynn came into the garage to say good-bye as he arrived. We kissed, and I said "I love you." Lynn responded, "I love you too. See you tonight." Later in the day, while I was on my way home, Lynn called and asked if I would be home for dinner. I reminded her that we were eating out and said I would be home by 7:00 p.m. Lynn always worried about me if I was late, so I padded the time by thirty minutes.

I arrived home at 6:30 p.m., and my friend left right away. I opened the garage door and passed Lynn's car, noticing a large pile of her clothes on the backseat. I opened the door to the house, and there was Lynn, running down the stairs with a suitcase in her hands. Shocked, I asked what was wrong, and she said, "I have to leave, I have to leave, I have to leave." I asked her why, but all she said was "I just need to leave for a few days."

Amazed and confused, I watched my wife get into her car and pull out of the garage. I cried out desperately, "Please don't leave. Talk to me!"

Lynn stopped, got out of the car, and repeated, "I just have to leave for a few days." I again asked why, and again she had no answer.

I then asked if she was having an affair and if that was why she was leaving, but she answered, "No, I just have to leave."

This was the beginning of the most painful experience of my life. Confused and tormented, I struggled to understand how a man and woman could live together for more than twenty-five years, enjoy deep conversation and physical intimacy in the preceding twenty-four hours, and then have the wife suddenly announce, "I just have to leave." Little did I know what was in store for me in the days, weeks, and months ahead.

After Lynn left, I was in a daze. I cried harder than I have ever cried in my life. I walked aimlessly around my development for hours. I then started drinking heavily and entertaining thoughts that no man should have, no matter how low he feels. I realized I needed to stop drinking, so I poured all the booze down the sink. But I didn't feel any better and was too proud to reach out to anyone, so I struggled alone through the evening, thinking about the future and what it might entail. Around midnight I wrote, texted, and tried to call Lynn about going to church with me the next day. I did get a response, but she declined my offer, saying she didn't want to put on a happy face.

I spent most of the evening thinking about the past: what we might have done differently, what we actually had done, and how we had gotten to this point. In all my thoughts, I was filled with regret for some of my behaviors and actions; however, I couldn't get my mind wrapped around the fact that Lynn was gone. It didn't feel right.

I wondered what Lynn was going through that same night. How long had she thought about leaving? How and why did our marriage get to this point? How had two Christians, people who claimed to be godly, let life take them to this crossroads? All these questions would be answered over the next several months, piece by brutal piece, as the closed doors opened little by little.

I had never before realized the deep, dark despair that could grab a soul and shake it to its core, even with God in the person's life. Maybe I needed that jolt, but did it require the breakup of my marriage to start me on a journey to God's perfect will? Sadly, I guess it did. Is that what it will take for you? I certainly hope not.

I went to church the next day, totally destroyed and not knowing what the future held. But God knows all things, and I knew I needed Him as much as I had ever needed Him. As I have often said, "I don't know how any person can go through something like this without God, especially if they never saw it coming and wanted no part of it."

The Trip to Wisconsin Starts the Healing Process

Lynn and I talked on September 28, and she said she needed to stay away for a few more days. I told her that my brother in Wisconsin was sick and going into the hospital, so he would not be going in to work for the next week. I suggested that I spend that week with him, and she could come back home while I was gone. She agreed to the plan, saying, "Okay, that makes sense," but she stayed at a hotel on the twenty-eighth.

The next day at work, I informed my employer of my brother's illness and asked for the week off, which was granted. I left for Wisconsin, and Lynn moved back home on the twenty-ninth. At my brother's house, I kept the issue of my marriage to myself. He and his wife enjoyed having me there, and although it was hard not to tell them what was going on, my pride prevented it.

During my stay in Wisconsin, I wrote the following words to God in my journal: *"As you know, it's been a very hard three days. Though I felt a pulling away by Lynn, I didn't realize how bad it had become for her and our relationship. My sins, my failure to follow You, and my flesh have harmed her in many ways. But I do not think it's too late for our marriage, because You are the great healer.*

"Lynn and I have many great memories together, and we share a great daughter in Kayla. But we have also allowed the evil one and the world entrance into our lives. Help us push them out, and give us hope, love, and forgiveness this day and going forward as we turn back to You. Open Your Word, and let us seek You together. Help us live according to Your ways, and talk to us this day and every day going forward."

In response, I sensed the Lord saying, "There is a battle going on, and it always has been. Arm yourself and fight! Fight for your life, Lynn's, and Kayla's as well. Put on the full armor, and pick up the sword of the Lord. Join the fight, and do not give up. The battle is fierce; do not give up the fight."

> "Because of the LORD's great love we are not consumed, for his compassions never fail. They are new every morning; great is your faithfulness. I say to myself, 'The LORD is my portion; therefore I will wait for him.' The LORD is good to those whose hope is in him, to the one who seeks him; it is good to wait quietly for the salvation of the LORD."
> —Lamentations 3:22–26

The journal entry for October 2 expressed my ongoing struggle: *"Lord, I go through cycles of doing my own thing and then walking after Your ways. Kayla calls it the 'God things' or 'God times.' I want and need every day to be a God day so I can be the person You called me to be many years ago. I know I am a much better person when I am serving You and Your ways. Pour forth Your Spirit in my life, and let me hear Your voice clearly now and every day. Grant me wisdom, knowledge, and understanding in my life, including in my marriage, relationships, and job.*

"Lord, there seems to be darkness over Lynn and me right now. Please send Your angels to help in the fight for our marriage and relationship. May Your Holy Spirit bind us together, and may nothing ever pull us apart.

"Lord, the days are flying by, and a reentry needs to take place. How can that happen in such a way as to make us both feel good about the future? We need Your guidance and voice in this time coming up. Drive out all fear, nervousness, and apprehension. Let this be an exciting union, and may we feel like a young couple again, with newness of life, love in our hearts, and butterflies in our stomachs."

"Two are better than one, because they have a good return for their work: If one falls down, his friend can help him up. But pity the man who falls and has no one to help him up! Also, if two lie down together they will keep warm. But how can one keep warm alone? Though one may be overpowered, two can defend themselves. A cord of three strands is not quickly broken." — Ecclesiastes 4:9–12

Daily Conversations for Purification and Cleansing

Lynn and I talked each day that week and cried together. Forgiveness and healing took place, and I talked about my reentry home, suggesting either Saturday or Sunday as the best option. To my great dismay, Lynn shared she was moving out of the house and into an apartment for three months. This shook me to the core, and we shared more pains, hurts, and fears. I told her she could come home anytime she felt ready. I didn't realize how far things had gone in her mind, heart, and life.

The next day I wrote: *"Lynn moves out tomorrow. This is a painful time for Lynn, Kayla, and me, Lord. Bring us out of this time whole and healed, once Your restoration process is complete.*

"In my flesh, I want to talk to Lynn; I want to touch her and never let her go. But other times I want to say or do hurtful things. How we got here does matter and will need to be worked through.

"We need You, Father, and we need Jesus and the Holy Spirit to help both of us to work on our marriage 24/7. I would also like to request a few warring angels to help in our time of need."

I sensed the Lord responding to my prayer with these words: "Lynn does love you and wants to be with you, but she fears losing herself and not being able to stand on her own. She wants to try to make it on her own for these three months so that she will know she can do it if forced to in the future.

"She will no longer tolerate the attention you give to other people and things, like you have done in the past. She will not tolerate being talked down to or demeaned in front of Kayla or other people. She will not tolerate inappropriate actions. She will give you the love, respect, and care that she has always given you in the past if you will give the same and even more to her. She is a tender person who has been harmed by many people, not just her parents and you. She needs to work through that as well."

On October 4, I wrote down the following about myself:

Who I Am and What I Do Today

Driven, compassionate, perfectionistic, kind, unbending, considerate, forceful, hard, cold, impatient, understanding, bold, fearful, competitive, close-minded, opinionated, loving, goal-oriented, generous

What I Need

Loyalty, trust, love, respect, patience, kindness, compassion, unity, relationship, my time filled, guidance, counsel, honesty

What I Need to Become in the Future

Compassionate; loving; unified; kind; flexible; open-minded; considerate of others' thoughts, opinions, and beliefs; patient; honest; my time filled with the right things that build me up, not tear me down; able to relax

"Lord, help me break through all barriers in my life and become the man of God You want me to be, the person I need to be, the husband and father Lynn and Kayla desire, and a friend to those being drawn to the person I am becoming. Direct my path, and lead me into Your righteousness as I read Your Word and go about building the future. Bring people into my life in the coming days to help me, to guide me, and to be friends with me. I need a miracle this day!"

Our First Time Together Since Lynn's Moving Out

As Lynn and I talked throughout the week, Lynn took care of things in the house, moved out many of her belongings, and prepared the house for the fall months. We also agreed to meet together on October 5 for dinner. I looked forward to that and bought her a nice necklace to show my love and to ask for forgiveness. We met for dinner and talked for two hours about life, Kayla, and the future. We left the restaurant together, and in the parking lot I asked for a kiss and a hug. Lynn consented, but that was the last time we ever kissed. I found out later it made her uncomfortable.

Realizing Change Must Take Place in My Life

"Lord, as You know, I have read through my past journals and listened to Lynn and Kayla. I can see that I have been asking for change, yet change hasn't come. Why? I haven't changed because I haven't pushed myself to move forward or asked for help. This is a wake-up call for me to move forward, painful as it may be. This coming week I need to seek counseling, to call Pastor Doug, and to join a short-term home group. Furthermore, I must continue to purge my life of the things of this world and replace them with the Word, prayer, and songs.

"Lord, I cannot stay in this place any longer. I need a miracle with Lynn, a change of heart, a spirit of love and forgiveness to prevail. We need to pray and read Your Word as we did before. I do not want this to be about me filling my time; I want true change.

"Cleanse Lynn and me of the world, sin, sickness, unforgiveness, pain, and doubt. Bring back our love for each other. Let Lynn feel Your love and guidance, let her feel my love and happiness, and let her feel completeness as a person and in Your kingdom.

"Lord, You say, 'Return to Me and I will return to you.' One day at a time, Lord, I need to serve You and remember all the great things You have done for Lynn and me. This day, bring us out of the desert place, Lord Jesus!"

Words Spoken Over Me at Church on October 5

"You are a man of integrity. Oh, how God loves you! And I saw a vision of you playing chess. I don't even know if you play chess; it doesn't really matter. But God has given you an ability to move with your mind; you carry intelligence, and you carry levels of understanding that not everyone around you carries.

"You have come out of a journey where you weren't given your identity as a young man, where you did not understand the level of love that God carries, because it wasn't served to you. It wasn't served into your journey at the level that God wanted to serve it to you. And you have had things spoken into your life and even favor removed by the hand of man.

"God is encouraging you that you are His son, that He delights in you, and that you carry the favor of God. You are a man of God, and God is proud of you. He is not looking at what you are looking at, and He does not want you to carry that weight of responsibility. I speak it off of you, in Jesus' name.

"He also wants you to know that you are a man of God, the son of the King. You carry finances from heaven, and your journey down here is insignificant compared to who you are in heaven. God is going to restore to you a new identity that He created and designed for you to carry.

"Father, I go back to this man of God, and with him I ask You to forgive him for judging those who brought betrayal and those who brought pain. Father, bring those names to his mind, and I ask You to forgive him for judging. Instead, help him shift these people into the hands of Jesus, for He is a righteous judge and will take care of that. I pull out bitter-root judgments, even on a situation that has happened. I pull out all bitter-root judgments from his life, and I ask You to open the heavens and loose power, love, and a sound mind.

"Sir, you are called to reign with the King, and you are called to be a man of God. I am going to speak a very difficult word over you. There have been three times that I have said in these meetings that you and two others are apostolic. Did you know that apostolic becomes a target? Did you know that apostolic becomes a forerunner? Did you know that apostolic has to die first? Did you know that apostolic carries new levels of pain because you have to go to the cross first?

"Did you know that apostolic is a platform that you have to walk on and give over to others? Did you know that apostolic is a place with God that requires you to pay a price to oversee others? Did you know that apostolic is a man of God who will oversee a younger generation? Did you know that apostolic is a man of God who moves in signs, wonders, and miracles? Did you know that apostolic is going to see the favor of God so the favor of God can be released through him to others?

"Did you know that you are going to partake in kingdom finances? Did you know that you are going to carry something so big that you have become an actual target for the enemy because you are going to bring damage to his kingdom? Did you know that apostolic means you are God's? Did you know that apostolic requires you to take the journey you have taken, but God is going to bring back to you everything the enemy has stolen, and the enemy is a big liar!

"I bind the torment that has come against you, and I bind the spirit of infirmity. There has been physical stuff that has been going on, but God wants you to understand that it has not been all physical; it has also been spiritual. And so I speak every assignment of the enemy off of you. I bind the spirit of infirmity that has come against your physical body. And I command it to go now, in Jesus' name, and I break free the healing for your body.

"You are going to experience healing this morning, and there is going to be freedom in your whole body. There is going to be an ability to sleep again. There is going to be an ability to digest food properly. There is going to be a rest, and you are not going to carry that pain any longer. I speak that the pain has to go now, in Jesus' name.

"And God speaks long life to you. You are a man of God who is going to have huge doors open to you. God is going to open doors to you, and you are going to step into a place where you will have actual joy in your life again. God doesn't want you to look so far ahead. He wants you to worship, and He wants you to stay in worship and just rest. And He wants you to rest because He is going to take care of everything that pertains to you and your finances."

"You can laugh again, you can laugh again! The devil is a big, fat liar, and everything he has been telling you is a big, fat lie. You need to get something to laugh at. I don't care what it is, but you have to laugh. You are going to laugh at the devil because he has no authority here. You are a man of God, and the devil can't touch you.

"Everything may look horrible, but that is just a big, fat lie from the devil. God is orchestrating your life. He has been networking, and even through the negative stuff, you have an identity that comes from the Father. God is going to reopen doors to you that man has closed, and He is going to reposition you. He is going to give to you the desires of your heart. I have to encourage you to die well."

Chapter 2

Communicating Through the Fire of Separation

"Everyone will be salted with fire. Salt is good, but if it loses its saltiness, how can you make it salty again? Have salt in yourselves, and be at peace with each other."
Mark 9:49–50

"*I praise You, Lord, for my wife, who she is and her decisions. She has made a stand for change, and I will make sure I change for the better too. This tremendous shock to my system, my marriage, and my friendships is a wake-up call to change my lifestyle, not short-term like so many times before, but a long-term commitment once and for all. Other men have done it by Your grace and mercy, so may I, too, find You, worship You, and be led by You so I can see the great things that Lynn, Kayla, my friends, and the people of this world are doing.*

"I love Lynn, and the changes she is making are wonderful; however, that is not surprising because she has always been a great lady. Throughout our marriage, she has always been beautiful, kind, caring, compassionate, and willing to help others. But I have not noticed some, maybe even most, of her growth because I have been so focused on my own wants and desires. That needs to change, and I have to change that part of me that competes against everyone, including Lynn. We are not competitors; we are to run the race together and win in life together, loving each other and the world

around us. How foolish I've been to need this wake-up call to realize my error!

"With a second chance, Your help, and Lynn's understanding, I can change and help make the rest of our lives and our marriage what we both want it to be: a relationship of respect, love, understanding, patience, support, and positive words that uplift. I love Lynn and thank her for this decision so that we can have a chance to live life to the fullest, not just go through it numb, lacking feelings and love."

"But as for me, I watch in hope for the Lord, I wait for God
my Savior; my God will hear me." — Micah 7:7

Earlier in 2008, Lynn and I had gone to the Dominican Republic and made a video of our trip, which I viewed again on October 10. After watching it, I realized how beautiful Lynn was and that I had become too comfortable with her. Over the years, I had stopped sharing with her, like I should have. I realized that we men must continue to share with our mates and not take for granted their beauty, help, wisdom, education, and knowledge.

Lynn had always been a great helper and friend to me and many others. I asked God to bless her and bless her schoolwork. She was a great lady, a wonderful wife, a devoted mother, and a faithful friend. I asked for new ways to show my love to her in the future.

"So I say, live by the Spirit, and you will not gratify the desires of the sinful nature. For the sinful nature desires what is contrary to the Spirit, and the Spirit what is contrary to the sinful nature. They are in conflict with each other, so that you do not do what you want." — Galatians 5:16–17

"When times are good be happy; but when times are bad consider: God has made the one as well as the other."
— Ecclesiastes 7:14

"Fear God and keep his commandments, for this is the whole duty of man. For God will bring every deed into judgment, including every hidden thing, whether it is good or evil." — Ecclesiastes 12:13

"Yet the LORD longs to be gracious to you; he rises to show you compassion. For the LORD is a God of justice. Blessed are all who wait for him." — Isaiah 30:18

From October 5 through 12, Lynn and I talked every day for hours and asked each other for forgiveness from past hurts, pains, and feelings. We then decided to meet for lunch, and we spent our time talking about many things, including Kayla. At the end of the lunch, we walked out to the parking lot and said good-bye. Lynn told me I could hug but not kiss her. It had been wonderful to see her, yet painful at the same time. The distance between us seemed to be growing, even though we were talking more openly than we had for years.

Shortly after the lunch, I read these words, and they spoke to my heart: "Sin, which can be defined as anything contrary to the character of God, always leads to the pain and degradation of injustice towards others." During this time of separation, I also read, "Righteousness, which may be identified as conformity to God's character, is exhibited in attitudes and actions of fairness, integrity, truthfulness, and honesty towards others." Stirred and challenged, I began declaring the words of Scripture: "But let justice roll on like a river, righteousness like a never failing stream!" (Amos 5:24).

Waiting on God to Move in My Marriage as He Works on Me

"I am waiting on You and Your justice, Lord. I cannot fix my marriage alone; I need You, and I need Lynn's commitment to make that happen. I need to let go and fix things within me. I pray that You can help me and help Lynn as well. I know You called us and want us to do Your work together. Forgive me for getting in the way and sinning. Forgive Lynn as well, and may she, too, be called back to You and Your work.

"As I meet with Pastor Doug, help me to put away sin once and for all. You know the sins I keep coming back to over and over again, like a dog returning to its own vomit! If there are things from my childhood that need healing, I ask You to heal them so I can make it through and have success."

"He has shown you, O man, what is good. And what does the LORD require of you? To act justly and to love mercy and to walk humbly with your God." — Micah 6:8

By this time, I had decided to talk to Pastor Doug, and Lynn had decided to see a counselor at her school. We were on the path to recovery, a path we should have walked long before the total breakdown of our relationship. But sadly, that is what it took. We both needed to come alive and live for something more than a paycheck and nice things.

"Father, may I have enough happiness to keep me sweet, enough trials to keep me strong, enough sorrow to keep me human, enough hope to keep me happy, enough failure to keep me humble, enough success to keep me eager, enough friends to give me comfort, enough faith and courage to banish depression, and enough determination to serve God better today than I did yesterday." As I read those words from an unknown author, I realized my life had been about more, more, more of everything, but all any of us really needs is just enough of everything. The only thing we need without limit is more of God. If we put God first in our lives, we will have enough of everything else.

On October 17, I wrote: *"The movers came to get several pieces of furniture Lynn wanted, and I was more than happy to provide them for her. It was a sad day to truly realize that Lynn and I are separated and more trials and tribulations await. I thought about the day when she said she snapped. Have I also caused that with other people in my life? Do I always push for more and try to control things when the world becomes stressful? I do not mean to break people down, but I guess I do.*

"Pastor Doug helped me realize I have three major issues to work on: selfish behaviors, control, and perfectionism. So I am

starting to work on these three issues with everything I have, but I also need the Lord to help me through the days ahead."

> "I, the LORD, have called you in righteousness; I will take
> hold of your hand." –Isaiah 42:6

I continued my writing: *We cannot obtain righteousness just by working for it. It is very difficult for us to change any part of our character by merely resolving to do so. What we need is a new heart and a new spirit. Righteousness comes from being joined with Christ. Christ calls us, and the righteousness comes because of our relationship with Him. We must be touched by Jesus!*

"God wants us to be happy. God can make us happy. I want to be humble and open to growth. I want to have true joy and an open heart. I must learn to be meek, gentle, and patient. I desire holiness and mercy in my life. I want to be pure of heart, and I want to be a peacemaker." This became my cry to God.

In Ephesians 6:10–12, the Word states: "Finally, be strong in the Lord and in His mighty power. Put on the full armor of God so that you can take your stand against the devil's schemes. For our struggle is not against flesh and blood; but against the rulers, against the authorities, against the powers of this dark world and against the spiritual forces of evil in the heavenly realms."

Meditating on this passage from Ephesians, I wrote: *"Both Lynn and I must understand where the battle is coming from and then attack the enemy. I will focus my energy and prayers against the kingdom of darkness."*

> "Wake up, O sleeper, rise from the dead, and Christ will
> shine on you." — Ephesians 5:14

Learning Outcomes at This Point of the Journey

"I must be a positive Christian; do things with gentleness and reverence; keep a clear conscience; help others with deeds rather than words; live a life of love, concern, and sensitivity to others; and have purity in my life each day."

"Since, then, you have been raised with Christ, set your
hearts on things above, where Christ is seated at the right
hand of God. Set your minds on things above, not on
earthly things." — Colossians 3:1–2

"Put to death, therefore, whatever belongs to your earthly
nature: sexual immorality, impurity, lust, evil desires and
greed, which is idolatry." — Colossians 3:5

On October 21, I wrote: *"Lord, I need Your help in reprogram-
ming my human nature to Your nature. My nature is always wanting
and doing more and pushing for further achievements. I need to
be more relationship-building, positive, and encouraging. You order
my steps, and I know I must let go and let You have Lynn, Kayla, my
job, and my will. Take these things, change them for the better, and
let me see Your mighty hand at work in love.*
*"As 1 Corinthians 13 says, my love for Lynn must be patient and
kind. It must not envy, boast, or be proud. It must not be rude, self-
seeking, or easily angered. My love for Lynn must keep no record
of wrongs. Real love does not delight in evil but rejoices with the
truth. It always protects, always trusts, always hopes, and always
perseveres. It never fails. And now these three remain: faith, hope,
and love. But the greatest of these is love."*

Termination of all Conversation

Another major blow now occurred in our relationship. We had
been talking or at least e-mailing each other daily since the separation. But on October 22, I came home from work to find an e-mail
from Lynn that assured me she was fine, but her counselor had
suggested she cut off all contact with me for three weeks. She had
decided to do it for only five or six days.

The message ripped me to the core, and I lost all faith and hope
for reconciliation. I felt like my flesh had been ripped off my body.
The woman I had loved, provided for, had a child with, and served
the Lord with didn't want to talk to me for several days. First it had
been just a day or two apart; then she rented an apartment; then she

allowed no more kissing; and now there would be no more conversations to rebuild what had been broken.

In desperation I left e-mails and voice mails with Lynn, and then I called her mother to make sure Lynn was truly all right. Her mother assured me Lynn was fine; I just needed to give her more time, she explained. That night, for the first time, I felt in my heart that our relationship was headed for divorce. How could this happen, and why?

Again I wondered if there was another man, so I asked Lynn's mother if Lynn was having an affair. She said she didn't know but didn't think so. Every time I thought about Lynn's cell phone, I felt pain. That night I tried to access the statement, but Lynn had changed the account to her name, and I no longer had access to it.

I found myself again questioning what was going on, and I was also tempted to resort to sinful ways to control the pain, hurt, and anguish in my soul. However, I did take a stand this time and firmly proclaimed: "I will not turn my back on You, God, or on Your ways. Even if the wife of my youth, my daughter, my family, and my friends turn on me, I will follow You until my dying day!"

I will admit, I was discouraged. It seemed that every time I thought Lynn and I were making headway, something happened to push us in the opposite direction. I knew I needed composure, presence of mind, cool-headedness, patience, self-possession, and restraint; and I also knew that was no easy task, for few people automatically display these qualities.

"For God did not give us a spirit of timidity, but a spirit of power, of love and of self- discipline." —2 Timothy 1:7

"But the fruit of the Spirit is love, joy, peace, patience, kindness, goodness, faithfulness, gentleness, and self-control. Against such things there is no law." —Galatians 5:22–23

"Finally, brothers, whatever is true, whatever is noble, whatever is right, whatever is pure, whatever is lovely, and whatever is admirable—if anything is excellent or praiseworthy—think about such things." —Philippians 4:8

Through this difficult time, I was discovering that God is God and I am not. I just had to let it be and let God work.

Words of Wisdom from Pastor Doug

I had a good conversation with Pastor Doug on the twenty-fourth of October. He helped me see that I needed to calm down and work on my issues while Lynn worked on hers. The area of control was the one area I most needed to resolve.

Later I recorded my thoughts: *"I try to move things my way too much, like I did Tuesday evening. I must relax and let God take over, and I must allow Lynn to exercise her free will and grow. Lynn wants freedom, peace, relaxation, and security. I want a wonderful partner who can stand on her own. The wants and needs align, but I must get out of my own way in our marriage, at work, and with friends."*

"Let us not become weary in doing good, for at the proper
time we will reap a harvest if we do not give up."
—Galatians 6:9

"I was foolish in running from God in the past. I will now run to God in all my ways. I need His leading!

"As Job followed You regardless, I will follow You and praise Your name. You are my God, and that will remain my steadfast focus going forward. Losing You, Your protection, or Your love and guidance is not worth anything in this world.

"Prepare both Lynn and me for the conversations ahead. They will be painful, but keep them from being hurtful. Let us build each other up and not tear each other down. Make us both whole, and bring us together in Your power and might. We will change the world together for the greater good as You bless us with Your Spirit. Bless this day, and may it be a positive day for our family."

"When calamity comes, the wicked are bought down, but
even in death the righteous have a refuge."—Proverbs 14:32

"The eyes of the LORD are everywhere, keeping watch on the
wicked and the good."—Proverbs 15:3

"The tongue that brings healing is a tree of life."
—Proverbs 15:4

"And we know that in all things God works for the good of
those who love him, who have been called according to his
purpose."—Romans 8:28

We Are Created to Become Like Christ

Slowly, little by little, I was learning the true goal of faith in
Christ. Its purpose was not so much what was in it for me—though
God does indeed bless His children—but how I could become more
like the Savior and represent Him authentically to a world that does
not know Him. In the process, I learned several key principles:

1. **God uses trouble to teach us to trust Him.** It takes resis-
    tance in our lives in order for us to grow. God exerts pres-
    sure on us to reveal what is on the inside waiting to come
    out. God already knows what is there, but we may not see it
    until pressure squeezes it out. We have to learn to trust God
    completely, even when everything around us is falling apart.
    As a matter of fact, that is exactly when we need to trust Him
    all the more.
2. **God uses temptations to teach us to obey.** The time of
    temptation is not the time to let our guard down, but the
    precise time to do the right thing. Like Joseph in the Old
    Testament, run when temptation comes your way. Get an
    accountability partner to help keep you on the right track.
3. **God uses trespasses to teach us to forgive.** Part of being
    like Christ is learning to relinquish our right to get even.
    Christ never retaliated, and neither should we.
4. **God orders our steps and open doors for us.** "Now if we
    are children, then we are heirs—heirs of God and co-heirs
    with Christ, if indeed we share in his suffering in order that

we may also share in his glory" (Romans 8:17). As His heirs, we can be sure that He is carefully watching over every detail of our lives.

5. **We go to Christ to become better, not bitter.** This principle can be summed up in the words of an unknown Confederate soldier: "I asked for health, that I might do greater things; I was given infirmity, that I might do better things. I asked for riches, that I might be happy; I was given poverty, that I might be wise. I asked for power, that I might have the praise of men; I was given weakness, that I might feel the need for God. I asked for all things, that I might enjoy life; I was given life, that I might enjoy all things. I got nothing I asked for, but everything I hoped for; almost despite myself, my unspoken prayers were answered. I am among all men most richly blessed."

Tough times will come to all of us, no matter how tight our controls, how much we plan, or how well things are going. A time will come when we can do nothing to change a painful situation. At that time, God can be trusted to meet our needs.

"Praise be to God! Praise be to God our Father! He answers prayers when we do not think there is hope. Lynn wrote me yesterday, just as I had resigned myself to three to four weeks without hearing from my best friend. Though Lynn originally said I would not hear from her for five or six days, Pastor Doug said I should prepare myself for three to four weeks, based upon my initial reaction to her mail message. Praise You, God, and I thank You for Your help in this time of need.

"Both Lynn and I have a long way to go to get whole, but we will move towards complete healing with Your help, God. I see growth in both of us and long for the day when we are under the same roof again. I will continue to support Lynn in her time of growth. When we talk or write in the future, give me wisdom, knowledge, and understanding to say and do the right things. I love Lynn and care for her so much, and I thank You for putting that love within me.

"I must remember that when my boat is tossing, I need to rock with it instead of against it. I must accept that there are areas I cannot control and understand that letting go can lead to submitting my will to God's. Job stubbornly clung to his faith even when those closest to him suggested he give it up.

"Silence and lack of communication with God or others is not always bad. It can be used for a purpose like self-examination. It can be used to think about our fears and inadequacies or to root out the flesh (control, selfishness, perfectionism). It can be a time to surrender to God's amazing love and will, a time to submit our will to His."

When I met with Pastor Doug, we talked about the need of both Lynn and me for a time of healing. During this time apart, I needed to work on control, selfishness, and perfectionism issues. I had to learn how to listen and follow through on issues that needed to be resolved, and I needed to focus on Lynn's growth rather than my own achievements. Pastor Doug cautioned that spiritual surgery would be necessary during this time, so I should be prepared for it and open to it as well. Pastor Doug's final words of wisdom were "The faster you go, the slower you will get through this time in your life."

Leaving his office, I thought about how Jesus relinquished His own will for the sake of doing God the Father's will, and I knew I must do the same thing. By doing this, I would become better and no longer be bitter. I did not know the reason or the purpose for my disappointments, but I did know that God could use them for His glory. Jesus trusted the Father was listening to His prayers and sustaining Him, and I, too, had to believe the same. What God had started, He would bring to completion. This was my belief, and it included my marriage; the calling on my life and Lynn's; other relationships in our lives; leading others to the Lord; and spiritual, physical, and financial health for both of us.

"Lynn wrote yesterday, so maybe that is a start to restoration in our marriage. I am going to let go and let God move in this area to produce love, forgiveness, and unity. There are better days ahead! God wants to bring me through and bring me out even better. He

wants to restore everything I have lost, plus give me more in the future. Becoming better is about growing, learning, and improving.

"God, You are so awesome, the maker of everything in my life. I will sing to the Lord all my life. Praise You, God, for being the Lord of Lords in my life. Thank You for calling me, blessing me, and living through me. May I follow Your voice today and seek Your shelter in the storms of life. Today I give You all of me!"

"He holds victory in store for the upright, he is a shield to those whose walk is blameless, for he guards the course of the just and protects the way of his faithful ones."
—Proverbs 2:7–8

"Thus you will walk in the ways of good men and keep to the paths of the righteous. For the upright will live in the land, and the blameless will remain in it."—Proverbs 2:20–21

God Opens and Closes the Right Doors

"I need to understand that just as God supernaturally opens doors, sometimes He supernaturally closes them. When God closes a door, it's always because He has something better in store. So just because you've come to a dead end, that doesn't mean it's time to give up. You've got to believe that God has a different route for you, and you've got to keep pressing forward. Out of rejection comes direction. When one door closes, God is about to open a bigger and a better door."

"Trust in the LORD with all your heart and lean not on your own understanding; in all your ways acknowledge him, and he will make your paths straight."—Proverbs 3:5–6

New Milestones in the Right direction— Or Maybe Not

"Lynn wrote on November 3 and gave me hope that we will be meeting in the coming days! I think we are starting to mark milestones

towards loving each other. Lord God, may this be the case. I love my wife and care for her so much. Protect her mind and heart as we walk this journey separate for now but together in the future.

"*I learned last night that I have made strife a part of our marriage and life. I pray and seek Your guidance to take the strife out and put You in the center of all my relationships. I need to be working on the following issues in my life: the need to always prove my point, pride, letting go of the past, and sarcastic behaviors.*"

"May your fountain be blessed, and may you rejoice in the wife of your youth. A loving doe, a graceful deer—may her breasts satisfy you always, may you ever be captivated by her love."—Proverbs 5:18–19

"For a man's ways are in full view of the LORD, and he examines all his paths."—Proverbs 5:21

Lynn called on the sixth and talked with me for an hour. She sounded great, and I enjoyed our conversation. I hoped this was a turning point and a new milestone in the right direction. We talked about Thanksgiving and what we wanted and needed to do for Kayla and ourselves.

I was feeling peaceful and calm most days now. I knew I was in God's hands! God was the one who would stand against the forces of darkness and break those strongholds that were threatening my family and keeping us in bondage. Nevertheless, there were several behaviors I needed to deal with.

Whenever anger problems or trust issues reared their ugly heads, I had a tendency not to treat other people with honor and respect and to tell myself that everything was okay. But now it was time to admit to that behavior and deal with it. It was time to learn to be honest enough with myself to confess my faults. Additionally, if not everything was happening in my timing or in the way I wanted, I had to keep doing my best. God was still in control. If I continued sowing seeds and living with excellence, I could know this: I was making a difference. In God's perfect timing, the fruit of my labor would be seen. Finally, I had to resist focusing so much of my attention on short-term goals and objectives that I overlooked the bigger, long-term picture.

"I need to think long-term in my relationship with Lynn. I need to continually lift her up to God in prayer. But I don't need to talk, share, and overpower her with attention, conversation, and lengthy e-mails. I must stay true, speak the facts quickly, and love her from a distance now. There will come a day when we will be together again as a couple, stronger than we ever were before—two distinct individuals, yet powerful as one in the Lord!

"Until then, bless this day, Lord, as I put You first in all things. You are my God and King. I will serve You all the days of my life! Let Your Spirit come and minister to me this entire day, Lord."

The Pain of Certain Unexpected Words

I often thought the Lord was telling me that Lynn and I would live together again and work together for Him. I knew He felt my pain and saw my ripped-out heart during this time. I knew He heard my prayers and loved both Lynn and me. As the days unfolded, I really thought we were moving closer together. One thing was working for sure—God in my life.

"I am having feelings that I have never felt before. God is truly working on me to become a new man, regardless of what happens with my marriage. I do, however, want to stay married, and I want to serve the Lord as well. Many days and milestones will continue to come, I'm sure.

"This day I thought God was sharing that Lynn and I would have a ministry when this time in our life is over. I will always believe there is a ministry for me and the lady in my life, but when I shared this with Lynn, she said, 'Maybe that person is not me.' Oh, that hurt me so badly! How could my wife of twenty-five years say such a thing?

"But I also felt the Lord was saying, 'You both need time to build up your strength because the journey ahead will require clear minds and hearts for each other as well as a passion for Me. During this time, have your eyes and ears open to help others succeed. Be not

afraid of these days; be open and willing to hear and do the Word. Your time to shine is coming quickly for My kingdom.' "

Everything Starts with Relationship with God

"I must remember that my vertical relationship with the Lord is the key to the horizontal relationships in my life. When I turn away from God and His kingdom, I invariably injure and pain those I love. That's what I did with Lynn and Kayla. But when I enjoy a growing relationship with the Lord, the quality of my relationship with Lynn and Kayla is also enhanced."

During this time, my relationship with Kayla was beginning to flourish; however, my relationship with Lynn continued to have its ups and downs. We spent hours and hours on the phone, and sometimes we talked in person. I asked for forgiveness for everything I had done throughout our twenty-five years of marriage. Every time I thought of something, little or big, I would write, call, or have a face-to-face meeting with Lynn.

During this time, I felt a pressing need to get involved with people at church and in home groups. Additionally, I started taking tae kwon do three days a week, as a release and way to get out of the house.

I also said to myself time and time again, "I am a friend of God's." To be God's friend, I needed to know Him more, so I spent hours praying and reading His Word. I also started reading a book called *The Power of a Praying Husband*. Each chapter included a prayer that I would pray and then pray again for Lynn and her life.

For a period of time, all I did was think, pray, and journal about Lynn and how much I needed her, loved her, and wanted to be with her. Many times I put my relationship with Lynn above my relationship with the Lord. I needed, wanted, and had to correct that going forward. It would take time, but I knew God's hand would be in it.

"God has made me to be a man who will serve Him all the days of my life. I will walk after His ways and listen to His Spirit leading and guiding me. I must remember that whatever I send out into the

world will always come back to me, whether blessing or cursing. I choose to bless others this day. I'm accepted, and I am the righteousness of God. I am more than a conqueror!"

God can and will restore anything that has been stolen from you, including your marriage and love for your mate. You may have failed a thousand times or lost everything you once held dear, but God has not run out of mercy. You can receive it today. It all starts by changing your attitude, so stop being negative towards yourself. Stop accepting the enemy's accusations, and start receiving God's mercy!

"The fear of the LORD is the beginning of wisdom, and knowledge of the Holy One is understanding. For through me your days will be many, and years will be added to your life. If you are wise, your wisdom will reward you."
—Proverbs 9:10–12

Everywhere we go, we should be encouraging people, building them up, challenging them to reach for new heights. When the people around us leave, they should leave better than they were before spending time with us. After being with us, they should feel challenged and inspired rather than discouraged and defeated.

"What the righteous desire will be granted."
—Proverbs 10:24

"When the storm has swept by, the wicked are gone, but the righteous stand firm forever."—Proverbs 10:25

I allowed strife to build in my marriage for more than twenty-five years. Finally, I realized the pain, suffering, and frustration that I had caused Lynn, Kayla, friends, and family. This prompted another journal entry: *Lord, I ask for forgiveness and freedom from this type of behavior. I just want to love, encourage, and help Lynn, Kayla, family, and friends to succeed and be at peace with me. Lord, help me be the man You have called me to be. I want to be an overcomer in Your kingdom and have victory over sin and death, including my flesh. I want to be a peacemaker and history-maker in this land!"*

"Submit yourselves, then, to God. Resist the devil, and he will flee from you. Come near to God and he will come near to you."—James 4:7

"Humble yourselves before the Lord, and he will lift you up."—James 4:10

"The wisdom that comes from heaven is first of all pure; then peace-loving, considerate, submissive, full of mercy, and good fruit, impartial and sincere. Peacemakers who sow in peace raise a harvest of righteousness."—James 3:17–18

"When pride comes, then comes disgrace, but with humility comes wisdom."—Proverbs 11:2

"For lack of guidance a nation falls, but many advisors make victory sure."—Proverbs 11:14

"A generous man will prosper; he who refreshes others will himself be refreshed."—Proverbs 11:25

The Wisdom of Pastor Doug

I met with Pastor Doug again, and he gave me many things to think about. First, I needed to learn discernment through the Spirit of the Lord in all things, both now and going forward. Each battle I faced would teach me more about using the gifts God had given me as well as the specific gifts provided for trying times. As I was learning, there is truly a fine line between direction from the Holy Spirit and discouragement from Satan and the world.

I also needed to water the righteous seeds that God was giving and spend time in positive thoughts from His Word. Regardless of what happened in my life, I needed to nurture my complete reliance on my alignment with God and strengthen my focus on putting

God first. It was time to break all cycles that took me high and then plunged me low. It was imperative that I learn to lean on God for all things, 24/7.

"This time I am going through isn't just for my marriage; it is also for my spiritual growth. Will I be a 'dock' or a 'raft'? A dock is steady when the waves come and go, but a raft is tossed about because it is unstable in nature. Today I choose to be a dock for the Lord, for me, for my relationships, and for my future.

"God's thoughts are higher and better than my thinking. May I hear God's thoughts, take up His cross, and follow His ways every day of my life."

"Whoever loves discipline loves knowledge, but he who hates correction is stupid."—Proverbs 12:1

"Be joyful always; pray continually; give thanks in all circumstances, for this is God's will for you in Christ Jesus. Do not put out the Spirit's fire; do not treat prophecies with contempt. Test everything. Hold on to the good. Avoid every kind of evil."—1 Thessalonians 5:16–22

"Lynn and I talked for over an hour about Thanksgiving and how to celebrate it with Kayla. We decided to do it together as a family. I was so happy to hear that. This is the first time in over a month that we will see each other and be together as a family. That can only mean great days are ahead!

"We also talked about celebrating Kayla's birthday at Applebee's the night before Thanksgiving. Again, that is great news, and happiness fills my soul.

"I have asked both Lynn and Kayla how they felt about my drinking wine over the past few years, and they both suggested I consider a change in that area. I have decided to stop drinking from this point forward. I went more than seventeen years without drinking anything, but then a slow fade happened in my life. The purging of sins continues, and the peeling away of bad habits is getting better

each day. I am growing as a person as well as preparing to be a better husband, father, and friend.

"We also talked about Lynn's advancement. It seems she is becoming much more self-aware, and her confidence in herself and her future is growing. I am so proud of who she is, what she is becoming, and who she will be long-term. Lynn is a wonderful wife, mother, student, and friend.

"I see much better days ahead for us as we both prepare for today and the future. God, continue to bring about positive change in both our lives, and prepare us for the future ahead when we will live under one roof, sleep in the same bed, and talk daily about the great things You have done."

Sharing the Separation with Accountability Friends

My accountability partners and I met, and I shared my situation with them. We prayed together for our marriages, companies, and decisions concerning the people we worked with.

"Thank You, God, for brothers in Christ who have been such a great sounding board for me. I have been blessed with a great wife, daughter, pastor, counselor, and brothers in Christ.

"I must remember this time and be there for others who are hurting. We have the power of God to set the captives free, to overcome the evil one, and to enjoy freedom in Christ Jesus who strengthens us. I can and will be an overcomer in this life! The days in the past have helped me be ready for the days in the future.

"God is so good to us all the time! We must just rely on Him and His ways, and He will make our paths straight."

Chapter 3

The Ripping of Flesh Through Vacation and Thanksgiving

"Haven't you read," he replied, "that at the beginning the Creator 'made them male and female,' and said, 'For this reason a man will leave his father and mother and be united to his wife, and the two will become one flesh'? So they are no longer two, but one. Therefore what God has joined together, let man not separate."
—Matthew 19:4–6

On November 15, 2008, I took my first vacation ever without Lynn. I went to see Kayla for the weekend in order to spend time with her. We had a great time together, and Lynn did not check in with us. It was a little weird because in the past Lynn had always checked in many times throughout the day.

I was looking forward to our time together as a family during Thanksgiving. I believed it would bring major restoration.

"The Lord tears down the proud man's house."
—Proverbs 15:25

"He who listens to a life-giving rebuke will be at home among the wise. He who ignores discipline despises himself, but whoever heeds correction gains understanding. The fear of the Lord teaches man wisdom, and humility comes before honor."—Proverbs 15:31–33

"Praise be to the God and Father of our Lord Jesus Christ, the Father of compassion and the God of all comfort, who comforts us in all our troubles, so that we can comfort those in any trouble with the comfort we ourselves have received from God."—2 Corinthians 1:3–4

Do We Always Get Second Chances?

"My nature has a tendency to try to reconstruct old ways and pick up where I left off. If I were wise, I wouldn't continue to go back to the way things were (I can't anyway, without Lynn's involvement). I must instead forget the old standard and accept a new normal. I really need to accept my new normal, but the pain is too great. I think about how I blew it and how much I want to make it better, both now and forever, if given the chance.

"I believe everyone should get a second chance, but time and time again, I see that is not the case. Should it be? Why can't we give and get second chances in life? I have realized each moment of my life should be lived as the last, so I must make the most of each and every moment. If I do that, only the best can happen, or at least the possibility is greater."

As I was walking through all this uncertainty and turmoil, I learned a valuable lesson: God answers prayers in His timing and in His perfect ways. Our God is a miracle-making God and performs miracles in our lives when it is in His plan. I want everyone to go to heaven, but more importantly, so does our God. My hope is that this book will bring newness in your relationship with God and others and that its influence will expand to the world as a whole.

For the longest time, I had no joy in my life. Each day I merely plodded forward, hopelessly enmeshed in the problems of the day. But when I started focusing on God and other people, I realized I did indeed have hope and purpose in life. Let's face it: Satan is a liar, and our flesh (our own thinking) is also able to fool us. It's easy to conclude things won't ever get better, even if God moves mightily. That, my friend, is in direct contradiction to the Word of God.

"So do not fear, for I am with you. Do not be dismayed, for I am your God. I will strengthen you and help you; I will uphold you with my righteous right hand."—Isaiah 41:10

My prayer on November 20 went something like this: *"Help me, Lord, be the person You want me to be! Life is getting interesting, to say the least. Pour forth Your blessings and open Your windows. I need You and Your Spirit in my life. I know You have helped me make changes for the better. I feel like a better man and a changed man, and I want to continue this transformation process. Help me continue walking the path I am on.*

"I must not give up on Lynn. I have to keep loving her, praying for her, and encouraging her. As I sow seeds to help her, God sees and will reward me. Sometimes we can get so focused on what we want that we let it consume us. I have done this many times and must then turn my focus back to God and His ways. Everything else will fall into place once I do that.

"God sets the priorities if we let Him. I am letting Him, but I am still praying, hoping, and fasting that Lynn comes back into my life as my wife and best friend."

God Can Do Everything at Any Time!

"Suddenly God can turn any situation around. Suddenly God can cause a door to open. All it takes is one touch of God's favor. Show me Your favor this evening, week, month, year, and lifetime, Lord.

"Why don't I trust God more every day? I must believe that He has me in the palm of His hand, and I must know that when it comes time for God to open a door, no person can keep it shut. No obstacle is too high for my almighty God."

The Need to Stay Pure in Every Area of My Life

"Lord, as I read Every Man's Battle, *I see how my sexual conduct affected my relationship with Lynn. It tarnished the way I viewed and treated her and led to the lack of respect I showed her. Lord, I confess now my sinful behaviors and ask for forgiveness. I ask that*

You cover Lynn with mercy so that when we talk on this subject, she can forgive me and also receive healing from the pain I have caused.

"Lord, You warned me back in 2006 to get pure and remain that way. I cleaned up my life for a while but then slowly reverted to my poor behaviors. I am now cleaned up again and on the right path, and I seek total freedom once and for all.

"Lord, return Your blessings and presence in my life and Lynn's. Bring her home so we can become one again, free in You and doing Your will 100 percent. Lead us, guide us, direct us this day in Your righteous path."

"To do what is right and just is more acceptable to the LORD than sacrifice."—Proverbs 21:3

"He who pursues righteousness and love finds life, prosperity and honor."—Proverbs 21:21

"He who guards his mouth and his tongue keeps himself from calamity."—Proverbs 21:23

"There is no wisdom, no insight, no plan that can succeed against the LORD."—Proverbs 21:30

"When I think about how far I went with sin, it is no surprise I am now at this point in my life. However, I recognize my sins, and I am dealing with them. Cleanse me, wash me, forgive me, and renew me, Lord.

"Lord, I want to stand before You white as snow and prepared for Your calling. I have let the world get into me piece by piece, and until this time, I have not been able to come out from under the sin, pain, and hurt. Now I have, and I am on a new course of correction; but I need You, Lynn, and Kayla working together with me so I can enjoy continued success."

Throughout the day, I felt a persistent need to talk with Lynn. When the feeling didn't go away, I prayed and received confirmation that a call that evening would yield a major breakthrough. So

I called, and Lynn and I talked for about ninety minutes. We talked about Thanksgiving, Christmas, Kayla, and the things we were both going through. I was encouraged that success would be the eventual outcome in our marriage.

"God, bring it about in the next few weeks, if that is Your will. I want and need Your will to be done, Lord. You can see the struggle of my flesh against my desire for Your will to be done. Let Your will come through loud and clear to both Lynn and me."

Meeting with Pastor Doug to Gain Wisdom

I met with Pastor Doug again, and he shared I should always be supportive of Lynn's decisions and thoughts. I should trust in her and, even more importantly, in God and His ways. He encouraged me to always consider how Lynn would feel about anything I might say.

As men, we often choose sin simply because we like our own way. Our mixed standards provide a relief from our dulling responsibilities. However, the pressure we experience from our work and family duties does not justify seeking release through sin.

As Pastor Doug explained it, to aim for obedience is to aim for perfection, not excellence, which is actually something less. Excellence is a mixed standard, while obedience is a fixed standard. I wondered how holy I could actually be.

"Because your heart was responsive and you humbled yourself before God when you heard what he spoke against this place and its people, and because you humbled yourself by me and tore your robes and wept in my presence, I have heard you, declares the LORD."—2 Chronicles 34:27

"A prudent man sees danger and takes refuge, but the simple keep going and suffer for it. Humility and the fear of the LORD bring wealth and honor and life.—Proverbs 22:3–4

"Naked I came from my mother's womb, and naked I will depart. The LORD gave and the LORD has taken away; may the name of the LORD be praised."—Job 1:21

Shall I accept good from God but not trouble? I had to ask myself that question and conclude, like Job, that both come from the hand of God for a reason. It is not up to me to dictate the course of my life. That belongs to God and God alone.

Stop the Flow of Sin in My Life

"Lord God, keep working on me, revealing my sins and purifying me. I want to be clean, focused, and used to bring glory to Your kingdom. Lord, I feel much better living focused on You and Your ways. Help Lynn and me to live according to Your ways and Your desires for our lives.

"This time will be different. I know it's my one chance to be whole with Lynn and Kayla. I know You will forgive time and time again, and You have; but times are short, and people need to hear and see Your love in action. May I put away my childlike ways this day and going forward."

Finally, at this point in my life, I made a clear decision, once and for all, to change. I determined in my heart that my life of sin and compromise had to stop here—had to stop now. I finally realized the people who win in life are the ones who hate their impurities and make a change. My victory and success in God's kingdom hinged on a series of right choices that I had to make daily.

Thanksgiving Week

"This is a critical week for our family, Lord, as You know. Grant me wisdom, knowledge, and understanding during this whole week when talking to Lynn and Kayla. Lord, bring our family back together, and make us whole in Your perfect timing. I want to serve You wholeheartedly, and I believe You called me to do that with Lynn as my married partner and fellow believer.

"Continue to do Your work in me, and bring out the Christlike attributes that You have started planting in me. I have seen amazing growth over the past two months as I have replaced my sins of the flesh with Spirit-led direction, as I have prayed and made myself

available to You. May my journey continue, and may it pick up speed as You continue to work in my life and in Lynn's and Kayla's lives.

"Lord, bless us with Your Spirit, protection, and angels this day. Please grant Lynn success on her exam at school and in the rest of her work."

> "Listen my son and be wise, and keep your heart on the right path. Do not join those who drink too much wine or gorge themselves on meat, for drunkards and gluttons become poor, and drowsiness clothes them in rags."— Proverbs 23:19–21

Breaking Habits and Changing Behaviors

"I have gone sixteen days without a drink, and I am breaking the habits in my life that caused such pain to me as well as to Lynn and Kayla. Lynn and I need a miracle to save our marriage, but that can come only from You and Your throne room. May I see the dawn this week as I follow after Your ways, Lord. I bless You today and ask for Your saving grace in our lives."

> "Who has woe? Who has sorrow? Who has strife? Who has complaints? Who has needless bruises? Who has bloodshot eyes? Those who linger over wine, who go to sample bowls of mixed wine. Do not gaze at wine when it is red, when it sparkles in the cup, when it goes down smoothly! In the end
> it bites like a snake and poisons like a viper."
> — Proverbs 23:29–32

As I pressed in to God, I prayed that He would keep me from wavering and stumbling. I prayed against opposition in the form of lies and possible spiritual oppression. On November 26, I took to my journal again: *"Lynn, you are still my one and only true love, the one I could never, ever leave or forsake for another. I need to show you that by keeping my mind, eyes, and flesh clean from looking at or thinking about anyone else."*

"For though a righteous man falls seven times, he rises again." — Proverbs 24:16

Birthday Dinner with Lynn and Kayla

"This day is the first time Kayla has been back in Minnesota since August. It is also the first time I have seen Lynn in six long weeks! Lord, bless our time together this evening as we celebrate Kayla's birthday and spend time together. We need the glue that binds us together, which is You, the Lord, in our lives."

"Through patience a ruler can be persuaded, and a gentle tongue can break a bone." — Proverbs 25:15

"I need more patience in my life. If I slow down and relax with the Lord in my midst, things will change for the better."

"Like a city whose walls are broken down is a man who lacks self-control." — Proverbs 25:28

"As a dog returns to its vomit, so a fool repeats his folly." — Proverbs 26:11

After the evening with Lynn and Kayla, I recorded the experience in my journal: *"Last night had many ups and downs. It was great seeing Kayla and picking her up for dinner. It was fantastic seeing Lynn and having dinner with both her and Kayla, but Lynn's love for me is missing, or at least it is very guarded. Is this God's will? Does He have us in this place for a reason? If so, is it to grow, heal, forgive, and release? Or is it the flesh or Satan trying to destroy what God has put together? Show us Your way, Lord, and what we should or should not be doing at this time."*

"We were under great pressure, far beyond our ability to endure, so that we despaired even of life. Indeed, in our hearts we felt the sentence of death. But this happened that we might not rely on ourselves but on God, who raised the

dead. He has delivered us from such a deadly peril, and he will deliver us. On him we have set our hope that he will continue to deliver us, as you help us by your prayers."
—2 Corinthians 1:8–11

Thanksgiving

We enjoyed a great Thanksgiving together as a family. We played games, enjoyed a great brunch, and talked about many things. The next morning, Lynn came to the house, and we had a good conversation for about an hour. Then we made plans to have dinner tonight at Old Chicago. And to make it even better, Lynn asked me, which was a real blessing.

I knew we still had a long way to go, but I felt like we were reaching milestones in our relationship. We were talking to each other, and a friendship was forming between us. Yes, there would be tests to face and deal with, but I believed the changes occurring in both Lynn and me would help our relationship to be better than ever.

In the meantime, I knew the Lord would continue to work within me on my issues, and I wanted that. Before I could be the husband He called me to be, I would have to be clean, pure, and holy, set apart for God and His kingdom.

"Lord, I feel such a peace over my marriage tonight. I know You are working, Lord, on my and Lynn's behalf. Your power, will, and purpose will win the battle Lynn and I are facing. Victory is taking place and will continue in the days ahead. Continue Your blessings, and continue the battle against the evil one on our behalf. May Your perfect will take place in our lives, and may You continue to pour out Your love and direction on our behalf.

"Lord, I have been a prideful man, doing my own thing regardless of how Lynn or Kayla felt. This should not have been so. How true is Your Word, 'A man's pride brings him low; but a man of lowly spirit gains honor' (Proverbs 29:23). My spirit is low, Lord, so may honor come my way in regards to my relationships. Forgive me my pride as I repent of it and turn away from it. Let me live according to Proverbs 29:11: 'A wise man keeps himself under control.' "

Prayer for Purity

"There are times when I know I am spinning out of control, and at those times, I try to control everything, including people. May I learn how to relax, be patient, and let go and let God. Remove the pain and suffering and the need for total control, Lord. Let love be my guide.

"Grant peace upon my soul, Lord God. May I enjoy life, living in peace with those around me, and may I find favor in Your eyes and man's. Continue to change me from the inside out as I search Your Word and Your Spirit. I want to continue to live in purity with my human nature and its weaknesses. When I fail, I will get to the root of my selfishness, controlling nature, and negative verbal communication. All these things are not rooted in Your nature and that of the kingdom I am part of. May I be a Christlike man living for You and doing Your will."

"You were brought at a price. Therefore honor God with your body."—1 Corinthians 6:20

"We demolish arguments and every pretension that sets itself up against the knowledge of God, and we take captive every thought to make it obedient to Christ."—2 Corinthians 10:5

"I must remember to always starve fleshly attractions and stay away from movies, TV shows, and situations that put my purity in question or cause me to sin. I must always stay away from one-on-one relationships with other women, married or single. My focus must be on God, Lynn, and my love for her. If I find another woman attractive, my first line of defense is a proper mind-set, which says, 'This attraction threatens everything I hold dear. I have no right to think these things.'

"I know spiritual maturity is always dictated by my willingness to sacrifice my own desires for the desires of God and others or for the interests of the kingdom. As I make sacrifices, as I lay down my own desires, blessings will flow. My spiritual life will experience new

joy and power, and my married life will blossom beyond belief as it reaches new heights of love, respect, and wholeness with my spouse.

"Lord, I feel a unity with You and a peace that I should not feel. But I have this peace because of You and what You are doing in my life. I am alive and renewed by Your Spirit. Continue to pour out Your blessings on Lynn, Kayla, and me. Let this weekend be a new and fresh direction for the future of our marriage and family."

Preparing for Christmas

"Kayla and I went to church today and also put up decorations for the first time ever without Lynn. We had fun and moved rather quickly. It is sad, though, to not have Lynn with us as we do these things, but I am learning to be content in the place You have me, Lord. The message today was timely, to say the least."

"For I have learned to be content whatever the circumstances. I know what it is to be in need, and I know what it is to have plenty. I have learned the secret of being content in any and every situation, whether well fed or hungry, whether living in plenty or in want. I can do everything through him who gives me strength." — Philippians 4:11–13

The Need to Be Content in Life

"If I am not content, I miss so much. Really, I miss everything in life, because I will never be satisfied. I want to be satisfied in life, Lord. I need to be content. You have given me so much, and I am blessed by Your hand. Thank You for the relationship You have given to Kayla and me. May I be content and focus on You and Your kingdom.

"Contentment is a learned behavior, I know. I am learning every day to be content. I have not yet arrived, but it is another focus I will develop in the days to come. The first focus I must have is to put You first, Lord, in all situations. The second focus I must have is to measure my needs versus my wants, realizing that as a human, I will always want more but must seek what You have for me at Your kingdom level."

The key to contentment, I was learning, lay in realizing that God had given me, in my present circumstance, everything necessary to remain victorious in Christ.

"But blessed is the man who trusts in the LORD, whose confidence is in him. He will be like a tree planted by the water that sends out its roots by the stream. It does not fear when heat comes; its leaves are always green. It has no worries in a year of drought and never fails to bear fruit."
—Jeremiah 17:7–8

"I have learned nothing in my life is arbitrary. It's all for a purpose. God never does anything accidentally, and He never makes mistakes. No, the separation, divorce, and other issues I face are not easy. I know the Lord is sorrowful that they are a part of my life, but they were allowed in order to shape me at my core so that I would grow daily into His likeness and be blessed because of that growth."

" 'For I know the plans I have for you,' declares the LORD, 'plans to prosper you and not to harm you, plans to give you hope and a future. Then you will call upon me and come and pray to me, and I will listen to you. You will seek me and find me when you seek me with all your heart.' "
—Jeremiah 29:11–13

"God, I live for You and You alone. You are my focus, now and going forward. I know You have called me and have a plan for my life. I will study Your Word, help build Your kingdom, and serve people on this earth.

"Thank You for watching over Lynn, Kayla, and me during this time of testing, reprioritizing, and cleansing from the sickness and sin in our lives. We are becoming stronger and more focused on You and Your ways, I think. At least, I know that I am!"

"However, as it is written: 'No eye has seen, no ear has heard, no mind has conceived what God has prepared for those who love him.' "— 1 Corinthians 2:9

"Do not conform any longer to the pattern of this world, but be transformed by the renewing of your mind. Then you will be able to test and approve what God's will is—his good, pleasing and perfect will."—Romans 12:2

Testing Times Come and Go

Trials, tribulations, temptations, refining, and testing are talked about hundreds of times in the Word of God. Our God continually uses these things to test our character, faith, love, obedience, integrity, and loyalty. Character is both developed and revealed by these testings.

All of life is a test. We are tested by major changes, delayed answers to prayers, seemingly unsolvable problems, criticism from others, and even major events that make no sense. However, when we understand that life is a test, we realize nothing happens in our lives that is insignificant. God will never, ever give us a test that is beyond our power to endure. He will provide the strength to persevere as well as a way out.

"No temptation has seized you except what is common to man. And God is faithful; he will not let you be tempted beyond what you can bear. But when you are tempted, he will also provide a way out so that you can stand up under it."
—1 Corinthians 10:13

The Lord has given us much, and He wants much in return. God didn't give us abilities for our own selfish gains and purposes. They were given to benefit others, just as others are given abilities for our benefit.

"Do not offer the parts of your body to sin, as instruments of wickedness, but rather offer yourselves to God, as those who have been brought from death to life; and offer the parts of your body to him as instruments of righteousness."
—Romans 6:13

"Therefore, I urge you, brothers, in view of God's mercy, to offer your bodies as living sacrifices, holy and pleasing to God—this is your spiritual act of worship."—Romans 12:1

God wants all of my life. He wants your life too!

Raising the White Flag of Personal Surrender

"I have found that the reason I am still troubled, still seeking, still making little forward progress is that I haven't come to the end of myself. I must surrender and obey God's Word, even if it doesn't make sense to me at the time. I know I have surrendered to the Lord when I rely on Him to work everything out instead of trying to manipulate Him, Lynn, Kayla, or others. I must let go and let God work through the issues. I do not have to always be in control. Instead of trying to control and manipulate, I must release matters into God's hands and trust Him more for the future.

"Lord, if this issue of Lynn and me, the pain, the problems, and the separation, is needed to fulfill Your purpose in my life and Lynn's, please do not take it away until Your perfect plan and perfect will are complete. I surrender to You, knowing that Your perfect will and plan will come to completion through my surrender.

"I know the greatest hindrance to God's blessings in my life is not Lynn, Kayla, or others. It is me—my self-will, my stubborn pride, and my ambitions. I cannot fulfill God's purposes for my life while focusing on my own plans for the future and how it should be.

"If I am just going through the motions, I shouldn't be surprised when the Lord allows pain to enter in. Pain is the fuel of passion to energize me with an intensity to change that I do not normally possess. Pain is the Lord's wake-up call. It is God's way of motivating me in my spiritual deadness.

"This does not mean the Lord is a God who wants to apply pressure and heartache to my life. No, He is a loving God, who is moving me into His perfect place. He is using circumstances to make me more Christlike and to prepare me for heaven."

"Love the Lord your God will all your heart and with all your soul and with all your mind and with all your strength."
—Mark 12:30

Giving My All to the Lord for His Glory

God is not interested in halfhearted commitment, partial obedience, and the leftovers of our time and money. He desires full devotion—not little bits of our lives.

"Lord, take my whole life and use it for Your glory now and forever. May I hear Your voice and obey the direction You would have me take going forward. May I be a blessing to You and Your kingdom! I want to be doing Your will and living by Your Spirit daily. I was fooling myself into thinking my ways were better than Yours. I am coming back to You with my whole heart, mind, soul, and body. I need You in my life now and forever. Guide me, direct me, fill me, and lead me by Your Spirit every moment of the day.

"If I seek God and what pleases Him instead of what pleases me or others, I will separate from the world and my own fleshly desires. Whatever I do, I need to work at it with all my might as working for the Lord, not for my own selfish desires, for Lynn, for Kayla, or for friends. God wants my best—everything I can give Him at all times. I might be able to fool others by words and deeds, but the Lord knows whether the desires of my heart are pure. I can never fool God or deceive Him with my thoughts or actions."

God calls us to nothing less than the excellence of Christlikeness, and this becomes possible only when we walk in the power of the Spirit.

"May God himself, the God of peace, sanctify you through and through. May your whole spirit, soul and body be kept blameless at the coming of our Lord Jesus Christ. The one who calls you is faithful and he will do it."
—1 Thessalonians 5:23–24

"Praise to the Lord who sits on high and at the same time is with His people in love and caring! He is my Lord and king.

"I know God is good. He loves me, He is with me, He knows what I'm going through, and He cares. He has a great plan for my life if I will but lean on Him and follow His calling."

It's About Loving God and Loving People

"I need to make love my top priority and greatest focus in life. After learning to love God, learning to love others is the second purpose in my life, starting with Lynn and Kayla.

"Love leaves a legacy for all eternity. I want to make sure that I spend time loving You and loving other people, Lord. I don't want to waste this day or any day not loving those around me. I need this day to be filled with love for You, Lynn, Kayla, family, and friends. Love means to give up my selfish behaviors and give my time and energy to others. May I pour forth my love today, Lord God."

New Pain and Confusion from a Phone Call from Lynn

Lynn and I had a phone conversation concerning the holidays and the next three months' rent. We decided to make different holiday plans from those in the past. Lynn and I would drive to Wisconsin separately, and she would celebrate with her family while I celebrated with mine. Kayla's time would be split between the two of us for those days. Furthermore, Lynn decided to continue renting her apartment for three more months. We had a productive conversation about these things and other issues. It was truly a sad time for both of us, at least from my perspective, and I was sure it would sadden our families when we shared our plans.

"God, I know You have a big plan through all of this. I see changes taking place in Lynn, and I know changes in me have taken place as well. As I told Lynn last night, I find contentment in You and Your ways. I also shared with her that I have surrendered all to You.

She forgave me for the past, and I will take that and move to higher ground in Your ways.

"Lord, reveal any way I can help Lynn find her way during this time in her life. Through her bright spirit, friendship, compassion, and smile, she has touched hundreds of women and men throughout her forty-five years on earth. She has also taught many women the wonders of Your Word and how to live by faith. They in turn have shared with hundreds more!

"Lynn has helped people in pain and those who were confused and needy. She has been a great wife to me, my partner and friend for almost thirty years. She has been a great mother to Kayla and a wonderful role model for her life. Finally, she is a very good student and will help change the world for the better!"

Forgiveness and Love Pour Forth from Me

"Lord, I forgive Lynn of all the decisions she has made that have negatively impacted my life. I know forgiveness must be immediate, whether or not a person asks for it. Trust, however, must be rebuilt in a relationship over time. Trust requires a track record, and I hope the changes in me and the conversations I have had with Lynn show her that I have indeed started a new track record of mutual trust between us.

"Over the years, with my words and actions, I have hurt Lynn repeatedly, and she has hurt me as well. I forgive Lynn as You, Lord God, have commanded me to do. I know I must rebuild trust in our relationship, and I also know it will take time to do that. May we both prove that we can trust each other, and may we share the pain that we have experienced so that You can remove the hurt over time.

"Lord, I pray that both of us can be humble enough to accept what the other shares and then to forgive. Let us both remember that humility is the oil that smoothes and soothes our relationship. Our own pride blocks Your grace in our lives, which we must have in order to grow, change, heal, and help each other as well as those around us, but especially our daughter Kayla and other family members."

The Pain Keeps Coming in Waves

I soon discovered exactly where I stood in my relationship with Lynn. She shared she had no wifely feelings for me at this time. She said she would try to be friends with me, but she didn't want to see me until the holidays were over. She was not happy when she agreed to a friendship with me and I responded that friendship would be a start. She also made it clear she did not want gifts from me whenever we did meet, and she did not want to hear how I felt about her. Needless to say, her words broke over me like waves of pain breaking on the shores of my heart.

"Lord, I truly need a miracle from Your throne room. If You do not intervene, I am afraid our marriage will dissolve. Kayla seems to be the only thread holding us together at this point.

"God, may Your plan and purpose for our lives come about in Your perfect timing. I know, I believe, and I see in Your Word that no man or woman should tear apart what You have put together. I will stay focused on You, Your ways, and will for my life. Reveal Yourself to me and also to Lynn and Kayla. We will overcome by the blood of the Lamb!"

Answers to our prayers may be hindered by unseen obstacles. During those dark days, I learned not to expect God's answers to come too easily or too quickly. Prayer is sometimes challenged by evil forces, so I knew I had to pray fervently and earnestly. Then I had to simply rest in God's power, expecting Him to answer at the right time.

"But seek first his kingdom and his righteousness, and all these things will be given to you as well. Therefore do not worry about tomorrow, for tomorrow will worry about itself. Each day has enough trouble of its own."—Matthew 6:33–34

Prayer to the Lord and His Words to Me

"I am broken in pieces, and my stomach is torn and spilled out, Lord. I am a weak man— broken, crushed, torn, and humbled like never before. This is the time for You to deal with me. I need You in my life, changing me, forming me, and preparing me for the big things to come. Show me the path I should take today and each day. I want to live for You now and forever."

After I wrote these words, I sensed the Lord saying, "My son, listen to the words I speak. I am with you; I guide your path and lead the way. You have not always followed after Me; you have put your selfish desires ahead of mine. That is changing, and I am well pleased.

"You must prepare yourself for the journey ahead. It will be intense, painful, and hard; but I will be there to bring about My glory, and you will see My mighty hand at work. Prepare, prepare, prepare, for the time is short. There are souls to win, victories to be had.

"Be the clay within My hands, and let Me mold you into a new person, the person I have been wanting you to be for a long time. Blessings will follow as you walk in the ways I have set before you this day. Stand strong, and use your voice to be a blessing!"

Comforted by these words, I began asking myself, *Is what I am doing really pleasing to God?* I needed to remember, as do we all, that God is God and I am not. I constantly reminded myself that God must be first, and everyone and everything else, including my wants and needs, a distant second.

"I know, O LORD, that a man's life is not his own; it is not for man to direct his steps. Correct me, LORD, but only with justice—not in your anger, lest you reduce me to nothing."— Jeremiah 10:23–24

Learning My Part of the Plan

At this point in my journey, I overwhelmed myself with other parts of God's plan that did not pertain to me. I struggled to remind myself to be fruitful to God's plan for my life and not be overly concerned with the parts that belonged to others. Deep inside, I truly desired God's plans over my own. After all, He alone holds the master plan, and He cares about our lives and how they fit in to His greater plan. His hand is totally unpredictable and unstoppable as He accomplishes His plan in and through us.

I knew in my heart that God always keeps His promises and is always working behind the scenes, even in His silence. Though there were many valuable components to His elaborate master plan, I was responsible only for my part. There would always be parts of His master plan that would not make sense to me. But that was okay—He was in control, not me.

> "Many are the plans in a man's heart, but it is the LORD's purpose that prevails."—Proverbs 19:21

I Give Up on Myself

"I put my life in Your hands, Lord God. I can do nothing on my own. I am lost without You and have no hope in this world apart from you. Lord, I surrender all to You—my life, my marriage, my finances, my daughter, my house, even my very being. I can do nothing apart from You and Your will.

"Lord, I give up! I give You my all to be used according to Your will. I am broken and spilled out. Use what You can, and then fill me with Your presence so I can change the world and the people in it to be more like Your kingdom—a kingdom filled with love, joy, and worship to You, the one who sits on the throne!

"From the very beginning, God, You knew what You were doing in my life. From the outset, You have worked to shape my life along the same lines as the life of Your Son."

> "You were taught, with regard to your former way of life, to put off your old self, which is being corrupted by its deceitful desires; to be made new in the attitude of your minds; and to put on the new self, created to be like God in true righteousness and holiness."—Ephesians 4:22–24

"I must remember that life is supposed to be difficult! It's what enables me to grow. I must never forget that life is not about me! I exist for God's purposes, not the other way around."

Time to Start Obeying God and His Ways

"As the Spirit of the Lord works within me, I become more and more like Him and reflect His glory even more. I cannot reproduce the character of Jesus in my own strength. Only the Holy Spirit has the power to make the changes God desires to see in my life. God is working in me, giving me both the desire to obey Him and the power to do what pleases Him. Obedience unlocks His power.

"God waits for me to act first. I must not wait to feel powerful or confident. Everything connected with that old way of life has to go because it's rotten through and through. I must get rid of it and allow the Spirit to change my way of thinking. Then I will be changed from the inside out. I will become more beautiful, and I will be free to soar to new heights as I develop the character of Christ and new, godly habits."

Meeting with Joanne

I met with Joanne, my therapist, and shared with her the conversations that Lynn and I had had over the past two weeks. She pointed out several interesting thoughts. First, Lynn left for Lynn's sake, so the choice was hers—not mine. We both recognized that we had individual issues to work on, and I needed to continue to work on the things that I could impact, but I did not bear total responsibility for the state of my marriage.

Second, Joanne wisely pointed out that my belief that I was the one who had failed in the marriage was a heavy load to carry. She shared her belief that I had not failed alone—it was both of us. We spent a lot of time talking about why I thought I had failed in my marriage. Joanne felt my view of failure was too harsh and one that I should not live with or, for that matter, could live with.

"Lynn has things to work on, and you have things to work on," Joanne explained. "You are two parts trying to be whole together.

Yes, you said things and did things, but Lynn didn't always speak up when she should have."

She continued, "You need to get over the idea that everything is your fault and that if you do this or do that, something else is bound to happen. If you stop drinking and control your thoughts and actions, there is still no guarantee that everything will be better."

At the end of the session, Joanne posed a question for me to think about. "How long can you live with ambiguity?" she asked. That is a tough question for anyone to answer and one that I struggled with for a long time to come.

After my meeting with Joanne, I wrote in my journal: *"I march forward in victory one step at a time. With the Lord, we win and have nothing but the best outcomes. They might not always be what we want, but they will be more than anything we could have asked for or imagined. God's plans are always much higher and better than ours.*

"I must be focused on the higher things of God and His perfect will. Then I will be blown away by the lovely hand of God. May the peace of God reside on me this day."

Time to Become Christlike in My Thinking

"I want to be like Christ, so I must develop the mind of Christ. The first half of this mental shift is to stop thinking immature thoughts, which originate from my self-centered nature. I need to continue to develop a mature mind-set. My walk must demonstrate clean conduct, and I must be a man of integrity.

"I must put Lynn, Kayla, family, and friends first in order to have the heart of Christlikeness. I know I must also saturate my mind with the Word of God. It creates life, develops faith, produces change, destroys the attacks of Satan, unleashes miracles, heals hurts, builds character, transforms circumstances, imparts joy, overcomes adversity, defeats temptations, infuses hope, releases power, cleanses the mind, brings things into being, and guarantees my future forever."

"If you remain in me and my words remain in you, ask whatever you wish, and it will be given you."—John 15:7

"Do not let this Book of the Law depart from your mouth; meditate on it day and night, so that you may be careful to do everything written in it. Then you will be prosperous and successful." —Joshua 1:8

"For our light and momentary troubles are achieving for us an eternal glory that far outweighs them all." —2 Corinthians 4:17

Chapter 4

Sharing with Family and Enduring the Holidays

"Do not be anxious about anything, but in everything, by prayer and petition, with thanksgiving, present your requests to God. And the peace of God, which transcends all understanding, will guard your hearts and your minds in Christ Jesus."
Philippians 4:6–7

The Fire of Suffering Brings Forth the Gold of Godliness

God has a purpose behind everything that comes into our lives, be it good or bad. In fact, He depends more on circumstances to make us like Jesus than He depends on our reading the Word. Life is a series of problems. Every time we solve one, another is waiting to take its place. But each one helps us grow more like Christ and prepares us for greater works on earth and eventually eternal life in heaven.

"I learn things about God in my suffering that I wouldn't learn any other way. I can never know that God is all I need until He is all I have in life. With all my challenges, I find myself relying on God more and more. Less and less do I experience the highs and lows. I am learning my 'God times' and my 'own times,' as Kayla tells me.

"When I need God and want God in my life, He is always there to help me. I must always remember to rely on God at all times in my life. Then and only then will my life be as He wants and as I need."

"Dear friends, do not be surprised at the painful trial you are suffering, as though something strange were happening to you. But rejoice that you participate in the suffering of Christ, so that you may be overjoyed when his glory is revealed." — 1 Peter 4:12

"The LORD is close to the brokenhearted and saves those who are crushed in spirit." — Psalm 34:18

"Indeed, in our hearts we felt the sentence of death. But this happened that we might not rely on ourselves but on God, who raises the dead." — 2 Corinthians 1:9

Shape Me, Lord, and Use the Tool That Does the Job

Like jewels, we are shaped with the hammer and chisel of adversity. If a jeweler's hammer isn't strong enough to chip off our rough edges, God will use a sledgehammer. If we're really stubborn, He uses a jackhammer. He will use whatever it takes to develop us into His likeness.

"It is vital that I stay focused on God's plan—not on my pain and my problem. The secret to my endurance is to remember that my pain is temporary, but my reward will be eternal. It has been said, 'God wants me to thank Him that He will use my problems to fulfill His purposes.' My cry to You, oh God, is 'What do You want me to learn?' One thing I know—I can't give up but must grow up!"

Oh No, a Dream About Divorce!

I dreamed Lynn told me that our marriage was over and she wanted a divorce. Needless to say, it was a hard night. But in the morning, while reading my Bible, I realized Satan was the one trying so hard to end our marriage. I could do nothing but look to God to overcome the enemy's attack. By the blood of the Lamb, Lynn and I were overcomers in Christ. With all my heart, I believed we were joined together as man and wife for a purpose in God's plan.

"Blessed is the man who perseveres under trial, because when he has stood the test, he will receive the crown of life that God has promised to those who love him."—James 1:12

"I will not be tempted to get a divorce, regardless of any fear that attacks my mind or anything Lynn might be thinking about. I will continue to pray, seek counsel, and walk in the new ways that I have learned.

"I need more of God and will move forward in His likeness. I want more of the Holy Spirit and His control over my life. I need His fruits: love, joy, peace, patience, kindness, goodness, faithfulness, gentleness, and self-control. To have the fruit of the Spirit is to be like Christ. God develops the fruit of the Spirit in my life by allowing me to experience circumstances in which I am tempted to express the exact opposite quality of the fruit being taught. I must remember that God develops real peace within me, not by making things go the way I want, but by allowing times of chaos and confusion. I learn real peace by choosing to trust God in all things in which I am worried or fearful.

"It takes time for new thoughts, actions, and godly desires to choke out the old nature I let flourish for so long. There are no shortcuts to maturity! The development of Christlike character cannot be rushed. Spiritual growth, like physical growth, takes time."

"Being confident of this, that he who began a good work in you will carry it on to completion until the day of Christ Jesus."—Philippians 1:6

Letting God Work to Completion in My Life

"I believe God is working in my life. At times it doesn't feel that way, when setbacks and disappointments come my way. But even when it doesn't seem like it, I must continue to believe God is working in my life.

"I am praying for a miracle, and I want it so bad. To be a family again is my hope and prayer. That would be by far the best thing that ever happened to me, other than accepting Christ and my wedding

day with Lynn. I am hoping through this time that gradual change is taking place in Lynn's feelings towards me.

"I have found that I am often in a hurry to get things back to the way they should be or, should I say, the way I want them to be. I must remember God is never in a hurry, but always on time. I need to be patient and let the goodness of God move in this situation.

"I know that I am growing through this my most painful period. I also know that God will take this difficult time in my life and turn it around for good in His kingdom. I am willing to let God use me, regardless of what happens in this part of my life or any future struggles I may face. Someone once said, 'Remember how far you've come—not just how far you have to go!' God has so many things He wants me to accomplish for Him, and I will not turn back to the sins and habits that were part of my life only a few short months ago. I will move forward with God's Spirit and His will.

"Lord, keep moving and keep pushing Lynn and me to a deeper level in Your kingdom. Continue to change both of us to be more Christlike. Help us to pour out love to others in this time, and fan the flame of love for each other while we are apart. May we love each other from afar and respect each other as well."

"May our Lord Jesus Christ himself and God our Father, who loved us and by his grace gave us eternal encouragement and good hope, encourage your hearts and strengthen you in every good deed and word."—2 Thessalonians 2:16–17

"Peace I leave with you; my peace I give you. I do not give to you as the world gives. Do not let your hearts be troubled and do not be afraid."—John 14:27

Words from God

"My son, the time is coming and is even at hand when you will know the truth and it will set you free. It is freedom you desire and need in order to move forward in the plan and purpose I have for your life.

"I am preparing you and equipping you to run the race I have set before you. Fear not, for I am with you during this time and the times to come. My love and compassion are new every day. I care for you, My son, and I am supplying your needs according to My Son's riches in glory.

"Walk uprightly and blamelessly, seeking the high ground. Stay pure, stay clean, and stay in My will, and you will marvel at the miracles I will perform while using you to build My kingdom. The desires of your heart will be granted, so fear not, My son. Love the Lord your God with all your heart, mind, soul, and body."

Kayla Comes Back to Minnesota for Winter Break

"Today is a great day: Kayla comes home for twenty-five days and will spend time with Lynn and me. I look forward to seeing her, talking to her, and hearing all the great things that are happening in her life.

"Thank You, God, for blessing Lynn and me with a wonderful daughter who will change the world for the better! Bless her, and keep her from all harm. Use Kayla, Lynn, and me in Your kingdom-building process. May You use the gifts You have already given us, and may You give us many more gifts and talents to build, save, and change the lives of others."

"For we are God's workmanship, created in Christ Jesus to do good works, which God prepared in advance for us to do."—Ephesians 2:10

We were placed on earth to make a contribution! We were created to serve God.

God wants to use us to make a difference in His world. He wants to work through us. What matters is not the duration of our life, but the donation of it. It is not how long we live that matters, but how we have lived.

God Gives Me Everything I Need to Accomplish What He Wants in My Life

All our abilities come from God and His Spirit. Every part of our lives can and will be used for God's glory if we allow Him access into our lives. What we are able to do, God wants us to do, and then, with the help of His Spirit, we can do even more.

I was blown away by the knowledge that God would allow painful experiences in my life in order to equip me for ministry to others. The very experiences I resented or regretted most—the ones I wanted to hide and forget—were the very experiences God wanted to use to help others. That is one reason I am writing this book: to share my pains, hurts, feelings, and sins so others can prevent this pain from entering into their lives.

It took months before I shared my situation with my family and friends. I should have allowed others to come alongside me and carry some of the weight, but I didn't. I was too ashamed and wanted to control what people knew or felt. This was wrong of me, and I shouldn't have chosen that path. For God to use our painful experiences, we must be willing to share them. We have to stop covering them up and must honestly admit our faults, failures, and fears.

Dinner with Lynn and Kayla

"I praise You, God, for all things, especially for bringing Kayla home safely and also for allowing me to have dinner with her and Lynn. I had a great talk with Lynn at dinner and with Kayla afterwards. I see breaks in the clouds but understand it will be Your perfect will that brings us together again.

"I now understand why Lynn doesn't want to celebrate the holidays together; she doesn't want to 'put on a face,' as she describes it. I can now see why that is not a good thing.

"I am praising You for having both Lynn and Kayla back in worship. Touch their hearts, and take them to a new level of worship and service to You. I believe we will serve You as a family in a deeper way in the future."

Opposition Will Come, So Be Prepared

Every time we start out in the right direction in life, we will likely soon face opposition. This is evident in the Bible in Joseph's life as recorded in the Old Testament. I have always been very interested in his story and the way he stayed strong no matter what happened. Regardless of the circumstance, he pressed through his feelings and confusion and trusted in God's plan. He always eventually broke through the waves, as should we in the storms of our lives.

Always remember, everything happens for a reason! Expect the waves of opposition, but fight through and don't give up. Hit the wave wall and keep going deeper. Don't sit on the beach, but get up, get in the water, and fight on!

> "God is my refuge and strength, an ever-present help in trouble. Therefore we will not fear, though the earth gives way and the mountains fall into the heart of the sea, though its waters roar and foam and the mountains quake with their surging. . . . The LORD Almighty is with us; the God of Jacob is our fortress. . . . Be still, and know that I am God; I will be exalted among the nations, I will be exalted in the earth. The LORD Almighty is with us; the God of Jacob is our fortress." — Psalm 46:1–3, 7, 10–11

We rarely see God's good purposes in the midst of our pain, failure, or embarrassment. Only in hindsight do we understand how God intended a problem for good. Extracting the lessons from our experiences takes time.

> "Jesus replied, 'You do not realize now what I am doing, but later you will understand.' " — John 13:7

Lynn Stopped By and Called—Baby Steps!

"Lynn came into the house and talked with me when she dropped Kayla off this afternoon. Is this another move in the right direction?

She could have just dropped Kayla off and left, but she didn't! It's little victories like this that give me hope for the future.

"*Today I feel peace about our future, though I know we're not anywhere near the final outcome. Lord, I do believe in Your Word and will hold onto the fact that both Lynn and I are true believers and worship You as Lord of Lords, and King of Kings. Bless Your name and who You are, Lord God!*"

A short time later, Lynn called, and I recorded my excitement and hope for the future: "*Praise Your name, oh God! Lynn called again this evening, and we had a great conversation! We made plans to have dinner with Kayla Wednesday evening. Baby steps and small victories work for me!*

"*Lord, thank You for the knowledge that Lynn needs time to heal, to find her place in You and in the world. I need to release that time to You, pray, and stand in the gap so her victory can happen. I have been selfish, thinking it has been only about me and what I did or didn't do, and trying to get her attention and time. But now I see it's about You and Lynn, and You and me.*

"*God, You are so good to us each day. I worship You and put You first in my life.*"

"But he said to me, 'My grace is sufficient for you, for my power is made perfect in weakness.' " —2 Corinthians 12:9

" 'For my thoughts are not your thoughts, neither are your ways my ways,' declares the LORD." — Isaiah 55:8

God Knows Better Than Me—Really!

"*I lean on God for my wisdom, knowledge, and understanding. My weaknesses are not an accident. God deliberately allowed them in my life for the purpose of demonstrating His power through me. I must depend on Him for all my strength and as the source to draw on. I must share my weaknesses and expand the works of the Lord.*"

"*My life is worth absolutely nothing unless I use it for doing the work assigned to me by the Lord Jesus. The work I do will further His kingdom here on earth as I use the abilities He has given me. I need to tell of the great things God has done and of His love and kindness. God, help me to do what You're blessing and calling me to do."*

Meeting with Joanne

I met with Joanne again, and we talked about the questions she had brought up in our last session, particularly the question of how long I could live in ambiguity. I had given it much thought and shared with Joanne that Lynn meant too much to me for me to impose an artificial time line, so I was willing to wait as long as necessary.

We also discussed whether I could have a relationship with Lynn as a friend, if that was all she wanted. She might get to the point where a friendship was fine, but not a husband-and-wife relationship. Joanne made it very clear that no one, including me, can control another person, though I had desperately tried to do just that with both Lynn and Kayla. A person cannot even control his or her own environment, much less another person.

The most difficult point Joanne made was that I must let go of Lynn. I had to let her live, breathe, and have space to decide the next step of her journey. This was not about us and our future; it was about Lynn and what she wanted.

> " 'You must go to everyone I send you to and say whatever
> I command you. Do not be afraid of them, for I am with you
> and will rescue you,' " declares the LORD.—Jeremiah 1:7–8
> "For our light and momentary troubles are achieving for us
> an eternal glory that far outweighs them all."
> —2 Corinthians 4:17

> "Above all else, guard your heart, for it is the wellspring of
> life. Put away perversity from your mouth; keep corrupt talk
> far from your lips. Let your eyes look straight ahead, fix your
> gaze directly before you. Make level paths for your feet and
> take only ways that are firm. Do not swerve to the right or
> the left; keep your foot from evil."—Proverbs 4:23–27

Prayer of Blessing

"Thank You, Lord, for Lynn and Kayla and how well they are doing in school. I am proud of both of them, and I know they will make a major difference in this world.

"Thank You for my place of employment, the owners and the employees; bless us with work and unity.

"Bless my time with Doug today, and may I gain insight. Continue to bless him, his family, and the Waters Church. Lead and guide me today at work, with Doug, and especially with Kayla at lunch and at the movie. Bless her time with Lynn for the next few days. Let them relax and have nothing but fun and a great time together!"

"Whoever has my commands and obeys them, he is the one
who loves me. He who loves me will be loved by my Father,
and I too will love him and show myself to him."
—John 14:21

Meeting with Doug

Life is like taking steps in the snow; though we move first to the right and then to the left, we eventually reach our destination. Our lives are not always perfect, but God is with us, moving us forward.

In my meeting with Doug, he encouraged me to keep working on my walk with God. I also needed to continue preparing my heart and life for the future. Doug felt I had successfully made it through the first wave of testing, but he suggested there might be more trials on the horizon, so I should prepare for them. Based upon all my feedback to him, he commented that everything was pointing to a positive outcome!

Hope for the Future

"I sense a moving together with Lynn each time we talk and meet. I have peace about our relationship! I praise God for His work in our situation. I appreciate God's healing of Lynn and me. I thank Him for stopping us in our tracks, because we were headed

for destruction. I ask that His love would come in like a flood tonight and each day going forward.

"I never want to take Lynn for granted again or treat her like an employee working for me. We are partners, friends, lovers, and fellow servants in God's kingdom. Going forward, I want to submit to the Lord, and I want to yield to Lynn when I should.

"Use this time, Lord, to build us up and to prepare us for the work of Your kingdom. Bless You, Lord God, the maker of today and every day. May my actions, thoughts, and behaviors line up with Your will today. Purify my mind, and help me to focus on Your holiness so I, too, can be holy in Your sight."

"For we are the temple of the living God. As God has said: 'I will live with them and walk among them, and I will be their God, and they will be my people. Therefore come out from among them and be separate,' says the Lord. 'Touch no unclean thing, and I will receive you.' . . . Since we have these promises, dear friends, let us purify ourselves from everything that contaminates body and spirit, perfecting holiness out of reverence for God."
—2 Corinthians 6:16–17; 7:1

The Need to Get Rid of Strongholds

"The weapons we fight with are not the weapons of the world. On the contrary, they have divine power to demolish strongholds."—2 Corinthians 10:4

"God, reveal strongholds in my life so that I can take care of them once and for all by using the weapons You have provided: Your Word, Your Spirit, Your truth, and the precious blood of Jesus. I want to be an overcomer, and I want You to use me to build Your kingdom and to lead people to freedom in Christ.

"Reveal Yourself today in a mighty way. I want changes in a holy and just direction to continue as I set my mind, heart, and spirit on the things of the Father. Lord, may You bless the work of my hands today."

Understanding Servant Leadership

"Lord, I have failed in the area of being a servant leader in my home, with Lynn, and at work. I know how critical it is to have mutual submission in a marriage, but I have not pursued it. I have been too busy worrying about what people might think or feeling like it is a weakness to rely on others, including Lynn. I need help overcoming these feelings.

"I do want oneness with Lynn in our marriage, and I want success at my place of employment and with all people. May my relationships with others be blessed and create opportunities so I can grow in life, Lord."

"I lift up my eyes to the hills—where does my help come from? My help comes from the LORD, the Maker of heaven and earth. He will not let your foot slip—he who watches over you will not slumber. . . . the Lord will keep you from all harm—he will watch over your life; the LORD will watch over your coming and going both now and forevermore."—
Psalm 121:1–3, 7–8

"There is no wisdom, no insight, no plan that can succeed against the LORD."—Proverbs 21:30

Working Through Issues with Lynn

"Lynn called this evening, and we had a great conversation and were able to work through some feelings. At one point, she said God told her I was a special person and a good man. Of course, she is the one who is special and the one God used to bring about His will in our life together.

"Lynn is working with Toys for Tots tomorrow; this is a start for her and an encouragement for me to be active and also volunteer in the community. I hope and pray that God open doors for us to serve together.

"We are both concerned about Kayla and her feelings. God, bless Kayla and grab hold of her heart and life! She needs You more

than ever before. Bring the three of us together under Your wings, and protect us from all evil, even our own flesh. Continue to talk to Lynn and also to me.

"I believe in You, Your will, and direction for our lives. May Your perfect will take place in our lives, Lord God."

Words from God

"Seek Me, desire Me, follow after Me, and listen to My voice. I am coming with the Spirit's power in My hand to fill you to overflowing. Cast Your cares on Me, and let Me overcome each one, for your sake.

"I am the God who owns ten thousand cattle on the hills. I am the God who opens the heavens and pours out blessings on you and all mankind. Prepare for blessings you have never imagined before. People will be shocked by the blessings I give to you. I am blessing you for one reason, and that is for you to bless others in My name.

"Prepare yourself, Steve Kirk, for My hand is at work in your life, and my thoughts are much higher than yours. Follow Me, follow Me, and then follow Me some more!"

"But he said to me, 'My grace is sufficient for you, for my power is made perfect in weakness.' " —2 Corinthians 12:9

Sharing the Separation with Our Families

As the holidays drew closer, I realized I had to call my family and share with them that Lynn and I had been apart since September 27. I knew it would be very hard to do this, but it had to be done since Lynn and I would not be together over the Christmas holidays. Making the calls would be painful, so I wrote a script so that each family member would hear the same thing. This is what I wrote and shared:

"I wanted to call and share with you that Christmas Eve will be different this year for Lynn, Kayla, and me. Kayla and I will be together on Christmas Eve, and Lynn is going to celebrate Christmas Eve with her family and Christmas Day with Kayla.

"Back in September, the decision was made for Lynn and me to separate. Lynn moved out and is living in an apartment at this time. This was Lynn's decision.

"We are both seeing counselors and working through our own issues. We have met several times to talk and to enjoy time together with Kayla. We are driving out together on Tuesday and going back together on the twenty-sixth. We will celebrate our own Christmas together with Kayla on the twenty-eighth.

"I ask that you pray for our marriage, for our friendship, and for God's perfect will. I also ask that you give Lynn time to work through her feelings without pressuring her through phone calls, and I ask you to do the same with Kayla and me on Christmas Eve. We just want to celebrate family, Christ's birthday, and friends. Please honor this request.

"The journey we are on is very hard for the three of us. It is something we are working through, and it will take time to resolve issues that have been around for months and years. I believe the outcome will be positive, and it will be God's perfect will for our lives."

The Drive to Wisconsin Together

"Today Lynn, Kayla, and I will drive to Wisconsin as a family, Lord. May we connect, enjoy one another, and relax as we drive and talk. Please move on my heart and Lynn's heart in the next few days as we are together for a longer period of time than we have been since September. Lord, may Your perfect will take place as You protect us and bring us together again.

"Lord, I have no doubt You are in control and moving on our behalf. I know You are a God of marriage and a God of restoration. May Your plan and will supersede any plan of man or woman. May Your will and ministry be complete in our lives. Your power, grace, love, and forgiveness are enough for me and my house. Direct our path, and may it be a pleasing direction guided by Your hand this day!"

"My son, if your heart is wise, then my heart will be glad; my inmost being will rejoice when your lips speak what is right."—Proverbs 23:15

"If you make the Most High your dwelling—even the LORD, who is my refuge—then no harm will befall you, no disaster will come near your tent. For he will command his angels concerning you to guard you in all your ways. . . . 'Because He loves me,' says the LORD, 'I will rescue him; I will protect him, for he acknowledges my name. He will call upon me, and I will answer him; I will be with him in trouble, I will deliver him and honor him.' "—Psalm 91:9–11, 14–15

"Lynn and I had a great time talking for eight hours in the car while Kayla slept in the backseat. I couldn't help but remember all those years when Lynn and I would take turns sleeping while the other one drove. Why do we fall into habits like that in marriage?

"Lynn and I had some of the best conversations that we have had in years. The conversation flowed so easily for both of us. It seems like everything is going in the right direction and that we are sharing as a married couple—which, by the way, we still are at this point."

Open and Direct Conversation with Bonnie

We arrived in Wisconsin, and I had a three-hour conversation with Bonnie my sister-in-law after the Christmas Eve celebration at their house. By the end of the conversation, I felt like a ship tossed back and forth on a raging ocean, and Lynn's hand was the one directing the ship.

"Have I fooled myself into believing our marriage will be healed? Is that what Lynn wants, or is she waiting until after the holidays to tell me otherwise? Has she already set the course for our marriage without my knowledge? Does she truly not love me as a wife, or can she in the future?

"Lord, I know what Your Word says, and I believe it. I must and will hold true to Your Word until Lynn tells me her thoughts and plans. I know Your thoughts and plans supersede ours, so Lord, tell me and show me what I should or should not do at this time."

Words from God

"Love Me with all your heart, mind, soul, and body. Love Lynn as you love yourself, and seek to love other people.

"I have set a course and direction for your life. Let My Spirit lead you and guide you on the journey. My plan will succeed, so take heart, My son, for I will never leave you or forsake you.

"Lynn is My child, a flower in My hand, and a daughter whom I love and cherish. I am working in her heart and life and making changes necessary for her ministry, just as I am doing for you. Do not lose heart, and do not lose sleep; relax and let Me do the work in both your lives.

"Come to Me as I come to you in this time of purging, healing, and setting apart. Trust in Me and know that I change the paths of the godly and ungodly alike. Allegiances, partnerships, and friends that bring destruction to your door will be confused, disciplined, separated, and cast out by My hand. Do not fear the future, for the future is in My hands.

"Oh, My son, I have a plan for you. Trust in Me, lean on Me, and watch My mighty hand move in both your lives."

"Trust in the LORD and do good; dwell in the land and enjoy safe pasture. Delight yourself in the LORD and he will give you the desires of your heart. Commit your way to the LORD; trust in him and he will do this: He will make your righteousness shine like the dawn, the justice of your cause like the noonday sun. Be still before the LORD and wait patiently for him; do not fret when men succeed in their ways, when they carry out their wicked schemes. . . . But the meek will inherit the land and enjoy great peace. . . . The days of the blameless are known to the LORD, and their inheritance will endure forever. In times of disaster they will not wither; in days of famine they will enjoy plenty. . . . If the LORD delights in a man's way, he makes his steps firm; though he stumble, he will not fall, for the LORD upholds him with his hand. . . . For the LORD loves the just and will not forsake his faithful ones.

. . . Wait for the LORD and keep his way. . . . The salvation of
the righteous comes from the LORD; he is their stronghold in
time of trouble!"
—Psalm 37:3–7, 11, 18–19, 23–24, 28, 34, 39

The dark moments of our lives will last only as long as is necessary for God to accomplish His purpose in us!

Remember the Lord First and Foremost

*"I need to keep my focus on the Lord at all times! He is the one
who leads and guides. He is my Maker, King, Lord, Savior, Deliverer,
Counselor, and Freedom-Provider! Lord, may I walk steadfastly in
Your ways and follow Your voice, no matter what the future brings.
I need, want, and must have total commitment to You and Your
kingdom, and I need a love that surpasses the love of this world.*

*"Hurts and pains will eventually cease, and I know joy comes
in the morning. Everything in my life must go back to 1982. That is
the year I became a believer in Christ and asked Lynn to marry me.
That was when we prepared for the future together, enjoyed holidays
together, and held such high expectations for our future.*

*"Now, twenty-six years later, I still walk with You, Lord. Lynn is
still my partner, and my hope for the future is somewhat bright. If we
stay fully committed to Your plan and love You first, above everyone
and everything else, our life together can be wonderful.*

*"I must obey You, Lord, in all things. I must remember Your
goodness and all the things You have done on my behalf."*

"Love the LORD your God with all your heart and with all
your soul and with all your strength."—Deuteronomy 6:5

Family and Friends Now Know of the Separation— I Am Done Hiding!

"When Moses' hands grew tired, they took a stone and
put it under him and he sat on it. Aaron and Hur held his
hands up—one on one side, one on the other—so that his

hands remained steady till sunset. So Joshua overcame the Amalekite army with the sword." — Exodus 17:12–13

"I need friends and family to help support me during this battle in my life. May I have those people holding up my arms. Most importantly, may Your banner be over me, Lord. My hands are lifted up to Your throne.

"Moses lifted up a snake for the nation of Israel, and Christ was lifted up for us. I must keep my eyes on the Lord and worship Him all the days of my life. Lord, I put You first, now, tomorrow, and into the future. You are my God, and I will not turn away from You all the days of my life!"

"Those who sow in tears will reap with songs of joy. He who goes out weeping, carrying seed to sow, will return with songs of joy, carrying sheaves with him. — Psalm 126:5–6

Great Conversation Back to Minnesota

We began the journey home, and it went great. Lynn and I talked all the way home, just enjoying the conversation and not touching on any sore spots. After arriving home, we made plans to join Kayla at a scrapbooking store. I continued my fervent prayers for my marriage.

"Lord, continue to break the ice in my heart and Lynn's. Let our relationship continue to grow. Let all the ice melt so the waters of our love can burst forth and enable us to live as lovers under the same roof in the home we have built together. Continue to work on both our hearts and minds even now, Lord. As we make plans to join our daughter today, I ask You to bless this time as a starting point in a new relationship with each other."

"For we are God's workmanship, created in Christ Jesus to do good works, which God prepared in advance for us to do." — Ephesians 2:10

"Be completely humble and gentle; be patient, bearing with one another in love. Make every effort to keep the unity of the Spirit through the bond of peace."—Ephesians 4:2–3

"Be kind and compassionate to one another, forgiving each other, just as in Christ God forgave you."—Ephesians 4:32

Christmas Celebration as a Family

"Lynn, Kayla, and I are going out to eat this afternoon, and then we will all go back to the house to celebrate Christmas together. I want our time to be blessed and our love for one another to break forth. Though I put God first in life and Lynn second, I still need her as a partner and friend. I need her in order to succeed in life's journey. The Lord joined us together twenty-six years ago, and may He bring us back together in love and forgiveness. I pray our time today in church, at lunch, and at the house will be blessed."

"Be imitators of God, therefore, as dearly loved children and live a life of love, just as Christ loved us and gave himself up for us as a fragrant offering and sacrifice to God."
—Ephesians 5:1–2

"For we were once in darkness, but now you are light in the Lord. Live as children of the light (for the fruit of the light consists in all goodness, righteousness and truth) and find out what pleases the Lord. Have nothing to do with the fruit-less deeds of darkness, but rather expose them."
—Ephesians 5:8–11

"For it is the light that makes everything visible. This is why it is said, 'Wake up, O sleeper, rise from the dead, and Christ will shine on you.' "—Ephesians 5:14

"Speak to one another with psalms, hymns and spiritual songs. Sing and make music in your heart to the Lord, always giving thanks to God the Father for everything in the name of our Lord Jesus Christ. Submit to one another out of reverence for Christ."—Ephesians 5:19–21

"Finally, be strong in the Lord and in his mighty power!"
—Ephesians 6:10

Oh No, Words That Hurt: "Good Provider," "Good Man," and a "Friend"

"With the holidays behind me, I cried like a baby this morning, feeling the sharp pain of separation from Lynn. Her words to me were kind. She said that I am a 'good provider,' 'good man,' and a 'friend.' But they were sadly lacking what I most yearned to hear: 'You are my husband, my best friend, and my lover.' In the past, Lynn so freely shared these words and the feelings that went with them, but now the words are no longer there outwardly and maybe not even inwardly. I cry out to the Lord for a change in our relationship and hope for the future."

Understanding the Cracks in the Foundation

As I thought about the past, I knew I had often followed my own ways and not done the things I should have. However, there were other times, especially earlier in our marriage, when I had been a leader in our home. In those years, Lynn and I prayed together, read the Bible together, and worshiped together. For years, we maintained regular morning devotions, but then we stopped after a move that kept us apart for eight months. When my job took me to Minnesota, Lynn stayed behind in Wisconsin until our house sold. Once we sold the house, Lynn joined me in Minnesota; but we never started up our devotions again, and it took a long time to find a church we both enjoyed. We both let the world into our lives and into our relationship. I no longer led my family; consequently, our spiritual life died first, then our feelings for each other. Ultimately, separation was the sad result of this process.

"I hope and pray the Lord gives us new hope, a new love for each other, a new spirit, and a new journey together. Lord, I know from Your Word that Lynn and I are meant to be together, flesh of my flesh and bone of my bone. Your hand must move for that to take place in our lives."

"Give, and it shall be given to you. A good measure, pressed down, shaken together and running over, will be poured into your lap. For with the measure you use, it will be measured to you."—Luke 6:38

Happy New Year

"How holy can I be in this year and beyond? How open, honest, and kind can I be in this year? How transparent can I be in this year and beyond?

"I want to line up with God's Word and serve Him like never before in this year and beyond. He is my life, my hope, my dream, my Savior, and my guide. He is God, and He holds the key to my future with the love of my life.

"Father, guide me, direct me, and show me the way to Your land flowing with milk and honey. You are maturing me, so please use me as You see fit. I am open to godly counsel and advice through the Word and godly people. I want God's Spirit to rest on me and guide my path this day."

"Every word of God is flawless; he is a shield to those who take refuge in him. Do not add to his words, or he will rebuke you and prove you a liar."—Proverbs 30:5–6

"Help us, O God our Savior, for the glory of your name; deliver us and forgive our sins for your name's sake."
—Psalm 79:9

Sharing at Church on Sunday Morning

One Sunday shortly after the new year began, I had the opportunity to share in church about my pathway to God. Here is the gist of what I shared that morning:

"I started off this past year with searching for a deeper relationship with the Lord. For days, weeks, months, and even an entire year, my prayers focused on my desire to grow closer to the Lord and to put away the things that were not pleasing to Him. Looking back over that year, I can say that my prayers continued with little movement until early September.

"In early September, I began sensing an extreme change in the wrong direction taking place in my life. Though it soon developed into a real sense of urgency, I still didn't make the changes that I knew were necessary to please the Lord, my wife, my friends, and even myself. Then, on September 27, my world changed dramatically.

On that dreadful day in September, the Lord fully captured my attention, and I finally began to change. In the process, I have learned the first key point in life, and that is God is God and I am not. My behaviors, actions, and lifestyle were not at a level, first and foremost, to please God. As a natural by-product, neither did they please my wife, my friends, or me. To be a Christian yet not be Christlike in word, action, and deed had major impact in every aspect of my life.

"In the *Purpose Driven Life*, it is stated that pain is God's megaphone to get our attention. It also says that God uses pain, trials, and tribulations as a way to help us grow. At times He uses these things even more than His Word, ministry, and prayer to accomplish growth in our lives.

"Over the past three months of my life, growth has taken place in me in a major way. I am closer to the Lord now than I have ever been, and I have spent much time in reading the Word, praying, seeking counsel, and worshiping Him by the minute, hour, day, week, and month. But remarkably, it hasn't stopped there. Deep-rooted habits and sins—things I have never been willing to face, allow the Lord to deal with, or, for that matter, to let other people in on—have been rooted out of my life. The victory has been won and complete healing restored. I am not 100 percent where the Lord wants me; however, I have gained much ground, and my prayer to start the year has been answered.

"Through the pain, trials, and tribulations, I have grown. Of course, I didn't want or think that the Lord would do it that way, but He has, and growth has come. The days ahead, I know, will bring more change to make me into the true person Christ wants me to be as I stand before Him. To be Christlike is simple in many ways, but in other ways it seems impossible. I must, therefore, believe, apply, and embrace the following words from Galatians 5:22 and 23: 'But the fruit of the Spirit is love, joy, peace, patience, kindness, goodness, faithfulness, gentleness, and self-control.'

"Through all my difficulties, I have learned to love God more than ever before, follow Him further, believe and lean on Him in all things, and trust that He has a better plan for my life than I could ever think of. I must and will believe God is God and I am not, and I will release all things into His hands for His perfect will and purpose to be accomplished.

"In closing, I share the words of Romans 8:28: 'We know that in all things God works for good to those who love Him, who have been called according to His purpose.' I am letting go and letting God take control."

Sharing with Lynn How I Feel

The next time we were together, I showed Lynn what I had written and shared at church. She read it with very little comment, which saddened me. I thought she might be touched or at least pleased that I had restored my relationship with God and was now moving in the right direction.

Lynn and I spent five hours talking about past hurts and pains. Following Joanne's advice, I shared my wants and needs with Lynn, as well as what I thought makes a great husband. I started out by telling her I felt empty inside and truly sad. I expressed my need for a relationship between the two of us that resembled a marriage in restoration. It was now going on four months since we had separated, and we had made some progress; however, most of that seemed to happen only when Kayla was present. I reminded Lynn that I had shared my heart, asked for forgiveness, changed in many ways, and now needed her to give me a chance.

I explained that I needed a relationship based on our marriage vows, which included physical touch such as hugs, holding hands, and, as time passed, a full physical expression. I told her that my feelings were equally as important as hers, but I wanted and needed to know her feelings as well.

Feeling as though I had stepped back and waited for Lynn to sort out her issues, I now expressed the desire for us to move forward together. We were past standing back to see what would happen, waiting for Kayla to return, or talking on the phone whenever a need arose. I wanted us to attend church together, either at Westwood or the Waters.

I had made a list of the traits of a great husband, and I now shared it with Lynn: A good husband is spiritual and godly. He supports his spouse's decisions, encourages her in her endeavors, and trusts her with all his heart. He has great verbal communication and openness, and he is a person of integrity. He gives his wife affectionate physical touch and is honest, selfless, and not controlling. He interacts with his family and is a great father. He is compassionate, peaceful, loving, joyful, faithful, kind, gentle, patient, caring, and respectful.

I told Lynn these were all areas I was working on, and with God's help, I was seeing success. I also went on to share that she and I were both good persons. We both loved God, we both hated the thought of divorce (or at least I did), and there was a plan for our future.

Lynn had told me that she often cried and was confused. She said she feared the future, as did I. But what was that future? She didn't seem to know, and neither did I.

Oh No, There Is Another Person!

In this five-hour conversation, I also discovered that Lynn was having phone and Internet conversations with a man from Canada. This knowledge didn't totally shock me, since we had been apart for a number of months now. But we were still married, so I did ask her to stop talking to the man. She never actually said she would, but I thought she would at least consider it in order to honor our marriage vows.

After five hours of conversation, Lynn said she wanted to leave and think about her wants and needs as well as mine. She said she would get back with me on our next step. Now it was up to God and Lynn to complete our path. Without God and His movement on our behalf, things looked grim, at least in my fleshly opinion. But I was still convinced that God had a plan for Lynn and me, and I believed His plan would be accomplished by His mighty right hand.

The words Lynn spoke that day and the feelings she shared were very difficult for me to understand, handle, and accept. I felt deep pain, sorrow, and sadness that I had been a part of the hurt she had experienced in life. We all have things done to us, but I had not realized the extent of the pain I inflicted on other people, especially Lynn.

This was another painful day for me. I couldn't help but wonder when the pain would stop and the healing begin. I set my hope on the days ahead!

"Jesus replied, 'What is impossible with men is possible with God.'—Luke 18:27

"But he said to me, 'My grace is sufficient for you, for my power is made perfect in weakness.'—2 Corinthians 12:9

"He will call upon me, and I will answer him; I will be with him in trouble, I will deliver him and honor him." —Psalm 91:15

"Trust in the LORD with all your heart and lean not on your own understanding; in all your ways acknowledge him, and he will make your paths straight."—Proverbs 3:5–6

"And my God will meet all your needs according to his glorious riches in Christ Jesus."—Philippians 4:19

"For God did not give us a spirit of timidity, but a spirit of power, of love and of self-discipline." —2 Timothy 1:7

"Cast all your anxiety on him because he cares for you."
— 1 Peter 5:7

"Keep your lives free from the love of money and be content with what you have, because God has said, 'Never will I leave you: never will I forsake you.' "—Hebrews 13:5

Chapter 5

What's in the Smoke Is Revealed

"For wisdom will enter your heart, and knowledge will be pleasant to your soul. . . . It will save you also from the adulteress, from the wayward wife with her seductive words, who has left the partner of her youth and ignored the covenant she made before God."

Proverbs 2:10, 16–17

Confused and in Need of Friends and Counsel

After my conversation with Lynn, I was very confused about our relationship, so I reached out to several friends. The first friend I called, a woman named Wendy, remarked, "When Lynn left, it was over in her mind, but you are working backwards to the beginning." Her words shocked me to the core. Never had I thought that the day Lynn left she already considered our marriage as totally over. Could I really have been fighting so desperately for my marriage when in reality it was over back in September? This was a hard message to hear and also to contemplate. I pondered the thought for many days and months, and I also shared these words with Lynn. But I am getting ahead of myself; I will share more on that later.

I also called another friend, Nikki, and she shared God was working in the situation and a foundation had been established. She commented, "Getting Lynn to open up about the man in Canada was helpful, and it was great wisdom on your part to share with Lynn that she needs to stop that behavior until your life together is settled." She encouraged me to remember that God was in the midst of this very hard time for both Lynn and me.

Pastor Doug and I talked as well, and he shared his thoughts. He started out by saying there was a breakthrough coming in God's perfect timing. He said he saw spiritual maturity taking place in my life, and he encouraged me to keep showing Lynn "Jesus with skin on" in all my actions and not to resort to past behaviors.

During Lynn's and my conversation, she had said that I had become the man she always wanted. Doug thought her sharing that was a great revelation and would help us in the future. He told me to ooze out the fruit of the Spirit, both now and into the future. However, I needed to remember that God was at work and was the one in control—not me!

Doug felt my conversation with Lynn had accomplished more than I would ever know. Lynn and I could never experience restoration without this conversation first taking place. Skeletons had to come out of the closet. Last of all, he reminded me to keep being the rock on the road to unity and to let the whole thing unfold in God's timing. His words of wisdom on not taking control and having patience, patience, patience, and more patience were just what I needed.

The last friend I talked to was Sara, who said, "I believe God will make His will clear in your eyes, and I pray that you will both have the strength to be obedient to what He reveals."

Prayer to God for Help

" "Lord, You know my heart, and You know Lynn's heart. We are both hurting. We both feel pain, we both feel loneliness, and we are both lost without You. We both need complete healing, restoration, and togetherness with each other and with You.

"God, pull the blinders off, tear down the walls, fan the flames of our hearts, and bring complete healing in our marriage. Only You can do this in our lives. Both Lynn and I have made decisions that are not pleasing to You. Forgive us, and then let us forgive each other and start fresh and new with You in the center of our marriage, life, and relationships.

"Lord, I pray that You would perform a miracle in Your perfect time—not a moment too late or a moment too early. I hold on to Your word: "If my people [Steve and Lynn], who are called by my name, will humble themselves and pray and seek my face and turn from their wicked ways, then will I hear from heaven and will forgive their sin and will heal their land [marriage]" (2 Chronicles 7:14).

"When I call on Jesus, all things are possible! The mountains will fall, and I will mount on wings like an eagle's and soar to new heights."

It's a New Day

Lord, I want You to keep doing in my life what You are already doing. I want to serve You, become Christlike, and walk in all Your ways. Even though this is a very painful journey, if You are in my life more and my flesh is under Your control, the outcome will be according to Your perfect will, plan, and purpose. I completely surrender all my actions to You—from my marriage to Lynn, to my relationship with Kayla, to my job, and to our financial well-being.

"I want to serve You and be used by You in any way You see fit. I want to be quick to respond as I hear Your voice and see Your move in my life today and every day. Grant me a double portion of Your love, mercy, grace, compassion, wisdom, knowledge, and understanding.

"I want this year to be the year that I walk with You, serve with You, and move with You each day. May I be that dock that Pastor Doug talked about; when the waters of life move up and down, may I be solid and unmoving.

" In this year, Lord, I ask for Your hand to move mightily in my marriage. Bless Lynn while we are apart, convict both of us of our sins, and expose the sin and darkness within us so that we can deal with it correctly.

"Bless Kayla in Florida. May she continue to do well in and out of school and in serving You. She is a great child, but grab her heart and cause it to yearn after You in all parts of her life."

Clarity of Mind, Clarity of Purpose

"Thank You, Lord, for revealing clarity of mind and clarity of purpose to me yesterday. I also thank You for giving me the chance to send Lynn a message. I know that You are doing a work in my heart and also in Lynn's heart. I turn everything over to You, and I will get out of the way. I know Your plans are clear and that they are plans to bless and to heal. Your plans are much, much higher than both Lynn's and mine. Reveal Your Word to me this morning as I seek You and Your plan for this day."

That morning in prayer, the Lord provided further clarity to me as He spoke to my heart: "Lynn will not be forced into meeting with you. She needs to make the choice, and then the walls will start falling down."

Looking in the Mirror and Seeing the Pain Inflicted

About this time, I read these words: "We learned earlier that achieving emotional closeness has little to do with emotions; it has everything to do with actions. Oneness has terms set by your wife's personal convictions and her soul essence. Comply with her terms and emotional closeness follows. If not, her emotions will die. You need to act right or, more precisely, act righteously. If you do, your wife's feelings of intimacy will follow."

Reading these words, I realized that Lynn's feelings for me had died because I trampled her by my leadership. I did not always love her as myself or act as if we were one. But if I could do this now, perhaps her feelings of intimacy would return. Regardless of the end result, I knew it was the right thing to do.

"For the LORD is righteous, he loves justice; upright men will see his face."—Psalm 11:7

"But I trust in your unfailing love; my heart rejoices in your salvation. I will sing to the LORD, for he has been good to me."—Psalm 13:5–6

A Vision of Lynn in My mind and a Vision of God's Righteousness

One day in prayer, I received a mental picture of a long corridor, with Lynn standing at the end, dressed in white. On each side of the hall were doors, and each door opened to certain sins and fleshly enjoyments. I walked past each door and reached Lynn; then together we walked out into God's fullness, pure white light surrounding us. Reflecting afterwards, I felt God was showing me the behaviors I needed to choose going forward and the ones I needed to leave behind.

"I believe this shows me my choices and my behaviors going forward. I choose Lynn, and I choose the Lord and His fullness over the sins of the flesh and the world. Let it be so, Lord Jesus, let it be so!"

Respect Is the Beginning and Not the End—Duh!

When Lynn and I discussed my list of what makes a great husband, she commented that I had left off *respect*. In response I had quickly added it to the end of my list, tacking it on to the other traits. Remembering that now, I realized that's what I had been doing for years in my relationship with Lynn. I showed her the respect she was due only as an afterthought, only when there was room in my life or I had the time. In particular, I had not shown her proper respect in the physical part of our relationship. I had pushed her to do things I wanted, even though she felt uncomfortable. This showed a deep lack of respect, and I prayed to the Lord and asked for forgiveness. I also felt a need to call Lynn and share my fault and sin.

Phone Call with Lynn on Respect and Feelings

Lynn and I talked, and she confirmed that she had felt disrespected for years in our marriage. When I was stressed and lashed out at her for little things, I made her feel bad. I asked for forgiveness and expressed my desire for change, knowing this behavior was unacceptable to Lynn, God, and me.

Lynn also admitted she should have said something at the time, but she felt like she could speak up now because we were on a level playing field. She told me she had shared all this with a friend, Jennifer, and stated that she would never be disrespected like that again. I wholeheartedly agreed that she must not allow me or anyone else to disrespect her.

"I hope this conversation brings about healing in our relation-ship. I am happy my sins are being revealed at this time. I did Lynn a disservice in our relationship, and we needed to get this issue in the open and resolve it. I want to treat her like the person she is: bright, loving, caring, understanding, patient, and pure in many ways.

"Lord, flood each of our hearts with forgiveness, compassion, healing, and oneness this day and going forward. Let a miracle happen in both our hearts today.

"Lord, I believe this revelation and conversation about respect is a huge step forward. Maybe that is why I sensed this morning in prayer that the dawn is breaking. May that be so!"

"However, as it is written: 'No eye has seen, no ear has heard, no mind has conceived what God has prepared for those who love him.' " — 1 Corinthians 2:9

A Prayer to God for More of Him and Less of Me

"In the name of Jesus Christ, I dedicate my body, soul, and spirit to the will and purposes of God, and I hold firmly to the truth of God. I ask, Lord, that You would give me a continual awareness of the power of the blood of Jesus Christ working in my life. I desire the mind of Christ so that I will have godly thoughts, motives, and purposes in all I do. I commit to walk where You would have me walk so that my steps are strong and steady in following Your will. I accept the work You did at the cross and all of Your mercy, truth, love, power, and forgiveness. Teach me, Lord, how to forgive those who have caused me pain, and help me to reflect Your love. I want to be a delight to You, Lord. I ask this in Jesus' name."

The Need to Get Rid of Fear and Control

"The words patient *and* freedom *came to me this morning. I must learn to be patient in all things, especially when it comes to Lynn. I am once again trying and pushing too hard to make something happen. I think that is why the word* freedom *came to me. I must have freedom in knowing the Lord is at work in this and all situations regarding my well-being and Lynn's.*

"I need to release the entire situation to the Lord, but how? Maybe that is where I am now: at the how-to-do-it question. Fear is at the core of my dilemma. I need to get rid of the fear, and then freedom will come. Fear is like worry; it will not change the place I find myself in. Perfect love casts out fear, so I seek perfect love."

"The LORD is my light and my salvation—whom shall I fear?"—Psalm 27:1

"Even though I walk through the valley of the shadow of death, I will fear no evil."—Psalm 23:4

"God is our refuge and strength, an ever-present help in trouble. Therefore we will not fear, though the earth gives way and the mountains fall into the heart of the sea, though its waters roar and foam and the mountains quake with their surging."—Psalm 46:1–3

"You will not fear the terror of night, nor the arrow that flies by day, nor the pestilence that stalks in the darkness, nor the plague that destroys at midday."—Psalm 91:5–6

"Say to those with fearful hearts, 'Be strong, do not fear; your God will come, he will come with vengeance; with divine retribution he will come to save you.' "—Isaiah 35:4

"So do not fear, for I am with you; do not be dismayed, for I am your God. I will strengthen you and help you; I will uphold you with my righteous right hand."—Isaiah 41:10

"For I am the LORD, your God, who takes hold of your right
hand and says to you, Do not fear; I will help you."
—Isaiah 41:13

My Destiny Is in God

*"My destiny is not tied to Lynn, Kayla, or any other person on
earth. It is in and all about God and His plan for my life. My success is
my ongoing achievement of becoming the person the Lord wants me to
be and accomplishing the goals the Lord has helped me set in my life."*

"But when he, the Spirit of truth, comes, he will guide you
into all truth."—John 16:13

"Be completely humble and gentle; be patient, bearing with
one another in love. Make every effort to keep the unity of
the Spirit through the bond of peace."—Ephesians 4:2–3

"Humble yourselves before the Lord, and he will lift you
up."—James 4:10

The Need for God's Spirit

*"I have found it is critical to be a godly person in everything I
do and to also obey the direction God has set in my life. It is only
when I am doing this that I find success as a Christ-follower. I do
not know why it took me this long to realize that God and His ways
are always best.*

*"I need to subdue Satan, the flesh, and the world every moment
of the day. My flesh pushes and pushes for more and more in life. I
must learn to be content in all things and with all relationships in
my life. God is opposed to me trying to be something that I can never
be apart from Him. Everything starts and ends with my relationship
with God, and that includes the inner man and as well as the outward man. It all starts with spiritual prosperity. I hope and pray that
the Lord pours out His Spirit on my spirit so I can flourish for Him
and those around me.*

"I know God has a plan and purpose for my life that includes Lynn. I hope and pray that God clearly reveals His plan to both of us so we will know beyond a shadow of a doubt which part of the plan is for each of us.

"I shared with Lynn yesterday that I believed God told me that He answers her prayers. I hope and pray that God shares His direction with her very clearly. Also, I hope He continues to reveal the pains and hurts I have caused Lynn and Lynn has caused me. I want to purge all the past issues and start on new ground with new love that pours from God's throne room.

"God, may You bless us today in church and with Your Spirit. Please do the same for Kayla."

Roller Coaster of Emotions

"Wow, the pain and grief continue. My life is like a roller coaster right now. One day I think I am seeing major breakthrough, but then the next day I perceive destruction at every turn. I know my desire is to serve the Lord first and lean on Him, but time and time again, I lean on my own understanding.

"Lord, I cry out to You for all things; help me in my time of need. Take the pain and turn it into a forward push for Your kingdom. I know, believe, and receive that all things work for good!

"Lord, I want to curl up and cry like a little baby, but I know I must keep the faith and realize You are molding me for a service in the future. Your heart is becoming my heart, and my heart is becoming Your heart. The ripping and tearing of my ways is painful, Lord, but do as You must do to change my ways and make me more Christlike in my actions.

"Lord, I want to serve You, walk after You, and worship You all the days of my life. This will not change as Your process continues in my life. Just be with me, comfort me, protect me, and pour forth Your Spirit within me! Lord, do the same for Lynn (flesh of my flesh, bone of my bone) and Kayla. I want our family brought back together, not broken apart in this process of change.

"Lord, show me my strengths and my weaknesses. Show me the way in and the way out of the battles ahead. May I be alert, ready,

and focused and know that I am loved for the journey. Prepare me as I prepare myself for the journey and battles ahead. May Your Spirit speak through me and consume me for this calling."

"Now to him who is able to do immeasurably more than all we ask or imagine, according to his power that is at work within us, to him be glory in the church and in Christ Jesus throughout all generations, forever and ever! Amen."
—Ephesians 3:20–21

The Desire to Fulfill God's Calling

"I am in the miracle zone because God is moving and will move for me, Lynn, Kayla, and all people who are called by His name. There is always more of God, and I want all of God poured forth in my life so I can be more like Him with every breath I take.

"I also know there is a lot to do on His behalf, and I want to fulfill the calling He has placed on my life. I will answer His call and be obedient and patient in all that I do each day. May I be an example to all the people around me, especially to Lynn and Kayla. Nothing, no one, not a thing should take my focus off what You are doing, Lord. I am looking towards You for all my answers."

"By this all men will know that you are my disciples, if you love one another."—John 13:35

The Need and the Desire to Let Go and Let God

"In the next two weeks, I will let Lynn have her space and let God have His way in her life. I am letting go, realizing God can do much more than I can in this situation. As a matter of fact, all my efforts could be doing more harm than good at this point. But if Lynn wants to talk, I will be there for her at any time, day or night.

"I want God to have His way this day and every day going forward, but oh, letting go is so hard! May my flesh come into alignment with God's Spirit this day and each day going forward. I want to and will serve the Lord all the days of my life. He is God and I am not!"

Meeting with Joanne

I met again with Joanne, and she shared her thoughts and insights with me. First, she pointed out that my backing away from Lynn and giving her space for two weeks was a major accomplishment. Lynn needed undisturbed time to wrap her mind around the consequences of future decisions, and I needed to release control over her and the decisions only she could make. This was not my chess board—it was God's. Only He could move hearts and minds.

Second, Joanne helped me to see that whether Lynn was aware of the changes I was making or not, I knew and God knew what I was doing during this time of quiet and separation. Lynn and I were adults on the same level, both making decisions for our lives.

Joanne complimented me on how well I was listening and responding to Lynn's thoughts and comments. Though I might not be able to completely control thoughts of fear, loneliness, terror, loss, and frustration, I had to focus on the positive things: home, health, happiness, family, and job. "Meditate on the Word, and think on God," she urged, "and above all else, think on positive things before falling asleep." In her last words to me for the day, she cautioned: "Stay in your own head. Stay in the moment, and don't try to predict the future. Remember, you cannot run Lynn's life."

Phone Call from Pastor Doug

Pastor Doug called, and I told him about my week and the words that Joanne had shared. He agreed that now was the time to back off and let God work things out. Now it was time to let Lynn process all the changes and words that had been demonstrated and spoken over the past few weeks. So I relinquished my control and made a conscious decision to let God and Lynn work together for the future. I acknowledged God as God, and I reiterated my belief that Lynn, whenever led by God, always made the right decisions for Him, the kingdom, and herself.

Do Your Work Within me, Lord God!

"Today is a new day, and I worship God and bow down to His wisdom, knowledge, and understanding. I have let go of Lynn so she can think through the future with God's help.

"I want God's surgery to continue in my life. I want God to continue to get hold of my life and set a new direction. I want perfect alignment with God and also with Lynn and Kayla. I need Him to share His goals and plans and the path I should be on. I need answers through His Word, Spirit, and fellow godly believers.

"Today Kayla returns to Florida, her home now. God, I ask You to protect her on her journey. Give her Your love and guidance in the days ahead, and give her Your Spirit of love, compassion, hope, and peace. I pray that she grabs Your hand and moves into right alignment with Your Word."

"Have I not commanded you? Be strong and courageous.
Do not be terrified; do not be discouraged, for the LORD your
God will be with you wherever you go." —Joshua 1:9

Looking Towards the Future

"Interesting thought: Am I willing to accept the belief that God desires my success? Absolutely! I know He wants nothing but the best for me, His child. The God of heaven Himself will prosper me now and into the future.

"My success is found in the way I live day in and day out. It is found as I pursue what God called me to do for His kingdom and as I follow His direction. I have wasted precious time and energy worrying about whether I have done enough, done well enough, or done the right things in the use of my talents and spiritual gifts. I need to get past the past life I have lived and look forward to the things I can change for the better with God's help. What I don't know, God knows. What I don't have, God has. God knows exactly what I am going through at this very moment, and He will help me overcome each issue if I let Him work in my life.

"With God working on each issue, I am setting new goals for this year. My goals are to walk in the Spirit daily, to experience the same kind of awesome Holy Spirit power that Jesus Christ experienced, to serve God in the fullness of the Holy Spirit's guidance and power, to maximize my full potential, to use all my talents and abilities in the way God created them to be used, to fulfill God's purpose for my life, to enjoy life to its fullness, and to live in the joy that comes from knowing Christ is in my life."

Finding Peace in God

"I feel that I must go through a peaceful, relaxing, unwinding stage with God and my relationship with Lynn. I have been pushing myself too hard, trying to control things and make something happen. I need to relax in both my personal life and professional life. I need to focus on my relationship with God and stay in His presence if I am to find the true essence of life and learn how to discern His leading."

In response to my prayer, the Lord said to me: "My son, I am with you on this journey. Lean on Me for your understanding. The training you are going through is needed. There will be pain and suffering ahead as you are obedient to the calling I have on your life, but there will also be peace and love. You will prosper as you walk through the calling."

"My son, keep my words and store up my commands within you. Keep my commands and you will live; guard my teaching as the apple of your eye." — Proverbs 7:1–2

"Give thanks to the LORD, call on his name; make known among the nations what he has done. Sing to him, sing praise to him; tell of all his wonderful acts. Glory in his holy name; let the hearts of those who seek the LORD rejoice. Look to the LORD and his strength; seek his face always."
— Psalm 105:1–4

I Need God's Plan, and I Need to Stick to His Plan!

"Today I must seek God's perfect will and perfect plan for my life and journey. I haven't always done that, and many times I have treated God like a quick fix to my issues. But thankfully, I am past that point in my life. I need the plan that God has. I need God to reveal that plan within, and I must walk in that plan daily. Anything short of what God wants is robbing Him, others, and me of His ways and His directions.

"Lord, direct my path into Your righteousness. May my ways become Your ways as they originate from Your throne room. Breathe on me, Holy Spirit, and may that breath change the world for the better today. I want to be holy, just, and a man after Your heart, Lord God. Bless this day with guidance from Your righteous right hand."

"Now then, my sons, listen to me; blessed are those who keep my ways. Listen to my instruction and be wise; do not ignore it. Blessed is the man who listens to me, watching daily at my doors, waiting at my doorway. For whoever finds me finds life and receives favor from the LORD."
—Proverbs 8:32–35

"I will remember the deeds of the LORD; yes, I will remember your miracles of long ago. I will meditate on all your works and consider all your mighty deeds. Your ways, O God, are holy. What god is so great as our God? You are the God who performs miracles; you display your power among the peoples. With your mighty arm you redeemed your people."—
Psalm 77:11–15

Finding Contentment in God and His ways

"Something good is going to happen this day! I know God is blessing us and filling us with His goodness and grace. I believe the skies will part and clarity will take hold of this situation. In the meantime, however, I must be content with where I am in life.

"Contentment is the realization that God has provided all that I need for my present happiness. I need to be content while at the same time pressing towards the goals I set a few days ago for this year and the years beyond. To be content means I must rest in the Lord and trust Him to help me with all my issues and situations.

"Contentment is living free of anxiety and worries. It is living free of anger, bitterness, and resentment towards Lynn or other people. It is living peacefully with God. Contentment knows that no matter what any person may do to me—leave, divorce, isolate, torture, persecute, ridicule, or even kill me—they cannot separate me from God's love and forgiveness.

"I have found that what matters most is my slow, steadfast, obedient pursuit of the goals to which God calls me. He is as concerned about my ongoing faithfulness, discipline, faith, obedience, and reliance upon Him as He is about my accomplishing the goals He helped me establish."

Meeting with Doug

I met with Doug again, and we talked about how the new year might unfold and what I should be doing going forward. We concluded I must stay the course with God every day, remain pure in all areas of life, grow in Christlikeness, seek godly counsel when issues arise, devote myself to prayer, and seek God's answers. God will give me the desires of my heart, but I must remember that He requires something from me in return. Never, never must I turn back to the world.

"You were bought at a price. Therefore honor God with your
body."— 1 Corinthians 6:20

Joseph, the Wonderful Example of Faithfulness

"I must go forward being obedient to the tasks at hand! I think about Joseph and how he knew that the Lord had planned and provided for his success. Vision, followed by years of faithful

preparation, trust, and obedience, resulted in years of service, authority, and reward. His trust, obedience, and faithful preparation brought results that saved his family and nation and brought about God's perfect will from so many years before.

"Just like He did for Joseph, God created me to be and to do very specific things in my lifetime. He is always guiding my life, every day, every moment, all day. I am becoming a man perfectly positioned for God's chosen success plan.

"What about all the setbacks that come into my life? Well, God uses them to help accomplish what He desires as an outcome in my life. For instance, the separation with Lynn has made me stronger and wiser. It has also made me more reliant upon God and His ways. I will never discount what the Lord is doing in me or dismiss what the Lord desires to do through me. God does have a success plan for me, and I am absolutely positive it will be accomplished.

"How can I help other people? I can create opportunities and open doors to assist someone in their time of need."

"The righteous man is rescued from trouble, and it comes on
the wicked instead."—Proverbs 11:8

"A generous man will prosper; he who refreshes others will
himself be refreshed."—Proverbs 11:25

"O LORD, do not forsake me; be not far from me, O my God.
Come quickly to help me, O LORD my Savior."
—Psalm 38:21–22

Blessings Are Coming

The Lord encouraged me with the following words: "The blessing are coming, the blessings are coming! I have opened up the windows of my storehouse and am pouring blessings out that you will not be able to contain; you will give to others and give even more.

"Blessings are falling even now. Rejoice, for these are given for you to bless others as I bless you. Rejoice, rejoice, and again I say rejoice!"

"God, I rejoice in You for the great things you have done, are doing, and will do in the future. You are my God, the one I serve all the days of my life."

How to Get Through Setbacks

How can we move through problems more quickly, or is it even possible? That is the question I pondered. I finally concluded that our role in any trial is to be obedient; trust in God; lean on His understanding and timing; seek and apply the Word; pray and then listen, listen, and listen some more; and always help others. At the end of the day, no matter what we do or don't do, it all begins and ends with our relationship with God and then with others.

My separation did not mean God didn't love me. It was about Lynn and me and how God would help us work through it. However, both Lynn and I had our own free wills to make our own decisions about how to handle our relationship with God and each other.

Don't Just Survive—Thrive!

When you are facing a trial, first submit yourself to God. Acknowledge that He is God and you are not. Then actively resist the devil, the enemy of your soul. As part of that spiritual resistance, you've got to put on your battle gear. No soldier would enter battle unequipped, and neither should you when you are facing a spiritual battle.

Ephesians 6:11–17 describes the spiritual armor we must wear as we engage the enemy: (1) The *belt of truth* keeps us from being controlled by our emotions. (2) The *breastplate of righteousness* guards our hearts. (3) The *readiness on our feet* comes from the gospel of peace that keeps us alert and ready. (4) The *shield of faith* repels the devil's flaming arrows. (4) The *helmet of salvation* guards our minds and protects our trust in our relationship with God. (5) The *sword of the Spirit*, the Word of God, is the offensive weapon we wield against the enemy.

So much of the battle takes place in our minds. We must always remember, "If God is for us, who can be against us?" (Romans 8:31).

Knowing this, to give up in the day of battle is foolish. Push on and find the place of your calling!

God Is a Mighty Tower in Times of Trouble

In the day of trouble, run *to* God, not away from Him. That may seem obvious, but it was a valuable lesson for me to learn.

"Is God capable of restoring my marriage? The answer is unequivocally yes! God is capable of all things. The truth is, in my own strength, I can do nothing of lasting benefit.

"God has promised to be with me every step of the way and to work in me and through me to accomplish His purposes. I can do all things God calls me to do because God is at work in me to do them. My confidence is valid only when I place my trust in God and rely on Him to get the job done.

"I'm placing all I've got in Him and His will for my marriage. I expect to have my marriage put back together and never to be the husband I was in the past. I must keep my emotions under control as I press towards the goal of restoration. I will have many opportunities to become frustrated and perhaps even angry. I must relax and know the battle is not against Lynn, but against the devil, the world, and the past.

"I am determined to keep my focus on God, His love, His help, and His approval. He is not going to disappoint me, fail me, reject me, or criticize the things that I do with a heart of love and a desire to obey."

Being a "God" Man by Applying the Lessons Learned in the Fire

"The changes I have made must be long-lasting, day-to-day changes for the better. Following the world's ways is not worth the pain it causes others. From this day forward, I must always walk after the Lord.

"I want to love God and love people so as to serve both for greater success. I want to serve the whole body of believers and to seek out the lost and share the great news of Christ with them. God

is impressed only by my obedience, faith, and reliance upon Him to guide me in all matters."

"Give, and it will be given to you. A good measure, pressed down, shaken together and running over, will be poured into your lap. For with the measure you use, it will be measured back to you." — Luke 6:38

"I must pursue righteousness, goodness, faith, love, patience, and gentleness rather than riches. Whether I have little or much, I must stay in the Word of God."

"The way of a fool seems right to him, but a wise man listens to advice." — Proverbs 12:15

"I waited patiently for the LORD; he turned to me and heard my cry. He lifted me out of the slimy pit, out of the mud and mire; he set my feet on a rock and gave me a firm place to stand. . . . Do not withhold your mercy from me, O LORD; may your love and your truth always protect me. . . . Be pleased, O LORD, to save me; O LORD, come quickly to help me. . . . Yet I am poor and needy; may the Lord think of me. You are my help and my deliverer; O my God, do not delay!" — Psalm 40:1–2, 11, 13, and 17

Count Your Blessings and Name Them One by One

"I took some time today to count my blessings and actually list them. At the top of my list were my relationships with God, Kayla, my mother, and the rest of my family. Also, I am happy in life and getting better. I have peace of mind and spirit. My meditations and studies of God's Word are bringing about fruit in my life. I am more relaxed, patient, and calm. I have my health. I truly love God and people more now than ever before. I have a good job with a good company, and all my bills are paid."

Meeting with Joanne

My next meeting with Joanne was quite productive. We talked about the five stages of grief and how they applied to me in my separation from Lynn: (1) The first stage is *denial*, characterized by the shock that something so catastrophic could happen to me. (2) Next comes *anger*, and I recalled my meltdown in November. (3) *Bargaining* follows, and this was the stage where I began giving up things and changing my life in hopes of reconciliation. (4) *Depression* comes next, characterized by crying and an inability or desire to take constructive steps towards resolving the grief. (5) Finally, *acceptance* comes in the final stage. At this point, I will be able to live life fully again, making good decisions as I walk into my future.

Joanne wisely pointed out that Lynn needed to feel separation from me right now. She needed this from the beginning, but all I had done was try to reconcile the relationship. She needed space and time to decide the future of our marriage.

We also had a conversation on control and my need to walk through actions in my head before acting them out. Though I was getting better in this area, I still needed to improve.

Furthermore, I still needed to work on breaking those cycles of thought that brought me pain. Joanne encouraged me to stay in the moment, focus on the things I needed to do and not do, and then take one step at a time. I couldn't afford to let my mind drift to negative thoughts that I could not control.

She ended the session by emphasizing that I needed to stay positive and realize that I was blessed. One way or another, everything would work out. Even if the marriage itself was not saved, I was growing stronger and stronger in God and becoming spiritually healthier.

All Changes Must Be Permanent

"I am at peace in my life because of the work God is doing. His Word, prayer, counsel, and the Spirit are helping me overcome my grief and pain. But I want and need more than that; I want to serve God and walk after His ways all the days of my life.

"Once Lynn is back home, it can't and won't stop there. I believe, Lord, that You have a ministry for both of us going forward. The past is the past. Open new doors, bring us new friends, and give us new relationships that build on our godly foundation.

"I ask for blessings of Your Spirit and right hand this morning. May our family have God's success today—Your way, the straight and narrow way!"

The Need for Hope and Faith in God—Not Fear

"When fear strikes, I need to face it head-on. I have been afraid of failure that would lead to rejection from Lynn. I have openly shared that fear with her, Pastor Doug, Joanne, and my accountability partners. I have been open with God as well.

"I am trying hard to overcome my fears, and I am building my faith. I know Jesus is my only real hope for the future. I cannot place my hope in Lynn and what she does; she will make her own decisions. I need my hope to be in the Lord alone!"

"So we say with confidence, 'The Lord is my helper; I will not be afraid. What can man do to me?' "—Hebrews 13:6

"Lynn or other people can do many things to me, but they can't take away my salvation, my relationship with Jesus, or my eternal destination in heaven. They cannot take away my joy, contentment, and the inner strength that the Lord imparts to me.

"Lord, help me right now in my situation. Help Lynn as well in her situation. As Your will is done, bring us together as one."

"So do not fear, for I am with you; do not be dismayed, for I am your God. I will strengthen you and help you; I will uphold you with my righteous right hand. . . . For I am the LORD, your God, who takes hold of your right hand and says to you, Do not fear; I will help you." Isaiah 41:10, 13

There are four things the Lord promises to give us: (1) His presence, (2) His power, (3) His provision, and (4) His protection against all our enemies. If we obey God and continue to move forward in pursuit of the goals He has helped us to set, He will find a way to work all of our losses into a pattern that is positive and of eternal benefit to us. He will make us strong in areas where we have been weak. He will turn all things to good! Seek to please God. Seek to fulfill what He has called you to do in every situation of life.

"I go through cycles of fear for the future. I fear Lynn leaving for good. I fear Lynn saying she wants a divorce. I fear she will reject all the changes I have made. I fear she will continue to be involved with the man from Canada.

"I also know that nothing good comes from fear. I need to confront these fears because they do not come from the Lord. I have faith in Jesus Christ; He knows what is going to happen, and He is in my life to help me through it and make something great out of it. I can overcome my fears through prayer, reading God's Word, and the power of His Spirit."

"I can do everything through him who gives me strength."
—Philippians 4:13

"And my God will meet all your needs according to his glorious riches in Christ Jesus."—Philippians 4:19

"Until now you have not asked for anything in my name. Ask and you will receive, and your joy will be complete."
—John 16:24

"Ask and it will be given to you; seek and you will find; knock and the door will be opened to you."—Matthew 7:7

"Haven't you read," he replied, "that at the beginning the Creator 'made them male and female,' and said 'For this reason a man will leave his father and mother and be united to his wife, and the two will become one flesh'? So they are not longer two, but one. Therefore what God has joined together, let man not separate."—Matthew 19:4–6

"God wants me to love Lynn, and He wants Lynn to love me. He wants me to leave my father and mother and cleave unto Lynn to nourish, cherish, admire, and respect her, as the Word of God instructs. Lord, I trust You to do this in my life and also in the life of Lynn."

The Need to Forgive Myself

"If God forgives me every time I confess my sins to Him, then I must forgive myself! I find it so hard to forgive myself for some of my behaviors, words, and actions of the past twenty-six years. I know I was not perfect, and I tried to make up for my shortcomings with gifts and vacations instead of what Lynn really wanted, which was to be treated fairly at all times.

"I keep confessing my sins and asking God for forgiveness, but I need to forgive myself of my shortcomings. I can never be perfect, but I can always be better."

Perfectionism or Christlike Nature?

"Over the years, my pursuit of the things of this world has hurt my ability to serve God and fulfill His perfect will for my life. When I sinned, I became negative and vocal about others' imperfections while I tried harder to be perfect.

"The key word is try; *only God can be perfect, and I am not Him. Over the years, my life, based upon my efforts to be perfect, became unbalanced; and that is when I fell even more for the world and its enticements.*

"I now realize that I must daily nurture a longing to be more Christlike. When I stay close to God's nature and His Word, my relationships are always better, and my conduct reflects Christ's nature better. I will never be perfect here on earth, but I can be pleasing to God, Lynn, Kayla, my family, friends, and all other people.

"I must continue to push forward in my quest for godly goals in my life. Then I will turn away from sin and reject every temptation. I have tried this before, and like a diet, it starts out well but soon ends in failure. I must make this a lifestyle this time, not a diet of short duration."

"Ask and it will be given to you; seek and you will find; knock and the door will be opened to you. For everyone who asks receives; and he who seeks finds; and to him who knocks, the door will be opened. Which of you, if his son asks for bread, will give him a stone? Or if he asks for a fish, will he give him a snake? If you, then, though you are evil, know how to give good gifts to your children, how much more will your Father in heaven give good gifts to those who ask him! So in everything, do to others what you would have them do to you, for this sums up the Law and the Prophets."—Matthew 7:7–12

God's Leading Is What I Need

"I need to always be asking God what He wants from me, my life, my family, and my work, as well as what is pleasing to Him in my actions, deeds, and focus. I know that obedience is what God most desires from me, now and into the future. That means I must listen to Him and go in the direction He wants me to go. I must also turn away from my sinful habits and turn to the Holy Spirit and the Word for my pleasures.

"I need to continue on this pathway of sowing only goodness into my life. I did not enjoy life to the fullest when I was sowing seeds of the fleshly nature. Life just kept moving along, but I lacked the joy, peace, love, kindness, goodness, gentleness, and patience needed to really enjoy life. Lynn saw that, Kayla saw that, and other people saw it as well. I don't fool anyone when I am away from God's goodness."

"Finally, brothers, whatever is true, whatever is noble, whatever is right, whatever is pure, whatever is lovely, whatever is admirable—if anything is excellent or praiseworthy—think about such things."—Philippians 4:8

Meeting with Accountability Partners

During this time in my journey, I regularly met with my account-ability partners. We discussed things going on in our lives and shared issues to pray for. It was great to know that God, not me, was in control of my life. I truly believed great victories lay ahead and the time was drawing near when Lynn and I would be back together again. However, I did continue to pray for God's perfect timing and perfect will, knowing it would not come a moment early or a moment late. Until then, I asked Him to continue blessing both of us and to build us up for the days ahead, days that would be filled with blessings from His throne room.

"I can do everything through him who gives me strength."—
Philippians 4:13

"My life today is the outcome of all I have thought about through the years to this very moment. That includes my thoughts while in the world, my thoughts while serving Christ, and my thoughts while married. I need to change my thought life through the Word of God and the things of God."

Chapter 6

God's Hand Moves! Marriage Counseling and *Fireproof*

"May the God of hope fill you with all joy and peace as you trust in him, so that you may overflow with hope by the power of the Holy Spirit."
—Romans 15:13

"Put to death, therefore, whatever belongs to your earthy nature: sexual immorality, impurity, lust, evil desires and greed, which is idolatry. Because of these, the wrath of God is coming. You used to walk in these ways, in the life you once lived. But now you must rid yourselves of all such things as these: anger, rage, malice, slander, and filthy language from your lips. Do not lie to each other, since you have taken off your old self with its practices and have put on the new self, which is being renewed in knowledge in the image of its Creator."
—Colossians 3:5–10

The Need to Change My Thoughts and Behaviors

Our thoughts and behavior determine our character. Our character, in turn, impacts our decisions, and our decisions determine our level of success. The reality is, the way we think and feel about ourselves will be projected in the way we behave towards God, our families, friends, and communities. The way men think about and treat their wives is the way their wives will feel about themselves as partners in the marriage.

"Lynn is a gift from God to me and the world. She is a beloved child of the most high God. She is developing and growing according to God's plan, and although she makes mistakes, she is trying to overcome them. Seeing her in this light, makes me treat her with much greater kindness, generosity, affection, acceptance, and forgiveness. The reality is, all this and so much more is the truth about her."

Lynn Is My Partner and One Filled with Wisdom

I prayed fervently for Lynn and me to reunite quickly. I truly missed my life partner, wife, best friend, and lover. I needed her counsel, wisdom, and knowledge. I needed her as a sounding board to bounce things off of. With her gone, it felt like half of me was missing.

"Lord, I pray for Your will to be done according to Your Word. Pour forth love into Lynn and me. May we be a couple again, but in a much better way than ever before. Bless our marriage, and perform a miracle today on our behalf."

Words from God

"Why do you let the evil one toss you back and forth? I have given you words of hope and promise for the future. I have given you the Spirit, the Word, and power to overcome the darts of Satan. Do not listen, take in, or dwell on defeat.

"I have blessed you, given you great gifts, and set your feet on the rock. You are gifted to do My work. Fear not, for My mighty right hand is at work. Renew your mind; keep hope and strength in Me and My words. Stay the course you have set with My guidance.

"I am well pleased with your growth and spirit. Continue to walk after My ways, continue to be obedient, and continue to search for souls that need My touch. When they present themselves to you, be prepared to minister to their needs."

"So if you think you are standing firm, be careful that you don't fall! No temptation has seized you except what is common to man. And God is faithful; he will not let you be tempted beyond what you can bear. But when you are tempted, He will also provide a way out so that you can stand up under it."—1 Corinthians 10:12–13

"Bring the Rain If That Is What It Takes"

"I hear these words in a song and feel strongly about them. I want God's rain in my life, and He is my only shelter from the storm. Lord, I draw closer to You through these times, so I pray that You bring me joy, peace, and a chance to be free. Bring me anything that brings You glory.

"I know there will be days when this life brings me pain. But if that's what it takes to praise You, Jesus, then bring the rain. I am Yours, regardless of the dark clouds that may loom above. You are much greater than my pain. You made a way for me by suffering Your destiny. So tell me, what's a little rain?"

It's All About the True Definition of Love

"Holy, holy, holy is my loving God, who cares for me and accepts me for who I am, who gives me a chance to redeploy my behaviors and grow within His own love."

"If I speak in the tongues of men and of angels, but have not love, I am only a resounding gong or a clanging cymbal. If I have the gift of prophecy and can fathom all mysteries and all knowledge, and if I have a faith that can move mountains, but have not love, I am nothing. If I give all I possess to the poor and surrender my body to the flames, but have not love, I gain nothing. Love is patient, love is kind. It does not envy, it does not boast, it is not proud. It is not rude, it is not self-seeking, it is not easily angered, it keeps no record of wrongs. Love does not delight in evil but rejoices with the truth. It always protects, always trusts, always hopes, and always perseveres.

Love never fails. . . . And now these three remain: faith, hope, and love. But the greatest of these is love."—1 Corinthians 13:1–8, 13

"I have not loved Lynn as I should have or could have in the past. Lord, make a way to her heart so I can have a chance to love her the way Your Word says to love and the way she wants to be loved. I know I have grown and can love the way I should. Break down the walls and make a pathway to Lynn's heart that is open to my love.

"I cherish Lynn in a new way based upon my growth and my putting away of my foolish sins. Pour Your love, for You and for each other, into our hearts. I see now what a wonderful person Lynn is and how badly I treated her. If given the chance by Lynn and You, I can make this up to her in the days, weeks, months, and years ahead.

"Open the floodgates, Lord God. I need a miracle to happen in my marriage and Lynn's heart. Grab hold of her heart, break the hardness, and turn her attention back to the loves of her youth, You and me. I ask in Jesus' name that this mountain move!"

"Therefore, my dear brothers, stand firm. Let nothing move you. Always give yourselves fully to the work of the Lord, because you know that your labor in the Lord is not in vain."—1 Corinthians 15:58

"Be on your guard; stand firm in the faith; be men of courage; be strong. Do everything in love." —1 Corinthians 16:13

"God, I know You are a God of second chances, and I need another chance with Lynn. I know she has free will and a mind of her own. But please speak to her spirit as I ask her to give me a second chance to make things right between us."

"The righteous cry out, and the Lord hears them; he delivers them from all their troubles. The Lord is close to the brokenhearted and saves those who are crushed in spirit. A righteous man may have many troubles, but the Lord delivers him from them all."—Psalm 34:17–19

Can That Which Has Snapped Be Mended?

"Lord, as You did with David, do the same with me! Deliver me from all my fears, and give me a spirit of love, power, and a sound mind. I put my trust, faith, and hope in You and Your ways. I want to walk uprightly every day of my life. I need Your angels encamped around me and all Your plans to come about in Your perfect timing.

"Lord, I do not want to continue in a broken marriage. Fill my heart and Lynn's with Your pure love and care. I want forgiveness to reign in our marriage. Help us both to find our true identity in You and to be centered in You going forward. Lord, I am crying out to You for our marriage. Bless it, unify it, break down the walls, and build up love. Seek out the lost, confused, and pained parts of our hearts, and give us peace, comfort, and wisdom.

"I take You at Your Word, Lord. Deliver Lynn and me from pain, fear, confusion, separation, hurt, unforgiveness, and lost feelings. Bind, blend, unite, and pour feelings into our hearts. Most important of all, give us love for You, ourselves, and each other, as well as for other people, starting with Kayla. May both Lynn and I take refuge in You and Your ways this day and every day going forward."

"Set your minds on things above, not on things on the earth."—Colossians 3:2

The Need for Peaceful Sleep

"I have asked the Lord to give me peace at night so I can sleep through the night without getting up several times and without thinking about Lynn constantly through each hour. Most nights I wake up hourly in sweats and torment. I need to forgive myself and Lynn, and I also need to daily let go of anxieties, troubles, hurts, and struggles within my own head. I need God to fill my mind with thoughts of His goodness, grace, and love towards me."

"Why, you do not even know what will happen tomorrow. What is your life? You are a mist that appears for a little while and then banishes."—James 4:14

Using the Righteous Tools of God

"I have just the right amount of time to do what God has ordained for me to do today. I want nothing but what God wants for me today and every day going forward. I must focus on the Bible, prayer, church, and sharing my faith. This is using my time wisely for the Lord. My success in marriage, life, and in Christ Himself is all wrapped up in my walk with Christ Jesus."

"I can do everything through him who gives me strength." — Philippians 4:13

All Journeys Come with God's Provision

God promises to be with us, provide for us, empower us, and give us courage to accomplish His goals. With God's help, we cannot fail; we will succeed in His perfect will and plan.

I truly believed God was on my side and that He was equipping me, providing daily for me, and empowering me to do what He was calling me to do in the days ahead. As I applied God's principles, I began discovering that the truths of the Bible worked.

God was requiring something of me, and that was to walk through the pain. He knew this day would come, and He also knew I would need His equipping in order to make it. I trusted He would provide all the knowledge, wisdom, and resources I needed to get through this ordeal. I was determined to learn and not fail in life, to succeed at the level He wanted me to succeed during this time.

"Lord, You will provide everything I need to successfully move through this period of my life. I will always ask for Your guidance each step of my way. The Holy Spirit will reveal all the details I need and where, how, and who will help during this event. I trust the Holy Spirit and His guidance. He will equip me fully for all He has called me to do!

"Lord, I do have doubts about what will happen in the days ahead. I do not want them, and I fight them daily. I know I must overcome them and believe in You and what You want. I must come

to grips with my doubts. If I do not, they will paralyze me and harm me long-term. I need to get my mind off the doubts and fears and turn to the Lord!"

"The one who calls you is faithful and he will do it."
—1 Thessalonians 5:24

"Give, and it will be given to you. A good measure, pressed down, shaken together and running over, will be poured into your lap. For with the measure you use it, it will be measured to you." —Luke 6:38

When we are incapable, God is able. When we are weak, He is strong. When we don't know, He knows. When we are powerless, He is all-powerful. When we don't have the answers, He does. The Lord is capable of handling any separation, the enemy that lurks nearby or within, and the loneliness we experience anytime or anywhere. God is with us always! He will never, ever, leave us or forsake us.

Meeting with Joanne

My next meeting with Joanne was productive, as always. She gave me a great deal of valuable advice. Right now, she said, it was all about me and the world. It was about me, the individual, so I needed to focus on myself and stay in the moment.

"Don't call Lynn," she cautioned. "Leave all calls, e-mails, and face-to-face meetings up to her. Stay in the moment; engage people, read the Bible, pray, help others, watch movies, and keep doing your tae kwon do. Keep everything centered on what is happening in your life."

Joanne continued: "The cycle of grief you are going through is normal. A person can work through all five stages and then go back through them, or they might just bounce through them. Be grounded and centered on who you are. Make decisions based upon where you are in life. Work from your own energy, not Lynn's."

During this meeting, Joanne also wisely pointed out that Kayla was not a part of this situation between Lynn and me, so we needed to leave her out of it. Kayla did not need to know how it was going between Lynn and me.

Additionally, Joanne warned me that I couldn't keep Lynn by giving her everything she wanted and needed, in regards to money and material items. Lynn needed to love me for me, not stay with me because of money or gifts I gave her.

Finally, she ended the session by saying, "Cut all ropes that are tethers to you and just see what happens!"

Raising the White Flag of Surrender

"I give up, Lord, and can do no more! I have prayed, had others pray, talked to people so they could connect with Lynn, changed myself, and sucked up to Lynn. I have given her space, attention, money, gifts, cards, pictures, and everything else—including control. I can do no more! It's Your turn, God—Your play! I have reached my end; I have no hope in myself. I know I can change neither the future nor Lynn's heart. If we are to get back together, it will come only by You, Lord God—not from me, not from Lynn, and not from the people around us. Help, help, help, Jesus!"

"The LORD is my light and my salvation—whom shall I fear? The LORD is the stronghold of my life—of whom shall I be afraid? . . . One thing I ask of the LORD, this is what I seek: that I may dwell in the house of the LORD all the days of my life, to gaze upon the beauty of the LORD and to seek him in his temple. For in the day of trouble he will keep me safe in His dwelling. . . . I am still confident of this: I will see the goodness of the LORD in the land of the living. Wait for the LORD; be strong and take heart and wait for the LORD."—
Psalm 27:1, 4–5, 13–14

Keep Looking, Keep Seeking, and Keep Believing

"There are better days ahead for me! God has an ever-growing plan and purpose for me. There is no justification in God's Word for remaining discouraged or giving up. When all others see no future

in my marriage, I will continue to believe God has a bright future for it tomorrow and the rest of my life."

"Suppose one of you has a hundred sheep and loses one of them. Does he not leave the ninety-nine in the open country and go after the lost sheep until he finds it? And when he finds it, he joyfully puts it on his shoulder and goes home. Then he calls his friends and neighbors together and says, 'Rejoice with me; I have found my lost sheep.' I tell you that in the same way there will be more rejoicing in heaven over one sinner who repents than over ninety-nine righteous persons who do not need to repent. Or suppose a woman has ten silver coins and loses one. Does she not light a lamp, sweep the house and search carefully until she finds it? And when she finds it, she calls her friends and neighbors together and says, 'Rejoice with me; I have found my lost coin.' In the same way, I tell you, there is rejoicing in the presence of the angels of God over one sinner who repents." — Luke 15:4–10

"My persistence is required if I am to overcome discouragement in my lack of relationship with Lynn. Persistence is vital to my success because pain, heartache, discouragement, and delays have occurred in the past four months. When it will end, I do not know; but I will persist in my quest to overcome the loss and reunite in the future.

"A friend told me recently that at times in his marriage, his wife had to carry the marriage while he did other things; then, in other years of their marriage, he had to put in the greater effort to carry the marriage. At the end of life, their marriage will still be intact because it had two partners working together to keep love alive.

"Over the years as we moved around the country, Lynn was the one who bore the greater burden of carrying our marriage. Now it is my turn to keep the marriage alive. I am willing to carry our relationship for as long as I have to. Lynn is well worth it, and I am willing to do everything necessary during this time. Fair is fair in marriage! We have not failed unless we give up."

"A man's steps are directed by the LORD. How then can anyone understand his own way?"—Proverbs 20:24

Regardless of My Problems, the Lord Must Be First

"I am now realizing I have placed so much focus on Lynn and our marriage that I haven't put the Lord first in all things. May I put You first, Lord God, from this day forward. I want to love You with all my heart, mind, soul, and body. May my focus be on You first, Lord, and then on the love of others. May Your commands, decrees, and directions be my direction and focus going forward. Bless me with Your presence, oh Lord my God!"

Out of the Blue, Lynn Calls

The hand of God fell one night, and perfect alignment occurred. For the first time in several days, Lynn called, and she asked about a book that I had loaned to a friend a year earlier (*Battlefield of the Mind*). Unknown to me at the time, my friend had lost the book, along with several other items. Somehow the police had come into possession of the book and used the address on the inside cover to track down Lynn and tell her she could retrieve it from them. She in turn called me, and I explained to her what had happened and said I would pick the book up in the near future. This was the first phone call and communication between Lynn and me in fifteen days.

While we were on the phone, we also had a two-hour conversation regarding the place we were in as a couple. We were at a fork in the road: we could seek marriage counseling, or Lynn could seek a divorce. After a long time, she said I could set up marriage counseling with a man or woman, Christian or not Christian, whomever I wanted. In my heart, I praised God for her decision, and hope for the future sprang alive within me.

Without a doubt, I knew we needed God's perfect will and guidance to make this work. We both agreed that if the counselor said, after meeting with us, that there was no hope, I would not stand in Lynn's way to obtain a divorce. My hope was in God and His Word, and deep down inside, I believed Lynn and I still shared a deep love for each other. I still felt sure that God had a plan and purpose for our life together, including some type of ministry. I prayed we could find a counselor for the very next day, a person that we both trusted and felt comfortable with.

After the phone call with Lynn, I immediately called several friends to have them start praying for God's will to take place and for doors to open, including getting into a counselor the next day.

"If you are pleased with me, teach me your ways so I may know you and continue to find favor with you."
—Exodus 33:13

"God will reveal Himself to Lynn and me. But before He does, we must come to a point where we surrender to Him in all aspects of our lives. I hope that Lynn and I are both at that point of total surrender."

"As the deer pants for streams of water, so my soul pants for you, O God. My soul thirsts for God, for the living God. When can I go and meet with God?"—Psalm 42:1–2

"For the Lord your God is a merciful God; he will not abandon or destroy you."—Deuteronomy 4:31

"Come near to God and he will come near to you."
—James 4:8

Everything Passes Through God the Father

"I must realize that whatever comes my way passes through the loving hands of the Savior first. Yes, God knows what is going to happen in my life and will be there to see me through the lowest of days as well as my best days."

"The LORD is my rock, my fortress and my deliverer; my God is my rock, in whom I take refuge. He is my shield and the hour of my salvation, my stronghold. I call to the LORD, who is worthy of praise, and I am saved from my enemies."
—Psalm 18:2–3

"God's love, strength, and abiding care are anchors to my heart and soul in times of great distress. I am in great distress, and I need an open door for the counseling that is ahead of both Lynn and me. We were in love for many years, and I believe we still have a future together if we will give each other a second chance. May this counseling time enable Lynn and me to reach back into the past to find the love we once shared or, better yet, a new and exciting love for each other."

Phone Call with Doug

I also talked to Doug late that evening, and he shared some wise counsel with me. "Be patient, and let things unfold as they will if given the time," he advised. "Let Lynn take the lead in the conversations ahead. Stay away from your own thoughts on her feelings because they might just be wrong in the first place! After counseling, don't automatically view Lynn's responses as negative."

"The great news is," he reminded me, "Lynn is willing to go to counseling and, better yet, Christian counseling. Also remember, you asked Lynn to go see *Fireproof* on Saturday night, and she is willing to go."

After our conversation, I felt sure better days were ahead in my relationship with Lynn.

Setting up Christian Counseling

I called the office of a Christian counselor the next morning at 8:32 a.m. Before making the call, however, I read the bios of the various counselors and selected two as my preferences. God provided a meeting at 1:00 p.m. with the woman I had selected, but we were instructed to come at 12:30 p.m. in order to first fill out forms.

When we arrived at the office, the receptionist stated, "It must be your day because we had a cancellation today." In fact, while we were there, another couple was told the time was double-booked and they would have to come back at 3:00 p.m. Lynn and I, however, were able to get in at 1:00 p.m. as planned.

I firmly believed that the hand of God was still upon our marriage and that success would take place for Lynn and me in the near future. Over the past five months, I had talked much, acted, pressured, used other people, and pushed Lynn, but with little to no results. I was done—I had no more to give and could not do another thing on my own. I finally yielded my marriage to God for His perfect plan and will to take place. As best I could, I surrendered completely to God and His timing. The results and outcome were now His alone. I purposed in my heart to accept His will and plan and to stay under His covering, regardless of what He wanted or Lynn decided.

Counseling Takes Place

In our first counseling session, Gwen, our counselor, asked a lot of questions. At the end, she shared with Lynn and me that she did not think we were ready for marriage counseling at this time. Needless to say, I was quite angry and upset with her remark. *Who is she to say that, and why did she even say it?* I fumed.

I had taken notes during the session, and when I looked at them later, I concluded that Gwen made her statement based upon the way Lynn had answered several questions. "Why counsel now, Lynn?" Gwen had asked.

"Because Steve wanted me to come, and other people said I should before making any other decisions. Plus, I owe it to Steve," Lynn had answered. Speaking again, she said, "I have no feelings towards Steve, and I do not know if I am in love or even can be again with him."

Gwen did say we could continue counseling, if we wanted to. It was up to Lynn and me to decide on our future.

What Does the Future Hold? I Do Not Know!

We walked out of the counseling session, and Lynn and I talked in the lobby for about an hour on what we should do. At one point, I thought Lynn was going to say she wanted a divorce, but then all of a sudden she said, "How do I know you've changed?"

I proceeded to share all the positive things I had been doing and finally said, "You just need to go all in and see for yourself." Gwen had suggested that we start going on dates together for Lynn to see the new me, and I shared my desire to do just that. But Lynn was reluctant, though she did agree to another counseling session next week, for which we made an appointment.

"How can I respect Lynn in the ways she wants? Until I learn how to abide in Christ, my life will be marked by moments of poorly orchestrated decisions about the future. Only God knows why He drew me aside, but I feel it was to bring focus and spiritual depth to my life. I do have my focus on Him now, and my spiritual man is growing daily as I seek Him and His ways through the Word. I know He wants me to do His will. For that matter, I know He wants Lynn to do His will as well. We both have things to learn through this time in our lives.

"I want to learn the right things, not continue the cycle of ups and downs that I have struggled with for most of my life. There are better days ahead if I put my trust in the Lord and behave like a true man of God with the Spirit inside me. That is my quest above all else, including what I want for Lynn and our marriage.

"However, with my first focus on loving God, my other relationships, starting with Lynn, will also become pleasing to all involved. When my life is committed totally to God, He will be able to take this separation and use it for His glory. I want to completely surrender to God and His will. This is what enables me to face each and every day with hope."

"The LORD will give strength to his people; the LORD blesses
his people with peace."—Psalm 29:11.

134

"Cast your cares on the LORD and he will sustain you; he will
never let the righteous fall."—Psalm 55:22

Words from God

"If you just knew what I have planned for you! If you could only
understand that the best lies ahead of you. If you could only realize
that walking outside My ways is very difficult. If you could truly
understand that My ways are better than your ways. If you could but
know that My plans and purposes are far greater than anything you
could do on your own for yourself! I have all the resources at My
command. I know your heart's desires. Many of these I have given
to you, but to enjoy them, you must walk in My ways."

*"Going forward, I will walk in Your ways. I do not want to miss
Your perfect plan for my life. Lord, open my eyes to see Your plan
and calling through all this. I want to obey You, follow after You, and
listen to every word You share with me. I will move when You want
me to move and stay when You want me to stay. I know You are an all-
knowing God. Open my mind so I can walk in perfect harmony with
Your Spirit.*

*"This is a new day with new blessings from You, Lord. I look for-
ward to Your guiding hand on my life today. I want to obey You completely. I want to focus on You and be about building Your kingdom!"*

In my daily time with God, I also took some time to evaluate
where I was and what God might be trying to teach me in the process.
These were some of my thoughts:

What can I gain from this experience with Lynn?

- A deeper love for God and right fellowship with Him
- A deeper love for Lynn and how to show her proper respect
- A deeper love for Kayla and developing my relationship
  with her
- A deeper love for others and valuing their opinions

- Reduced or no desire for the world and its pleasures
- Helping out mankind by using the blessings God has given me

"Inspired by Lynn's involvement with Toys for Tots over the holidays, I decided that I, too, need to be involved with serving others. I signed up to serve meals to the homeless. This is the first time I have ever done something like this. In the past, I have given money and thought that was enough; however, I now realize God wants more from me. I have now served twice, and it is a real eye-opener to see the hurting in my community."

What does God want me to learn?

- Obedience to Him and His ways—always
- Belief that He has a plan for Lynn and me
- Realization that it's not always about me, but it is always about God working through me
- Knowledge that God is God and I am not!
- Forgiveness to everyone, starting with myself
- Respect for others, but most of all, Lynn.
- Lesson of leaning on the Father in all things

What is God saying to me?

- He is in control.
- My marriage will be healed.
- Lynn and I have a ministry in the future.
- Relationships will be rebuilt.
- Obey, obey, obey, and when I think I have obeyed, obey God and His Word even more.
- Never, ever turn back to the world or the things in it.

"Even in my darkest hours, I know God hears my heart-wrenching prayers to Him. I know through His Word that His promises are based upon His conditional promises to me as well as His absolutes. Concerning the conditional, I must do something and then God will

do something. I believe God works in my life mostly through conditional methods. But there are also the absolutes, the things God has planned and will do what no matter what. For instance, He decided to bring Christ into the world, and it took place at just the right time and location."

Never Give Up on God's Promises!

"I woke up this morning crying out to God and surrendering all. God did His surgery in my whole body, and I will not be the same man I once was. I am becoming more Christlike by the day. Jesus is the one I seek first and foremost in my life. I am now getting to a level I have never experienced before!

"Lord, take me to higher levels, and continue to show me Your ways and the path for my life. I want all of You before I seek anything else in this world. Show me who You are, and open my eyes so I can see completely Your will for me life."

Words from God

"My son, write down these words I am about to give you. Do not turn to the right or left to seek the answers for your life. I am the answer-giver, and I am the one who blesses your path. The journey has been long, but the journey is not yet complete. I am getting you to a place where you can rely completely on me for every aspect of your life. I am burning out the old nature and burning in the new. The time is coming when you will rise up and take the place I give you at that time. My hand of blessing will be on the words you speak and the direction you go, and My Spirit will flow out of you. Prepare yourself for the journey by the Word, My Spirit, and My love.

"The time of blessing is coming. My storehouse windows are open, and the blessings are flowing even now into your soul. Your pocketbook will be filled, and people will be amazed how the filling continues. It will be like the widow and her son of old. The flow will continue, and people you don't even know are preparing to bless you! These blessings are coming from My throne room, so the praise and glory are due to My name.

"Fear not, My son, for I am with you always and will not leave you or forsake you. I see the desires of your heart and will fill those that are due you and part of my plan and will. Miracles are coming, and doors are opening. Fear not, for I am in total control and will not allow destruction to come to your household. Walk free, walk upright, and walk in boldness."

"I must trust in the Lord, always do what is right, and follow Him no matter what man tells me. When I do, all will be well. Yes, trials and tribulations will come, but His glory and blessings will be there as I fight through the dark days and temptations."

I Cannot and Will Not Give Up on Lynn and Our Marriage

"I believe Lynn's hard heart will melt and is melting over time. I must give Lynn time to heal as I share my love in a respectful way time and time again. It's going to be a long road back to the early days and on to even better days, but it will be worth it in the long haul. I won't give up on Lynn, and I hope Lynn won't give up on me!

"Lynn and I are meeting at Sartell Middle School to watch the movie Fireproof. *We will not be sitting together, but at least she will be there. Afterwards, we are going out to the Blue Line restaurant. I wrote the following letter that I will give her tomorrow night at the restaurant":*

Dear Lynn,

I write this letter on Friday night, January 24, not knowing what tomorrow brings. I want you to know a few things, so please bear with me. First off, for many years I thought we had a good marriage and good relationship. We built a life together, full of nice things, great vacations, and good conversations, as well as raised a wonderful daughter together.

However, since you left, I have realized my view of marriage and my view of you were lacking in many ways. At times my actions towards you were more like those of a boss to an employee, and other times I was shortsighted, uncaring, and demeaning. Of course, as you stated this week, you felt you had to be at my beck and call, and my actions supported that view. All in all, I could have and should have done much better.

I regret many of my actions, my bold statements, and my attitude. The measuring stick I used to judge our marriage was the wrong one, and as a result, we are now separated. This pains me, and from our conversations, I know it has pained you as well. But I believe there is still hope for our marriage. We can change the path we are on and also change our future to have a marriage and partnership that can be the best for both of us!

The question you asked me the other day, "How do I know you have changed and will not go back to being the old Steve?" is a valid question, based upon my past. All I can say is that this time I have resolved the many issues that caused me to behave like I did, and I have once and for all put away the things that led to my poor behaviors. I now know what true love is; it is burned into my heart and soul daily.

Respect is the first and foremost thing I can give you. Respect is treating you like an equal, because you are. Respect is talking things out calmly and not getting upset and insisting on getting in the last word. Respect is treating you like a person who is loved and cherished, not as an employee. Respect is understanding that you have goals and plans and not demanding that you always be at my beck and call. Respect is speaking caring and kind words when you're down and need encouragement. Respect is not pointing out things that make you feel bad about yourself, but always looking for the best in you and our relationship. Respect is saying "Thank you," "I appreciate the help," and "Without you I couldn't have done this task," instead of yelling "I wish I had done it myself!" And last of all, respect is treating you with proper expectations in the bedroom. I have failed here many times over the years, and I am truly sorry. To always remember the importance of respect, I told you I would always open your car door in the future as an outward reminder to both of us of this commitment.

I also know I have lacked patience in many ways. When I am patient with things, I can handle life's twists and turns calmly and with the proper frame of mind. When I let this area of my life get out of control, I become controlling and angry and lash out. Counseling has helped me get to the root of this issue. Also, my quiet times and tae kwon do have helped center my mind. I also realize that caffeine and sugar have had a major impact in this area of my life.

I have learned to be kinder to people and to look for the best in them instead of being so picky about everything. Kindness is being positive, encouraging, and thoughtful, and it means going above and beyond, just "because." Kindness has replaced my many selfish ways; it has displaced my thinking that life is all about me, what I want and when I want it.

To help me go this deep into my soul, I began helping others and continue to look for ways to do this daily. I will never veer from the new course I have walked on for months now. It has given me peace, but even more important, it has given relief to those I work with and assisted people in the community.

Over the years, I have protected you from outside harm whenever possible. At the same time, I did not always protect you from my own behavior. My emotional relationship seven years ago with another woman was wrong and unbecoming for me as your husband. I know I hurt you badly and did not protect you as I should have. I realized that far too long in the process, but when I did, I knew the love I had for you was far greater than an emotional relationship with another. What made me realize that was not the hair you colored, the nails you painted, the weight loss you achieved, or the exercise we did together. It was the inner beauty, compassion, love, and care you had always shown in so many ways. I could never go for fool's gold when I had the real gold in you!

Lynn, your question this week spoke to me in many ways. I want you to see the real Steve of today and tomorrow, not dwell on the old Steve of the past. I believe I have established a track record over these past months, and I only wish you could see me on the inside and know how I have changed for the better in so many ways. To do that, however, you will need to have faith, and you will need to trust me at a deeper level than ever before.

I have kept the things you loved about me and added the things you always wanted from me. I want to love you for who you are on the inside. I want to love you with kindness, gentleness, and joy in our being together. Loving you on the inside is the highest level of respect I know. I have also made major improvements in my old tendency to try to control you. Freedom and goodness are needed by both of us in order to have fun together in life.

In closing, I have heard your concerns, pains, and frustrations and want to build a bridge back and a highway to the future together. If you let me into your life again and trust these words I have penned to paper, you will see that I am, always will be, and am becoming a man you can be proud to call your husband. If you will give me and yourself a chance to pursue a new life as a couple, I know great days are ahead for us.

Push all in, and see the great days ahead! That is my prayer for you.

Steve

The man you have always wanted and prayed for

Eyes of Love and Compassion

"I feel great headway has been made in the last twenty-four hours. After the movie, Lynn and I cried together over parts of it. It was some of what we have been through, and the feelings came out. We then went for a soda, and I gave Lynn the letter and told her to read it later.

"As we talked, I saw love, or at least compassion, in Lynn's eyes for the first time in months. I believe the movie broke off pieces of the wall around her heart, and I believe my letter will break off other pieces. But even more, I believe God is moving on Lynn's heart and mind.

"Lord, continue to move in both Lynn and me, and let the walls come tumbling down. In Your name I pray this. May the church service today continue the healing process, and may Your glory reign in our hearts and minds."

God Is Great All the Time

I slept great that night and woke up feeling wonderful the next morning, assured that God was in control of everything. Once more I purposed to obey Him and walk after His ways all the days of my life. It was freeing to walk in the ways of the Lord and to trust Him and His perfect timing.

I was also happy because Kayla had shared some great news the day before: she was coming home for all of spring break! It would be such a blessing to have her around for nearly ten days.

"Thank You God for giving Lynn and me such a blessing in Kayla. Continue to bless her in school and relationships, and draw her to You daily, Lord. Let her find her way back to You this day."

"I knew that you are a gracious and compassionate God, slow to anger and abounding in love, a God who relents from sending calamity."—Jonah 4:2

"I will trust God and believe that He is working, regardless of what I see or do not see. My God's ways are not limited to the way things seem on the surface. There is absolutely no limit to what my Savior can do when I give Him access to my life. When I give God everything, He has everything He needs. My obedience to Him and His ways combines my everything and His something to make a perfect plan achievable."

"Be still, and know that I am God; I will be exalted among the nations, I will be exalted in the earth."—Psalm 46:10

"No matter how much pain and suffering I go through, I must always remember God's love is deeper. He always has a fantastic purpose in mind for every trial and tribulation I face."

Meeting with Joanne

At this meeting, Joanne and I discussed the idea that if I consumed Lynn or she consumed me, then one of us would no longer exist. Over the years, I had consumed Lynn, and she had not liked it. But now I was working hard on the things in my life that needed to change, and I was going in the right direction. My actions over the past two weeks were making those changes obvious to Lynn. I had to remember that we were bone of bone and flesh of flesh, not spirit of spirit and soul of soul.

Letting God Lead the Way

"I have all the faith and hope in You, Lord, to cleanse me, change me, direct me, and open doors of faith for me. The days ahead will be blessed because You are leading me and I am focused on obeying Your will and ways. Thank You for saving me and putting me on the road to serving You with all my heart, mind, soul, and body."

"I love you, O LORD, my strength. The LORD is my rock, my fortress and my deliverer; my God is my rock, in whom I take refuge. He is my shield and the horn of my salvation, my stronghold. I call to the LORD, who is worthy of praise, and I am saved from my enemies. . . . In my distress I called to the LORD; I cried to my God for help. From his temple he heard my voice; my cry came before him into his ears. . . . As for God, his way is perfect; the word of the LORD is flawless. He is a shield for all who take refuge in him."
—Psalm 18:1–3, 6, 30

"I know beyond all doubt that nothing is coincidental in life. God is involved in or aware of every single event that takes place. He always keeps His Word and delivers on it in His timing and in His

way. God is going to use this time in my life and Lynn's to develop a fantastic testimony for His sake.

"I must have holiness and purity in my life daily and be totally committed to God and His plans. God has used this time as a means to get my attention. I will obey Him and serve Him the rest of my life. I may think this separation is unfair, but the Lord knows its value in my development. At times I think it is more than I can bear and is a mistake, but God can use it to encourage me to fulfill the plans He has for me."

"Create in me a pure heart, O God, and renew a steadfast spirit within me. Do not cast me from your presence or take your Holy Spirit from me. Restore to me the joy of your salvation and grant me a willing spirit, to sustain me."
—Psalm 51:10–12

"I want to find the center of God's love and then have it poured into me in a complete way. I seek the Lord and His will for my life. I want to obey and trust God in every way possible. I want my ears and eyes to be opened to His will and ways. I want my heart to be cleansed and my hands to be clean. Once this happens, I want to break free and share love, compassion, and caring with the world in ways it has not seen."

"Trust in the LORD and do good; dwell in the land and enjoy safe pasture. Delight yourself in the LORD; and he will give you the desires of your heart. Commit your way to the LORD; trust in him, and he will do this: He will make your righteousness shine like the dawn, the justice of your cause like the noonday sun."—Psalm 37:3–6

"God has never failed to keep a single promise. I must trust God, trust God, and trust God even more. That trust I have in the Lord will show me exactly what I need to do and when I need to do it.

"There are times when God's plans and methods make no sense whatsoever to me. When those times come, I must remember that I live by faith and not by sight."

"I am the LORD, the God of all mankind. Is anything too hard for me?"—Jeremiah 32:27

"I know, O LORD, that a man's life is not his own; it is not for man to direct his steps. Correct me, LORD, but only with justice—not in your anger, lest you reduce me to nothing."—Jeremiah 10:23–24

Chapter 7

Pushing Through the Embers with Counsel and the Word

" 'I will be a Father to you, and you will be my sons and daughters,' says the Lord Almighty. Since we have these promises, dear friends, let us purify ourselves from everything that contaminates body and spirit, perfecting holiness out of reverence for God."
—2 Corinthians 6:18 –7:1

Meeting with Doug

At my next meeting with Doug, he shared that this time in my life was a birthing process, so I needed to know when to push and when not to. I had to get rid of cycles in my relationship with God; that is, an up-and-down relationship that varied according to circumstances and outward influences. Lynn wanted and needed a man of God who was stable and solid every day of his life, not just six months a year.

Doug warned me not to let my guard down as time went by. Satan was not going to just stand passively by and let victory take place. In the past, my spiritual life included God, me, and the Spirit. This equated to selfish behavior because I left Lynn out, rather than walking hand in hand, shoulder to shoulder with her. When we are truly close with God, He pours out His love through us as demonstrated in the fruits of the Spirit.

I Want to Be More Christlike in Nature

"I feel victory is at hand in my journey. The coming days will have God's blessing, I am sure. I will follow God's plan. I must never turn away from God's calling again. I want to be Christlike and have the fruit of the Spirit pouring out of me daily.

"Speak to me, Lord, and I will obey and trust Your leading. Search me, call me, and seek me as I seek You. I want to be about Your work, and I want to turn my back on the world and the things of the world. May Your will become my will as I chase after You and Your kingdom. I must not, will not, and cannot give up ground in my life any longer."

"The LORD will fight for you; you need only to be still." — Exodus 14:14

"I will sing to the LORD, for he is highly exalted. The horse and its rider he has hurled into the sea. The LORD is my strength and my song, he has become my salvation. He is my God, and I will praise him, my father's God, and I will exalt him. The LORD is a warrior; the LORD is his name. . . . Your right hand, O LORD, was majestic in power. Your right hand, O LORD, shattered the enemy. In the greatness of your majesty you threw down those who oppressed you. You unleashed your burning anger; it consumed them like stubble." — Exodus 15:1–3, 6–7

"I will not and cannot give up on Lynn and our marriage. She is the partner God gave me when He sealed our life together almost twenty-six years ago. I know God wants us together doing His will, and because He does, I know it will happen when He sees fit and Lynn opens her heart.

"Bless Lynn even now with Your Spirit, Lord. Walk with her today, tomorrow, and every day after. Bless her with Your gifts and Spirit for the days ahead."

Rest Assured, God Is Always Moving and Working

"I encounter pressure and stress when I want to see something happen with Lynn and believe it is part of God's will for our lives, but then nothing happens. There are seasons in my life when God wants me to rest in the fact that He is on the move, even though I do not see the evidence of His work. He may not move the way I think He should, but He is nevertheless moving and accomplishing what He desires.

"God says in His Word that we should be still and wait on Him. We can be certain that He is going to do something fantastic. When He tells me He is working in a certain area, I can rest in Him, knowing that He is working and His will is being accomplished. I know the purpose in my life is to love Him and follow His direction. My goals should reflect this by working on His behalf with Lynn. I know something good is going to happen for us in the future if we put Him first and follow His Word.

"I must keep telling myself that I need to trust God and let go. When I do that, I will experience the presence of God with a new sense of hope. I need to learn how to wait on God and live according to His timing; then hope will spring forth like never before. God is never in a hurry! He is always on time—not a moment early or a moment late."

God Leads, and I Follow

"I am setting goals from this day forward to do exactly as God leads. I believe if I do that, I will be in the center of His perfect will. My challenge is to give myself totally to His control and guidance. I will have hope, encouragement, and growth by living in total obedience to His plan. I realize God wants the best for me. He also knows how to prepare me for the future much better than I know how. Why? Because He knows the future and I do not!"

"But those who hope in the LORD will renew their strength. They will soar on wings like eagles; they will run and not grow weary, they will walk and not be faint."—Isaiah 40:31

"When I trust God's schedule, something great happens. His blessings begin to flow my way, and I travel much further and do so many more great things for His kingdom. When God is opening doors, it is much easier to navigate life's course. When I am always fighting against God's perfect will, I am trying to force things to happen. Then it is hard work, and the rewards are much less satisfying."

Second Counseling Session

Lynn, Gwen, and I met for our second session of marriage counseling. Lynn shared that when she viewed *Fireproof*, she felt like our life was on the screen. She had felt much the same way in our marriage as the woman in the movie: as though she did not measure up much of the time. Lynn explained that she had just taken in things without sharing her thoughts and feelings, that she had always caved into me and whatever I wanted.

Lynn's hope for counseling was to become a whole person, rid herself of baggage, evaluate whether she wanted to proceed with the marriage, learn how to deal with Kayla during this time, and establish necessary boundaries. I was willing to examine each of these issues.

Gwen seemed to be gathering facts at this stage of the process, and I worried about Lynn and her feelings. After the session, Lynn and I talked, and she said she felt better about Gwen this time as compared to the previous session. In that first session, she had felt Gwen was on my side when she suggested we start doing things together.

But we had been separated for months now, and we still did not do things together, not even simple things like having dinner or going to a movie. We seemed to be spinning our wheels, and I couldn't help but wonder if Lynn had already made a decision. I was growing more confused and worried with each day that she stayed away. Was this counseling just so Lynn could say in the future that we had tried, thus providing relief from guilt for both of us? I did not know the answers to this and many other questions; however, I knew clarity would come in the days ahead. In the meantime, I purposed to make things right with all the people in my life, starting with my father.

Travel to Wisconsin to Meet with My Father

Carrying through with my plan, I traveled to Wisconsin and went to breakfast with my dad. We talked about his marriage, separation, and divorce from his first wife and his feelings about it. We also talked about the death of his first son at birth.

I also wanted my dad to know the great example he had set for me concerning the way he had raised my two older brothers, Jeff and John, children from my mother's first marriage. From the time Jeff was two years old and John was six months old, Dad had raised them as his own, never treating them differently from his three biological children. We talked about the death of my mother's first husband and also her father's passing.

Although it was many years in the past, we talked about his drinking and smoking, and I shared how proud I was that he had quit both habits cold turkey. I thanked him for the great father, role model, and provider he had been all his life. Dad, in turn, shared his thoughts on my marriage and what I might decide to do in the future.

We had a great time together, and I was so happy that I had made the effort to have such a conversation with him before it was too late. He is a great man that I am proud to call my father!

Meeting with a Close Friend

On that visit to Wisconsin, I had lunch with a good friend of both Lynn and me, a woman named Michelle. I asked for advice on our marriage, and she candidly shared much insight about Lynn and how she had felt throughout the years of our marriage. At the time, I had not known of these feelings that Lynn had obviously shared with Michelle, and it hurt to find out now about so many things that I could do nothing about. If Lynn had brought these issues up in the past, would I have changed my behavior? I honestly did not know, but now we certainly would never know. Michelle and I spent four hours together, and it was healing.

"The path is long, but one well worth traveling if it ultimately provides release and freedom in my life and the lives of those I have

hurt. I believe this is part of God's will for my life that He wants to accomplish during this separation time."

Follow God, Obey God, and He Will Guide and Direct into Paths of Righteousness

"Blessed are they whose ways are blameless, who walk according to the law of the LORD. Blessed are they who keep his statutes and seek him with all their heart. They do nothing wrong; they walk in his ways. . . . How can a young man keep his way pure? By living according to your word. I seek you with all my heart; do not let me stray from your commands. I have hidden your word in my heart that I might not sin against you. . . . I delight in your decrees; I will not neglect your word. Do good to your servant, and I will live; I will obey your word. Open my eyes that I may see wonderful things in your law. . . . Give me understanding, and I will keep your law and obey it with all my heart. . . . You are my portion, O LORD; I have promised to obey your words. I have sought your face with all my heart; be gracious to me according to your promise. . . . I will hasten and not delay to obey your commands. . . . I have kept my feet from every evil path so that I might obey your word. . . . Your word is a lamp to my feet and a light for my path. . . . Sustain me according to your promise, and I will live; do not let my hopes be dashed. . . . Your statutes are wonderful; therefore I obey them. The unfolding of your words gives light; it gives understanding to the simple. . . . I obey your statutes, for I love them greatly. I obey your precepts and your statutes, for all my ways are known to you. . . . May your hand be ready
    to help me, for I have chosen your precepts."
—Psalm 119:1–3, 9–11, 16–18, 34, 57–58, 60, 101, 105,
    116, 129–130, 167–168, 173

"Lord, may I walk after Your ways and be obedient and quick to respond to You. I trust You have my best interests at heart for me and my journey. I ask for Your perfect will and Your perfect timing

in my life. May I hear Your voice clearly and know it is coming from Your throne room."

Purity in my Soul

"I so want this to be a blessed day in which I follow after God and become more like the person He wants me to be. I choose love, kindness, and joy over my flesh and getting my own way. I want to love You, Lord, and love people rather than thinking of myself.

"Thank You, God, for the conversations with my father and Michelle; they were both helpful in many ways. I have an opportunity few people take, and that is to make all my relationships right with all the people in my life."

Conversation with My Godly In-Laws

That afternoon I spent several hours with my in-laws, and we had a wonderful conversation for the first time in years, maybe ever. We talked about God, our relationship, my relationship with Lynn, and my growth. My mother-in-law said she could see great changes in my life, and regardless of the outcome, she hoped it continued. She remarked that she saw a life in my eyes that had not been there in years.

I laid it out there with them so they could see the man I was becoming and know that the man who had taken care of their daughter in the past could do a better job in the future if given the chance. At the end of the day, I walked out of their house feeling renewed in our relationship.

"Say to God, 'How awesome are your deeds! So great is your power that your enemies cringe before you.' . . . Come and see what God has done, how awesome his works in man's behalf! . . . Praise our God, O peoples, let the sound of his praise be heard; he has preserved our lives and kept our feet from slipping. For you, O God, tested us; you refined me like silver. You brought us into prison and laid burdens on our backs. You let men ride over our heads; we went through fire and water, but you brought us to a place of abundance. . . .

Praise be to God, who has not rejected my prayer or withheld
his love from me!"—Psalm 66:3, 5, 8–12, 20

Looking for Peace from the Throne Room

*"I am looking for true and lasting peace in my life: peace that
includes contentment, completeness, harmony on all sides, rest, and
quietness in every aspect of life. The reality is, God is peace! True
and lasting peace comes only from the throne of God, and that is
Jesus Christ in complete control of my life."*

"May God himself, the God of peace, sanctify you through
and through. May your whole spirit, soul and body be kept
blameless at the coming of our Lord Jesus Christ. The one
who calls you is faithful and he will do it."
—1 Thessalonians 5:23–24

"Peace I leave with you; my peace I give you. I do not give
to you as the world gives. Do not let your hearts be troubled
and do not be afraid."—John 14:27

"I have told you these things, so that in me you may have
peace. In this world you will have trouble. But take heart! I
have overcome the world."—John 16:33

"If it is possible, as far as it depends on you, live at peace
with everyone."—Romans 12:18

*"With peace in my heart, it is time to have perseverance in the
faith. I need to push through, hang on, and blow the flesh out of
my life. When I do this, I will see doors open, walls fall down, and
clouds lifted by my God who is in control."*

The Three Steves in My Life

A friend shared with me that there have been three Steves in
my forty-eight years of life. The first was the old Steve, the Steve

before Christ; the second was the old Steve, but with both Christ and sin; and the third was the new Steve, the Steve with the Christlike nature. He shared this to remind me of how close the old nature always lurks.

"I must never go back to the old ways! Lord, continue this process within me, and never let me turn back from the growth that has taken place. I want, need, and must have more of You in my life! I love You and want to serve You and Your kingdom."

Lynn's Healing

My friend and I also discussed Lynn's remembrance of the many things I had said and done in the past. He had a different view on it than did I. He helped me to see that maybe she needed to pull these things out one by one. Maybe she wasn't just rehashing old history or picking the scabs off old wounds; maybe it was a necessary part of her healing process. With that new insight, I began praying protection over Lynn so the evil one could not use these thoughts to destroy, but rather that God would use everything for His glory in the future.

"Therefore, I urge you, brothers, in view of God's mercy, to offer your bodies as living sacrifices, holy and pleasing to God—this is your spiritual act of worship. Do not conform any longer to the pattern of this world, but be transformed by the renewing of your mind. Then you will be able to test and approve what God's will is—his good, pleasing and perfect will."—Romans 12:1–2

A Daily Walk with the Lord

I was learning to daily lay aside my fleshly desires and to instead pick up my cross and follow God. I laid all my energy and resources at His disposal and trusted Him to guide me. I gave Him complete control of my life, knowing He had a great, pleasing, and perfect plan for me. I was determined to put away all worldly behaviors and follow God always. I was slowly learning the lesson that God's grace is enough.

"I love the Lord for who He is and what He is doing in my life right now. I love the fact that I am getting my life back in order— maybe more than I have ever done before. Lord, may I walk further and seek Your love more than ever. Pour forth Yourself on me this day. I want to live for You!"

Whenever I trusted God and obeyed Him, my moments of extreme exhaustion and confusion were replaced by clarity and hope. I was certain God had a plan and a purpose for my suffering. It is in difficult times when we are at our lowest that we gain the greatest insight into God's wonderful faithfulness, and that was true for me. In my case, the battle was not really with the problem itself, but with my need to control the situation. I desperately needed to put to death once and for all my desire to control. Unless I let go, the battles and fights would only increase. God was calling me to relinquish my need to control and instead to trust Him completely. He wanted to work on my behalf, but He could not do that if I insisted on relying on my own strength.

"God's abilities are far greater than mine—all the time. God is not the author of separation, but He will use this tribulation to teach me about Himself and to build a bond between Him and me. No matter how deep my valley, God reaches even deeper to pull me out of it in His timing. God wants me to say no to sin and to be trained for His service by doing the things that lead to a closer relationship with Him."

"No discipline seems pleasant at the time, but painful. Later on, however, it produces a harvest of righteousness and peace for those who have been trained by it." —Hebrews 12:11

"Fighting on my own behalf without God's strength and ability is totally foolish. Jesus, show me what You want to teach me through this time in my life. I need to see things as You see them,

regardless of the pain, suffering, and hurt that might come from seeing through Your eyes."

God's Pruning Is the Best Way and Only Way—Really!

If God had not taken drastic measures and moved me from Wisconsin to Minnesota in 2006, I fear I would have kept going in the wrong direction and ended up far from God and His kingdom. But God, for reasons known only to Him at the time, made a way for my family and me to relocate to Minnesota. The first year there, I grew closer to God, but I soon regressed in my spiritual walk. Now, two years later, Kayla was in Florida, Lynn was in an apartment, and I was faced with the trial that drove me to my knees. There were still steps I needed to take in my spiritual journey.

"Lord, please reveal Your plan as I seek Your ways. I know You are pruning me so that I may bear fruit for Your kingdom. My goal in life is righteous and holy living in front of my Lord and Savior. You will prune but not kill me in the process. Once the pruning and learning are complete, my life will produce an abundance of fruit for Your kingdom."

"The LORD blessed the latter part of Job's life more than the first."—Job 42:12

"God sees what I will never be able to see. He knows so much more than I could ever know. He knows what will happen in the future, while most of the time I see only the present and fear the future. This present suffering is training me to trust God and know that He is always at work in my life. He is not done yet and never will be as long as I walk on the face of this earth."

God Is for Me, So I Can Accomplish His Plan

"I have come to realize there is only one way to demonstrate my trust in God, and that is through total surrender in every aspect of

my life. If God is for me, who can be against me? I'm not quitting and I'm not giving up, no matter what happens in life.

"If I want to know why this separation with Lynn has happened, I need to move towards God and seek His wisdom in the matter, not blame Him for the separation and walk away from Him. I need to seek His forgiveness for all the times I sought after my own pleasures throughout my marriage. I need to ask for forgiveness for the days, weeks, and months I didn't read His Word faithfully. I need forgiveness for all the days we didn't have devotions as a family, pray together, or seek His direction for our lives.

"Too many times I have followed my own path in life, even though I know God's pathway is so much better. I cannot continue to mix my will and God's and expect His perfect plan to be achieved. So, away with sin and my own selfish behaviors, and onwards to seek God's purity! With God's purity come the fruits of His Spirit: love, joy, peace, kindness, goodness, faithfulness, and self-control. I can no longer ignore God's universal principles but must be obedient to His calling and direction. Your will be done, heavenly Father. I am letting go and letting God!"

Words from God

"Seek Me, My son, seek Me! I want to reveal Myself to you in so many ways. I hold the keys to your heart, and I am about to unlock hidden passions and power to do My will in this land. You have prepared well, My son, and I am well pleased with your progress. Keep pushing forward regardless of the world and the changes that are taking place. There is a ministry that I have for you in the coming days. I will use your voice to bring great blessings to My body.

"Do not fret or lose sleep during this purging time in your life. I am in total control, and My will is already being accomplished behind the scenes. Have faith, My son, and do not give up hope in Me regardless of what you see or feel around you. My hand is at work, and My will is going to be accomplished. Hear and believe My word to you this day."

"Your love, O LORD, reaches to the heavens, your faithfulness to the skies. Your righteousness is like the mighty mountains, your justice like the great deep. O LORD, you preserve
both man and beast. How priceless is your unfailing love! . .
. Continue your love to those who know you, your righteousness to the upright in heart."—Psalm 36:5–7, 10

Meeting with Joanne

This time Joanne encouraged me to keep changing and keep
focusing. "You must remember you are doing these changes for
you," she reminded me. "Stop doing things so quickly, like returning
Lynn's phone calls and e-mails. In fact, keep your mind off Lynn!
Don't focus on her or what she is doing. Remember, you are separated, and Lynn is the one who made that decision. You are the one
on the sidelines, not the one in the game, so sit back and relax."

If our marriage was to have a chance, both Lynn and I would
need to change. If only one changed and we got back together, , we
would eventually revert to the same old marriage we had always
had, and that was not an option.

"He gives strength to the weary and increases the power of
the weak. Even youths grow tired and weary, and young men
stumble and fall; but those who hope in the LORD will renew
their strength. They will soar on wings like eagles; they will
run and not grow weary, they will walk and not be faint."
—Isaiah 40:29–31

Seeking God's Perfect Will

*"Lord, Your perfect will, Your perfect plan be done! Show me
what You would have me do in this world. I need Your revelation
knowledge and direction for the future. I need You to speak to me
through Your Word, and I will obey, trust, and seek the path You
have planned for me. I know Your ways are better and Your thoughts
are clearer and higher than mine. Pour forth Your plan for my life
as I seek to follow Your ways."*

Words from God

"I am the Lord your God. I am with you and seek to have you know Me better. You will move in the flow of My Spirit. You will seek the deeper knowledge that I will reveal to you in the coming days. Fear not, fear not, My son, for the desires you have will come to pass in Me. Be obedient, be prepared, and seek only My face and hand during your journey. Protection will come from Me and through you."

"But I trust in you, O Lord; I say, 'You are my God.' My times are in your hands; deliver me from my enemies and from those who pursue me. Let your face shine on your servant; save me in your unfailing love."—Psalm 31:14–16

Love Is Changing Me for the Better

"Love has changed me! It has changed the way I view life, the way I respond to others, and the way I view my circumstances. Love, forgiveness, and restoration are the very heart of Jesus. I cannot lose Jesus' love, and I cannot gain more of it. The moment I accepted Christ as my Savior, I gained all that Jesus had for me. That means Jesus loves me without any restrictions.

"There are two universal principles of God that I know to be true: I cannot outgive God, and obedience always leads to blessings. There is absolutely never a time to disobey God. I should obey Him regardless of what I think and how I feel. I disobey God when I refuse to do what He has gifted, trained, and called me to do."

"Do not be wise in your own eyes; fear the Lord and turn away from evil. This will bring health to your body and nourishment to your bones."—Proverbs 3:7–8

"The Lord will guide you always; he will satisfy your needs in a sun-scorched land and will strengthen your frame. You will be like a well-watered garden, like a spring whose waters never fail."—Isaiah 58:11

Releasing the Pains of Life

"My healing will never take place if I am holding on to my hurts and frustrations. I need to totally surrender to the God who loves me and has a plan for my life. The circumstances that come into my life will help make that happen sooner than later if I continue to walk after the Lord.

"I need God to make His will absolutely clear so I will not take a wrong turn. If I obey His direction, all aspects of my life will be pure and aligned with His will. If I am not obedient to Him, my life is filled with disappointment, suffering, and failure in jobs and marriage.

"I need to let go of the what ifs *about my past. I cannot change the past, but if I am obedient to God in all things going forward, my worries will fall by the wayside. He is in control, and I must trust Him. Nothing just happens in my life. He always has a plan, and that plan reflects His ways."*

Marriage Counseling for the Third Time

Gwen, Lynn, and I met for the third time, and it went well. Gwen hit the nail on the head concerning our issues. She also hit me hard about the way I handled stress and anxiety. She talked to me about my place of employment and their recent decision to reduce pay by 10 percent. Lynn had not known about that and seemed genuinely concerned.

I was hoping that everything would turn out like the end of *Fireproof*, but unfortunately, that did not happen. However, Lynn and I did talk some more after the session and set up more appointments. I accepted the fact that we would probably have no conversation between counseling sessions, which meant I wouldn't talk to her again until the next Wednesday.

Prepare to Answer God's Call

"This is what I need to remember in walking more closely with God: First, I must be available to His call 24/7. Second, if I desire to please Him, He will make sure I am in the center of His will. Third, though I am in a deep valley with this separation, I am waiting on

God to perform a major miracle. I am trusting Him 100 percent. I cannot change the fact of the separation; only He and Lynn can do that. Fourth, I must answer His call from this point on.

"The Father, Jesus, and the Holy Spirit never change. They never leave me and never abandon me. I must walk more closely to God and seek Him more every day of my life."

Words from God

"My son, I see that your heart is broken and your hands are empty. I will mend your broken heart and fill your hands with blessings. Seek Me and continue to walk a pure walk, loving people and having compassion.

"Understand, My son, My timing is not your timing. I am healing, I am setting apart, and I am clearing the way to the future. Do not give up hope and happiness. I want to fill your heart and life with abundance. My fruits and My Spirit reside in you, but you must push them out, release them, and use them for My glory. It is all about bringing attention to My kingdom and glory.

"We have great days ahead together. Walk with Me as I walk with you. Love Me, follow Me, search My hidden places, and you will be rewarded mightily."

"Each of you should look not only to your own interests, but also to the interests of others." — Philippians 2:4

Opening My Ears and Closing My Mouth

"I am surrendering myself, my ways, and my behaviors to Jesus, first and foremost, but also for the good of Lynn and Kayla. I must maintain an attitude of willingness, flexibility, and humble submission. This means laying down what I have the right to claim for myself for the good of others. The wise and loving thing to do is to start approaching disagreements with a willingness to not always insist on my own way. Sadly, for many years I have done just the opposite with Lynn, and I am ashamed that I didn't learn this lesson sooner. Lynn is

very intelligent and knowledgeable in so many areas, but throughout our marriage, I didn't listen to her when I should have."

> "But the wisdom that comes from heaven is first of all pure;
> then peace-loving, considerate, submissive, full of mercy
> and good fruit, impartial and sincere."—James 3:17

"Going forward, I will be patient, I will listen, and I will give Lynn's words full weight before I speak. Walk by faith, Steve Kirk, and faithfully obey God with courage and confidence! Whatever appears to be a loss will be a gain! There is a vein of silver coming into your life, Steve Kirk. The darkness will end, the sun will shine, blessings will come, the Spirit will be there, and Jesus will pour forth Himself into your life. God Himself sets an end to the darkness."

> "Haven't you read," he replied, "that at the beginning the
> Creator 'made them male and female,' and said, 'For this
> reason a man will leave his father and mother and be united
> to his wife, and the two will become one flesh'? So they
> are no longer two, but one. Therefore what God has joined
> together, let man not separate."—Matthew 19:4–6

The Tide Turns in a Negative Direction

"I trust in God, I have faith in Him, and I will walk with Him all the days of my life! Lynn told me she wants to counsel with Gwen alone, and she also shared she is going to talk to a divorce lawyer in the next two weeks.

"This is my darkest hour, but I believe by faith our marriage will be restored by God's mighty hand. I trust in God's perfect will and perfect plan, and I will walk according to the life He has set before me. I will not be shaken by the outward signs, knowing full well that God, my God, is in full control of my life.

"God uses trials and tribulations brought on by the world, my flesh, and others to test my knowledge and character. When this happens, it lays everything open and shows me what I am made of."

"His divine power has given us everything we need for life and godliness through our knowledge of him who called us by his own glory and goodness. Through these he has given us his very great and precious promises, so that through them you may participate in the divine nature and escape the corruption in the world caused by evil desires." — 2 Peter 1:3–4

God Is Walking with Me; I Will Fear No Evil

"What agreement is there between the temple of God and idols? For we are the temple of the living God. As God has said: 'I will live with them and walk among them, and I will be their God, and they will be my people. Therefore, come out from them and be separate, says the Lord. Touch no unclean thing, and I will receive you. I will be a Father to you, and you will be my sons and daughters, says the Lord Almighty.' Since we have these promises, dear friends, let us purify ourselves from everything that contaminates body and spirit, perfecting holiness out of reverence for God."
—2 Corinthians 6:16–7:1

After reading these verses, I asked myself, *Do I believe I can be this type of man? Can I be clean and purified in perfect holiness?* Yes, if the Lord and His Spirit were filling me each and every day of my life, then I could be that man of holiness, I concluded. However, that would happen only if I opened His Word, sought His face, and walked in obedience each moment of each day. If I failed to do this, I would only hurt those around me.

"Be strong and courageous. Do not be afraid or terrified because of them, for the LORD your God goes with you; he will never leave you nor forsake you." — Deuteronomy 31:6

Meeting with Joanne

I met with Joanne, and she gave me some homework as well as her usual advice. She instructed me to write an essay on who I am, focusing on my journey only. She shared the thought that a man is measured by his belief system and values, not by his failures. Despite the problems in my marriage, I had not lost Kayla and never would. If Lynn could not love me, that was her decision. True, I owned a piece of Lynn's pain, but not all of it.

By far this was my most difficult meeting with Joanne up to this point. For the first time, I cried and couldn't stop sharing my pain. Knowing that Lynn was moving towards divorce and was not willing to give me a second chance broke my heart, and I simply fell to pieces.

Later, as I looked back in my journals, I began to think that Lynn had never planned to move forward together. We had not kissed since October, and we had not gone on a date since the night before she left in September. The only time we saw each other was when Kayla was in town or when we did counseling together. It wasn't looking good at all, and when I finally started to face it in my session with Joanne, I just couldn't handle it.

Phone Call from Gwen

Gwen called, returning my phone message to let her know that Lynn wanted to counsel with her alone. I soon realized, however, that Gwen already knew, because Lynn had seen her that morning. While we were on the phone, I asked her what I should be doing. She said I needed to be a magnet; if I stopped chasing Lynn, she just might be attracted to me. She also said Lynn was very confused at this point, and if I kept chasing her, she would be pushed in the wrong direction.

Gwen encouraged me to seek my own help, and when I told her what I was already doing with Doug and Joanne, she encouraged me to continue seeing them. She suggested that I ask Lynn for "do overs"; that is, asking for a second chance when I said or did something inappropriate. She also advised me to give Lynn time to heal. This was the last time Gwen and I would ever talk, since Lynn wanted to see her alone from now on. I eagerly took in her every word and moved forward.

Life Group and Conversation with Doug

After talking to Gwen, I attended a Life Group meeting at a friend's house, where we were studying the book *Becoming a Better You*. It was a great group of people helping each other out. We all go through things, and we all have abilities to help others in their problems. That's what we did in the Life Group.

After the Life Group meeting, I was getting ready to leave when Pastor Doug arrived for a meeting with the church board. I was able to spend a few minutes with him and share about Lynn's decision to not meet with me in counseling again. He suggested that I give Lynn all the space she needed in order to make the right decision. That might mean I needed to adjust my boundaries. For example, if I normally called her on a certain day and that day fell on Valentine's Day, I could change the day I called so she would not have to deal with my feelings and the holiday all at once. He also told me to relax and heal myself. He observed that Lynn's comments about seeking a divorce lawyer were primarily about her need for protection. Though I was not happy with Lynn's decision to seek counseling alone and did not see it as a positive sign, at least she was continuing counseling, he pointed out. Great things were ahead if I would wait for Lynn to heal, he encouraged.

Don't Forget God on the Mountaintop

It had been a hard day, very painful in some ways. I liked Pastor Doug's positive nature, I appreciated Gwen's sweet spirit, and I was blessed by Joanne's help; but in the end, it all came down to what Lynn decided to do. Apart from the deep valley facing me, I was doing so many great things to clean up my life, deepen my relationship with Kayla, help people in the community, get involved in the church, form new friendships, and, most importantly, live for God. However, I also knew all those positive things probably would not have happened if not for the valley I had been forced to walk in. I needed to get to the place where I could enjoy the mountaintop yet continue to build and never turn back to the old ways.

Let Healing Take Place in Lynn's Life and Mine

"I need to relax and let Lynn heal completely. I know leaving it up to God and using Gwen as a tool are much better strategies than my pushing and trying to fix Lynn. I know only God and Lynn can get her completely healed and on the right path. God, I release Lynn to You for Your work to be done!"

"I planted the seed, Apollos watered it, but God made it grow. So neither he who plants nor he who waters is anything, but only God, who makes things grow." — 1 Corinthians 3:6–7

"You have loved righteousness and hated wickedness; therefore God, your God, has set you above your companions by anointing you with the oil of joy." — Hebrews 1:9

"Jabez cried out to the God of Israel, 'Oh, that you would bless me and enlarge my territory! Let your hand be with me, and keep me from harm so that I will be free from pain.' And God granted his request." — 1 Chronicles 4:10

Build Those walls for Protection

We can learn many things in life by studying the lives of biblical characters who went before us. Nehemiah is one of those people who stood for God and fulfilled his purpose in life. When Nehemiah saw that the walls of Jerusalem were broken down, he decided to do something constructive and rebuild the walls. Sometimes, through a slow fade of our beliefs and corresponding actions, the walls in our lives become broken down. Like Nehemiah, we need to rebuild them through obedience, focus, and the willingness to follow God rather than the world. Part of this is accomplished by hearing God's voice and standing firm in our faith.

"I must be open to the supernatural events of God's plans in my life. I do this not only through reading His Word, but also by hearing His voice and doing what He says—always. When the voice inside

cries that it is no use, I must arouse a fighting spirit within to understand that my marriage and future are worth the battle."

"After I looked things over, I stood up and said to the nobles, the officials and the rest of the people, 'Don't be afraid of them. Remember the Lord, who is great and awesome, and fight for your brothers, your sons and your daughters, your wives and your homes.' " —Nehemiah 4:14

Loving and Caring for the Lord, Family, Friends, and Community

"Steve Kirk can be called a man of great faith, character, and obedience if he walks after God each and every day of his life and carries out God's will and plan. Let it be said that Steve Kirk did everything exactly as God commanded him!"

"I ask that we love one another. And this is love: that we walk in obedience to his commands. As you have heard from the beginning, his command is that you walk in love." —2 John 1:5–6

"I am now on a quest to become loving and caring to a level that I have never been before. I have heard that the word trampling *can mean sinning against those around me. I have trampled on both Lynn and Kayla throughout the years. At times I even trampled on Lynn's intimacy. Lord, forgive me, as I ask for Lynn and Kayla to forgive me. It wasn't right, it isn't right, and I will not tolerate this behavior ever again."*

" 'I hate divorce,' says the LORD God of Israel, 'and I hate a man's covering himself with violence as well as with his garment,' says the LORD Almighty." —Malachi 2:16

It is not that we can't love our spouses; it is that we won't love them. I shared this thought with Lynn, but she protested that it was not true. She insisted she did not have the ability to turn love on or off. I didn't understand why she would say that, but it was nevertheless how she felt, and it was affecting our marriage relationship.

"God always loves to reclaim, renew, and restore a marriage tottering on divorce, and He will always put His full attention and power into such marriages." When I read those words, they seemed to leap off the pages of the book and into my heart. For the next several months, I read them time and time again. Throughout that time, I also used the words as a prayer, believing them to be true because they lined up with God's true Word.

> "Whoever has my commands and obeys them, he is the one who loves me. He who loves me will be loved by my Father, and I too will love him and show myself to him."—John 14:21

"Am I willing to play out my life before an audience of one? Intimacy with God means oneness with God, oneness with His character and His ways. Intimacy with others means freeing them to play out their lives before their audience of one as well. Yes, yes, yes, I am willing to play out my life to my audience of one. I am also willing to stand aside and let others choose what they want to do in life and with God."

> "The entire law is summed up in a single command: 'Love your neighbor as yourself.' If you keep on biting and devouring each other, watch out or you will be destroyed by each other."—Galatians 5:14

"When I obey God's commands, I love those around me, especially Lynn and Kayla. Living a holy and blameless life is not dull, distasteful, and restricting. It is the only path to real love, real peace, and real life!"

Growing New Fruit for God and Myself

"Some of my fruits in the past were lust, faithlessness, selfishness, self-absorption, and the love of money. Of course, my fruit should be

that of the Spirit. The fruit of the Spirit is love, joy, peace, patience, kindness, goodness, faithfulness, gentleness, and self-control. I am in waiting mode for the Lord to move, for Lynn to reach out, and for my flesh to come under complete submission to God's will."

"Yet the LORD longs to be gracious to you; he rises to show you compassion. For the LORD is a God of justice. Blessed are all who wait for him." — Isaiah 30:18

"I wait patiently for the LORD; he turned to me and heard my cry." — Psalm 40:1

"Delight yourself in the LORD and he will give you the desires of your heart." — Psalm 37:4

"I say to myself, 'The LORD is my portion; therefore I will wait for him.' The LORD is good to those whose hope is in him, to the one who seeks him; it is good to wait quietly for the salvation of the LORD." — Lamentations 3:24–26

"Wait for the LORD; be strong and take heart and wait for the LORD." — Psalm 27:14

Prayer to God for My Family

"I will wait for the Lord and His mighty move over this time in our lives. Only God can heal, restore, blend back, and refresh both Lynn and me. I believe God wants us together, serving Him and sharing Him to others in this world.

"Lord, bless Lynn with Your Spirit, love, and joy this evening. Let her feel and see Your healing hand in her life. Bless her with Christian friends and with counsel that breaks the shell around her heart and lifts the veil from her eyes. Bless me with Your wisdom and guidance when Lynn and I talk so I can build a bridge back to her heart and life.

"Lord God, we need a miracle from Your hand, in Your timing and perfect will. Both of us need to align our wills with Yours and conform

to Jesus Christ. We need Your mighty right hand moving, even this evening, on both of us to make us whole in You and in our own minds. Change us, renew us, and be with us this evening and also in our dreams. Speak loudly so we hear You clearly and obey completely Your spoken and written Word. In Jesus' name I pray. Amen."

Chapter 8

Valentine's Day and God Is Moving Mightily

"What is more, I consider everything a loss compared to the surpassing greatness of knowing Christ Jesus my Lord, for whose sake I have lost all things. I consider them rubbish, that I may gain Christ and be found in him, not having a righteousness of my own that comes from the law, but that which is through faith in Christ—the righteousness that comes from God and is by faith."
—Philippians 3:8–9

Praying for Lynn's Body, Mind, and Spirit

"*I feel a real need to pray for Lynn's body, mind, and spirit this morning. She is under a tremendous amount of pressure from her own thoughts as well as from the dark one. By her own admission, she is not sleeping well, feels under the weather, and is struggling with what steps to take in life. She needs release, Lord, in the spirit realm and in her mind. I need the same, Lord, in a mighty way. Oh God, please don't leave me like this. I want more of You. Please don't leave us like this!*"

"Now may the Lord of peace himself give you peace at all times and in every way. The Lord be with all of you."
—2 Thessalonians 3:16

"With this in mind, we constantly pray for you, that our God may count you worthy of his calling, and that by his power he may fulfill every good purpose of yours and every act prompted by my faith."—2 Thessalonians 1:11

Words from God

"My son, it is time to rise up and take your rightful place in My kingdom. I have chosen you for a purpose and plan. Walk with Me regardless of what the world and the people of the world do. We have a relationship, and this relationship must continue to grow.

"Yes, you have been faithful for many months, but can you go the distance? Do you have the long-term commitment and focus that are needed? Search Me, find My ways, and find My source of strength and help. I am with you always; never forget that, Steve Kirk.

"My ways are perfect, and My plan will succeed to bring about change in you, Lynn, Kayla, and the world. The time is at hand when blessings will fall on you, My son. Be prepared and know why you are being blessed. My hand is opening even now and releasing such blessing into your life. Receive it, accept it, and use it for My glory.

"Do not be fooled, My son, into believing the lies of the evil one. This time is almost over, and the outcome will bring glory to My kingdom and to hurting people. Fear not, for I am with you until the end of this age and into eternity. Fear not, My son, and do not believe everything you hear and see during this trial. More is happening for My glory than you can comprehend. My glory and power will prevail. My victory and plan will be accomplished. My love will show, not only for you and Lynn to see, but for the whole world. Many shall come to know Me because of this time in your life and Lynn's.

"I will change the heart of stone into a heart of flesh—flesh that loves, flesh that forgives, flesh that is attracted to you, and flesh that is yearning for Me and My love. Seek first My kingdom, and seek to have Me always as your first priority so things can be accomplished. Fear not, fear not, fear not, but trust in Me and believe in Me above all else this day."

"For God did not give us a spirit of timidity, but a spirit of power, of love and of self-discipline."—2 Timothy 1:7

"By wisdom a house is built, and by understanding it is established; through knowledge its rooms are filled with rare and beautiful treasures."—Proverbs 24:3–4

"Today I have heard God's Word, read His Word, and felt His moving in my life. I continue this mind-set today and every day going forward. I need God so much in my life to direct me and move me along my path.
"I want to serve God and my fellow man. I want to walk, talk, and hear the things of God. I need God's love, peace, and joy flowing out of my life daily. I want to love and see people with God's eyes."

"However, each one of you also must love his wife as he loves himself, and the wife must respect her husband."— Ephesians 5:33

True love is *agape* love, which is best described as unconditional love. Respect, like love, should be unconditional.

Valentine's Day Letter to Lynn

Valentine's Day was the perfect day to gather my thoughts and share them with Lynn. I hoped my letter would give her a glimpse into my heart and the work God was doing there.
Here is what I wrote:

Dear Lynn,

I write this letter to share the love I have for you. It is a different, better, more understanding love than any love I had in the past. I have been pushed, pulled, pruned, and purged of my old nature and grown in my understanding of how to love you and other people. I know (or think) it's hard for you to understand, accept, and believe that I have changed to that degree. I know you find it difficult to believe that the changes will be long-lasting and pure, the kind of changes you are seeking. But I truly believe I can be everything you desire in a husband, while keeping all the things you enjoyed about me in the past.

Over the months, I have read, soaked in, and oozed out the truth of 1 Corinthians 13 (verses 4–8, 11): "Love is patient, love is kind. It does not envy, it does not boast, it is not proud. It is not rude, it is not self-seeking, it is not easily angered, it keeps no record of wrongs. Love does not delight in evil but rejoices with the truth. It always protects, always trusts, always hopes, and always perseveres. Love never fails. . . . And now these three remain: faith, hope, and love. But the greatest of these is love."

The two questions that I have—and I think you have them too—are, am I a better person than the man you left on September 27; and can I continue to be a better person each day going forward, or will I fall back into my old ways? I leave the first question to you and others to answer, but I think only I can answer the second question. Yes, I can continue and will continue my spiritual growth, because the focus this time is totally different from past spiritual highs. I am now focused on my love for you and others, not on me and my selfish nature. In the past, it was more about me and how I felt, and then it was about you and others. But this time, with that perfect alignment, we cannot lose as a couple.

You are not a trophy, a possession, or anything else that I might think I want or need. You are a beautiful, loving, caring woman, and I want to spend the rest of my life loving you and being a part of your life. I ask that you open your heart and let my love in at a level never seen before in our marriage. Better days are ahead if we will love each other and share our feelings at the level we have these past few months.

Seeing your growth and my growth, I know we are both different people from the people we were for the first twenty-five years of our marriage. Now we have a chance to show ourselves, Kayla, and the world what a marriage built on a solid foundation, mutual respect, and love can do to change the people involved as well as the world.

Only you can make the decision to let my love in and trust that I will be the man you always wanted. And that is a man who loves you, wants to be a part of your life, and will continue to seek higher levels of love in the future.

Love,

Steve

P.S.: Happy Valentine's Day!

Thirst for God and Love from the Throne Room

"I have such a feeling of love for God, Lynn, and Kayla. My thirst for God's love, knowledge, and revelation is deeper than ever before. I feel compassion, peace, and rest like never before. I have a thirst for reading books about God and books about how to be a better person, mostly a better husband.

"God, You know my cry to be one with You and one with Lynn in our marriage, together in the same house. First, continue to work within me to make me whole. Second, heal Lynn's emotions, spirit, and mind; help her break free of the bondage of her mind. Then, in Your perfect timing and plan, bring us together like never before. I look forward to Your blessing in this area while all the other areas of my life continue to grow."

"If you remain in me and my words remain in you, ask whatever you wish, and it will be given you."—John 15:7

"Now to him who is able to do immeasurably more than all we ask or imagine, according to his power that is at work within us, to him be glory in the church and in Christ Jesus throughout all generations, forever and ever! Amen."
—Ephesians 3:20–21

"Be self-controlled and alert. Your enemy the devil prowls around like a roaring lion looking for someone to devour. Resist him, standing firm in the faith, because you know that your brothers throughout the world are undergoing the same kind of sufferings. And the God of all grace, who called you to his eternal glory in Christ, after you have suffered a little while, will himself restore you and make you strong, firm and steadfast. To him be the power forever and ever. Amen."— 1 Peter 5:8–11

Love from Me or Love from Another?

In my readings, I came across this powerful statement: "Practically every woman I have met or counseled would be willing to say, 'I just want somebody to love me, to make me special, to make me the most important one in his life.' " I wanted to be that person with Lynn. For months I had been sharing that sentiment face-to-face, over the phone, and in e-mails. I did not know what else I could do to show her my love.

Lynn had shared two times now that she was talking to a man in Canada. Was she developing an emotional connection with him and was thus totally disengaged from me? Or was there another root cause of our separation? I prayed fervently for understanding and acceptance that would enable me to move forward. I decided that when Lynn called in the future, I would make sure I understood completely her boundaries, her decisions, and her thoughts. Plus, I needed to limit the phone call to thirty minutes or less, unless Lynn herself extended it.

The Best Beauty to Seek and Desire

"I want the supernatural experience of being completely known and unconditionally loved by Lynn. I must continue to learn about her and her interests. Neither Lynn's outer beauty nor my own eyes should dominate my sexuality. My visual side may be a natural part of my sexuality, but it is not my only side and certainly not how God created me to walk. I need to look past Lynn's outer shell and gaze

deeply upon her inner beauty. I need a strong prayer life with Lynn if we are to succeed in our marriage going forward.

"Throughout my life, when I read my Bible less and didn't stay close to the Word, my behaviors changed and became more aligned with the things of the world. The lust of the flesh, the pride of life, harsh treatment of Lynn, and the love of money characterized a large portion of my nature. But when I stayed close to the Lord and His Word, I shared my faith, gave of my time and money to build the kingdom, and treated people with love and kindness, starting with Lynn and Kayla. I therefore need to stay in the Word always and give myself completely to God, Lynn, and Kayla. My right feelings and actions have always translated into right actions and feelings of love towards God and others."

Praying Together Changes Things for the Better

"I feel the love of God this morning and love for Lynn as well. I had a great night with my Life Group. After the meeting, Trevor, Beth, and I talked for two hours about what is going on in my life. It was good to share with them, and I look forward to hearing more about Trevor's and Beth's walk.

"I feel such love for Lynn and can't wait for the day when she opens up and lets love for me come back into her life. Our lives will never be the same—in a very good way! Love, joy, and peace will reign in God's perfect timing and plan.

"In the future, Lynn and I need to start praying together as a couple. We did that on and off for years, and when we did, our marriage was much better."

I had read these ten "prayer chillers" in the past and knew from personal experience how true they were:

1. Men are rebellious by nature.
2. The male ego is bigger but more fragile than the female ego.
3. Men are relatively less sensitive to the needs of others than are women.

4. Men are generally less able to verbally express emotions and feelings than are women.
5. The male brain is more oriented to facts and logic than to emotions and intuition.
6. Men are sexually stimulated visually.
7. During courtship, males will initiate the prayer relationship, but after the wedding, things are different.
8. Men need less romance and intimacy than women.
9. The male shield from feeling inferior is his work.
10. Men desire peace from marriage; women desire oneness and intimacy.

Prayer is hard work, and it takes courage, dedication, concentration, and steadfastness from all parties involved. That is what I had learned and hoped to initiate with Lynn once we were together again.

"Therefore confess your sins to each other and pray for each other so that you may be healed. The prayer of a righteous man is powerful and effective."—James 5:16

Is This Storm Coming to an End?

"It is 11:07 a.m., and I sense a major breakthrough in the spiritual realm on behalf of my marriage! The battle has been intense and hard fought, but victory is breaking forth. A newness of life is being brought forward at this time. A new heart of flesh, love, kindness, and care is being realized. Wave after wave of blessing keeps washing over my heart.

"A unity is being birthed in Lynn and me, even at this hour, minute, and second. Our spirits are coming into alignment with God's Spirit. A flow of love and respect is breaking free and flowing on me. Let it be so, Lord God, let it be so!"

"One day Jesus said to his disciples, 'Let's go over to the other side of the lake.' So they got into a boat and set out. As they sailed, he fell asleep. A squall came down on the lake, so that the boat was being swamped, and they were in great danger. The disciples went and woke him, saying, 'Master, Master, we're going to drown!' He got up and rebuked the wind and the raging waters; the storm subsided, and all was calm. 'Where is your faith?' he asked his disciples. In fear and amazement they asked one another, 'Who is this? He commands even the winds and the water, and they obey him.' " —Luke 8:22–25

Storms happen in our lives, even though we may be very close to God. Sometimes the winds blow ferociously, and Jesus puts us in the boat to face them even though He could direct us to stay on shore where it is safe. But if we always seek what is safe and secure, we will miss out on the lessons we can learn in a major storm.

Although we hate to face the waves crashing against our boats time and time again, we still do not usually change course quickly. Sometimes it takes something more, like a tidal wave of pain, before we finally surrender control of the boat to God and allow Him to steer it. God does not cause these waves and storms in our lives, but He allows them as a means to help us grow.

Boy, had I grown through my storm of separation!

"I have told you these things, so that in me you may have peace. In this world you will have trouble. But take heart! I have overcome the world." —John 16:33

Another Letter to Lynn

Dear Lynn,

I have been inspired today to write to you based upon *The Love Dare* book I have been following for twenty-two days. I didn't plan to write another letter to you, as I stated in my E-mail message yesterday, but this just poured out of me onto paper, and I wanted to share it with you.

Lynn, you have been my greatest help, and if I am wise going forward, I will honor you always. I need to humble myself and accept your valuable role in my life. You have been the greatest partner I could have hoped for, the special person God planned just for me. You are an equal (50-50) in all things, including matters with Kayla, finances, the house, cars, and retirement.

My love for you flows from the throne room of God and into my heart. I have such a new love for you. Though I have always loved you, this new love is deeper, wider, and more sincere. It is more about your essence, your inner beauty, rather than your outer beauty. No doubt about it, you're beautiful on the outside, but on the inside your beauty is like a precious gem. Throughout our marriage, your compassion, joy, peace, and kindness have often balanced my rougher edges. Though I am developing those traits in my life now, it can never replace the true balance you have brought to our relationship. How the Lord has blessed me with the time we have shared since 1981!

As I now walk forward in life, I know I am a much better person for having known you, Lynn Marie Kirk, for the past forty years. If we are able to come back together, our marriage will be so much better because we will each be whole. And two whole people with new love for each other can change themselves and the world. Just think, in our life together we could be married for seventy-five years! The first twenty-five were good, the next twenty-five can be great, and the last twenty-five can be awesome if we continue to change for the better and keep God in our lives.

If we come back together, I want us to talk daily before retiring for the evening. We need to share our wants, dreams, frustrations, and beliefs. I think we also need to pray together and cry out to God together. Last of all, we can't let the sun go down on our anger if one of is upset with the other. If we do these things, living in peace and partnership without control or selfish intents, we will succeed in some of the things we started in the past but failed to follow through with.

I am not seeking a decision from you. I am just pouring out my heart to the woman who has my love like never before. The changes I see taking place in you—the self-assurance, the openness and directness, the new, independent nature—make me love you even more, knowing you are your own person.

Better days are ahead for both of us, regardless of what happens with our marriage. You are on your road, I am on my journey, and we are both better for this time of separation. We can succeed in life outside of marriage, but oh my, what we could do together inside of our marriage! We would rock the world!

The Bible says, "One can put a thousand to flight; two can put ten thousand to flight." There is strength in numbers. May our number—two—be blessed by God's hand!

Love,

Steve

Loving God Is More Important Than Loving Anyone or Anything

Though I deeply loved both Lynn and Kayla, I also had a couple of questions running through my mind. *What do I love even more than Lynn and Kayla?* I asked myself. I could truthfully say that I loved God the Father, Jesus, and the Holy Spirit more than I loved life itself and anyone in it. *What are the by-products of this love?* I further wondered. Living like Christ, following His Word, and becoming holy in nature were the natural results flowing from learning to live in the love of God.

For the first part of my life, I had been harsh, selfish, controlling, and downright mean at times. In the second part of my life, I wanted to be loving, caring, kind, peaceful, patient, faithful, and self-controlled. I knew I needed the Lord to help me in my quest each day going forward.

"Only be careful, and watch yourselves closely so that you do not forget the things your eyes have seen or let them slip from your heart as long as you live. Teach them to your children and to their children after them."—Deuteronomy 4:9

"I do need to remember the past and how I have acted, but I need even more to change and continue to change in the future for the sake of both Lynn and Kayla. I also need to change for my future grandchildren and the generations to come. Lynn and Kayla need to see my flaws as well as my finer points. I want them to watch me closely to see how I walk each day. I have committed my heart to change."

A Phone Call from Lynn

"Lynn and I talked this evening, and it was probably our best conversation in weeks. She is becoming a new woman, with help from God and Gwen. I praise You, God, for Your movement in Lynn's life! She is much kinder and more positive towards me and what I say to her. She is more confident and more verbal as well. I do love her and look forward to our future together.

"Lord, may I not push Lynn and may Lynn not pull back during this time, but may we both let go and allow You to perform Your healing in our marriage. I ask You to heal both of us during this time, emotionally, spiritually, and physically, and I ask that both of us will show more of Your nature."

Visit from My Father and Brother

My dad and brother John were coming to visit for the weekend. I asked God to touch them during the visit and give me words for both of them, but especially for John, that he would understand God's plan for him. Lynn was in Florida with Kayla, and I prayed they would have a great time enjoying each other's company. I hoped they would have meaningful conversations, enjoy beautiful weather, and create many fun memories.

Though I was excited to have family coming to visit, the trial of separation from Lynn continued. I knew I had to learn to become a better man and better Christian, living as a child of God. I had to resist the temptation to try to work my way out of the problem through my own strength. I had tried that many times, but this battle was far beyond my strength and ability to handle. Only God could solve it.

Many times throughout those months of marital separation, I was very confused. Though Lynn's behavior was quite unusual for her and out of place for our marriage, I knew God often allowed this type of testing. But as I began writing this book, I discovered that Lynn's behavior was not as unusual as I had thought. Over the past few years, more women than men have been leaving their mates to search for their true identities. As I talked to people knowledgeable about family life, I learned that more than 50 percent of all marriages today end in divorce. In my own Life Group, close to 75 percent of the members had been or were currently going through separation and divorce. This is happening in marriages all across the country and even within the church.

"These are trying days for all marriages, not just mine. With that said, I need to pray hard to God for His intervention. For weeks now, I have prayed consistently for Lynn and our marriage. I plan to continue to pray and fast for the Holy Spirit's guidance now and going forward. God will lift me out of this valley in due time as I learn from the trial and apply the learning in my life in general."

"His divine power has given us everything we need for life and godliness through our knowledge of him who called us by his own glory and goodness. Through these he has given us his very great and precious promises, so that through them you may participate in the divine nature and escape the corruption in the world caused by evil desires." — 2 Peter 1:3–4

Developing the Mind of Christ

"I need to get on my knees and recognize that my approach to life is reflected in my attitudes and behaviors. Over the years, I have taken on behaviors learned from the world, but I must take these off and put on instead the nature of Christ Jesus.

"My happiness should not depend on whether Lynn calls or people visit (though both are very nice). True happiness comes from God and the choices I make in life. I believe that is why Joanne wanted me to write down who I am. I must magnify the Lord and put all trials and tribulations in the light of that knowledge, which means I shouldn't magnify them. My true source of happiness, joy, and direction must always come from the Word of God. That is where my wisdom, knowledge, and understanding are found, and what better place than the throne room of God the Father.

"I need to reprogram my mind and move back to the center of God's will with new and better habits. I need to get rid of the phrase as soon as and start every day and every thought with now. My life should be active and moving, not waiting for something to happen to get me moving. Through the Scriptures, I already know that I need to be moving on God's behalf.

"God is in control of my life. Nothing depends on my circumstances; everything depends on His perfect will and direction. As long as I follow Him, I can do no wrong. These thoughts are mine alone and work for me. I cannot change another person, including Lynn; only they have that ability.

"I want people to see that I have changed and that the fruits of the Spirit are coming out of me more now than ever before. I want to love, honor, and cherish all people and help them along the journey of life. I know the changes in my life so far have made a positive impact on others, including nonbelievers, because over the past few months, they have told me they can see a change in me. Many great things have happened in the past five months, and I know many more are ahead, even for this weekend!"

"There is no wisdom, no insight, no plan that can succeed against the LORD." — Proverbs 21:30

"All my victories and successes rest in the Lord! I trust Him for all victories in my life. That trust includes victories over sin, death, my marriage, my relationships, work, and battle against the evil one. Victory comes by following God all the days of my life and seeking His wisdom, knowledge, and understanding.

"I will trust in the Lord in all things and obey His call and leadership over my life. I want and need to hear His voice today so I can share with my father and brother. I also need direction in the way I should go in the other areas of my life. Guide and direct my path and the words of my mouth, Lord.

"In order for me to have victories, I must walk with God and keep His favor by staying clean before Him. I want to stay clean before the God who sees and knows all things; I also want to stay clean in my marriage, even during this separation from Lynn. I do not want to, nor will I, go back to the pit to satisfy my sinful nature. I am a new man, and I want to please God, Lynn, and the world in all that I do."

Another Letter to Lynn

Dear Lynn,

I wanted to tell you what a wonderful conversation I had with you on Thursday evening. To hear the energy level in your tone of voice, your positive thoughts on Gwen and your counseling, and your overall thoughts on how you feel about yourself and your progress was thrilling.

I am happy you're taking the approach that other people do not know how you feel—only you do. I do not know if we will find our place in life at this time. Because of what we have done, it's hard to know if our current situation is God's will or if Satan is in it. But I do know, regardless of what happens with us, you have changed, I have changed, and both changes are for the better.

I am so happy to see you in a much better place, even in the past two weeks. You seem so confident, so positive, and so calm. Your words were already compassionate, but now they are coming out as kind. Even in tough conversations, both our spirits are calm, peaceful, and understanding.

I cannot explain or put into words the happiness I feel for the changes you are making. May all the changes that you want gather steam in the coming days, weeks, and months. Better days are ahead for both of us!

God has told me several times that you are His flower. I see His flower being restored and stretching to new heights. You are straighter, taller, and wider in nature than I have ever seen you, and I realize your work, His work, and Gwen's work is not yet complete. Wow!

Have a fantastic time with Kayla, and enjoy yourself in Florida.

Steve

Sharing God's Love with Family

"I have peace today and feel better days are ahead, based upon the Lord and His calling. I thank You, God, for the time with my father and brother this weekend. It has been good to share with and hear from both of them. I want our time to continue to be blessed the rest of today and into the evening. I pray once again that our families will all be back together again, including my relationship with Lynn and Kayla."

My father, brother, and I had gone out to eat the night before and talked about my marriage, their marriages, and what we men need to do to make our marriages more fulfilling. I knew God was calling me to speak up more than I had done in the past. I was already trying to do that at work, and some of the men there had told me they were treating their wives better because of our conversations. I had also noticed some other men wearing their wedding rings, when in the past they had not. If part of God's plan was to use me as a voice to speak up for marriage, then I was willing to be one. I was open to sharing what I was learning about being a better husband and better friend, and I asked God to use me to share with other men the upsides and downsides to our behaviors.

My father, brother, and I had also watched the movie *Fireproof* together in my home. Afterwards, both had called their wives. Interestingly, when things happen in other people's lives, especially those close to us, we often observe and learn from these events, not wanting the same thing to happen to us. Everything happens for a reason, and I was determined to make the best out of my situation. It sickened me to hear of so many couples splitting apart, and many of them for trivial reasons, so if God wanted to use me as a tool in His hand to keep love alive in marriages, then so be it. I was willing.

"Is anything too hard for the LORD?" –Genesis 18:14

"I will praise the LORD, who counsels me; even at night my heart instructs me. I have set the LORD always before me. Because he is at my right hand, I will not be shaken." — Psalm 16:7–8

"May he give you the desire of your heart and make all your plans succeed. We will shout for joy when you are victorious and will lift up our banner in the name of our God. May the LORD grant all your requests. . . . Some trust in chariots and some in horses, but we trust in the name of the LORD our God. They are brought to their knees and fall, but we rise up and stand firm." — Psalm 20:4–5, 7–8

"I want to be changed, Lord, even more today, and I want to be more Christlike in nature. Purify me and prune me into Your likeness. I want to truly be a man of God, a husband with the godly traits talked about in Your Word, a friend and person filled with the fruits of the Spirit. Change me as I desire more of You and less of the world."

Stopping Poor Behaviors

"I know I need to stay pure in my life and treat people with love and respect. I want to walk through this day seeking to obey and hear God's voice. My dad and John return to Wisconsin today. I hope God has used me to facilitate change in both their lives. Grab hold of them, Lord, and let Your love take hold in their lives.

"Bless Lynn today as well. I hope she had a great time with Kayla this past weekend. Cover her, protect her, and let Your love move through her this week, Lord."

My decision to let go of some bad habits and to lay aside certain sins, including drinking too much wine, was doing wonders for me. I did not want to ever go back to the place I had been last summer when I was sinning against, God, Lynn, Kayla, and my own flesh. Though indulging my flesh, I was not happy at all. That's because sinning and happiness do not go together. The world thinks it does, as did I at the time, but loving God and happiness work hand in hand now and forever.

Meeting with Joanne and Sharing Who I Am

When I met with Joanne again, we went over the document I had put together and titled "Who I Am." This is what I listed:

"I am God's child and Christ's friend and have been justified and united in the Lord Jesus. I am a member of Christ's body and a saint of God. I have been adopted as God's child and redeemed and forgiven. I am the salt and light of the earth. I have been chosen and appointed to bear fruit. I am God's coworker.

"I am the loving husband of Lynn and the father of a wonderful daughter, Kayla. I am the son of great parents, Bill and Janet Kirk. I am the son-in-law of John and Suzie, who are great, godly people. I am the proud brother of Jeff, John, Scott, and Kim. I am the brother-in-law of Jenny and Tom.

"I am the close friend of Steve, Joe, Doug, Andy, Wendy, John, Nikki, Daren, Chris, Danny, Kent, Steve, Dave, and many others.

"I am a person who cares deeply about my daily walk with God. I am a person who helps people through life, making it easier for them and a better world for all.

"I am a person who realizes that I make mistakes, and I try to right the wrongs when I understand the magnitude of my actions.

"I am a leader at a printing company in the role of vice president of manufacturing, and I am also plant manager.

"I am blessed, anointed, empowered, and strong in the Lord.

"I am a person who works hard on his spiritual, mental, emotional, and physical state. I am a person who tries to do good for mankind, his family, and his own well-being.

"I am a servant of the most high God and have a calling on my life that I must fulfill."

After going over this list, Joanne commented, "See, you are so much more than just a husband. Yes, it's important to be a husband, but if in the future you are not, you can still go on and be productive." She was right; I was more than one-dimensional and could thrive into the future.

Joanne also recommended that I continue serving the homeless, attending my Life Group, reading, and relaxing through tae kwon do and golf.

Living in Accordance with God's Honor Code

"I talked to Kayla last night and had a great conversation with her. She is such a wonderful young lady. She seems to be very happy with friends, family, and school and is looking forward to coming back to Minnesota to visit Lynn, me, and friends at other colleges. Lord, please bless Kayla with Yourself, in her school and with her friends.

"As a leader at home and at work, I have to adjust my values so that they are in line with God's perspective. I must live with God and for God, and regardless of the world and other people's decisions, I will follow the Lord my God all the days of my life.

"I must live by God's honor code and do what is right in the eyes of the Lord. I must not turn to the right or the left in my journey. I will listen always to the Lord and follow after His ways, and He will make my path straight and cause the work of my hands to prosper all the days of my life."

Words from God

"You have made Me proud! You are walking after My ways and seeking Me all your days. I want to show Myself to you in deeper ways, and I will. Seek My ways, seek My will, and seek My desires for you and this world.

"The cup has tipped; the sins of man are too great. I am angry and will pour out My judgments on mankind. Know this, My son, you will be used as a spokesperson for My message to mankind. The days ahead will be days for you to prepare. Strengthen yourself in the Word and through prayer, and seek Me all the more.

"The time is at hand when I will release My plan. Be strong, and be of good courage, for the path will be filled with resistance, no doubt. Step by step, the journey will lead you to a different land for your voice to be heard. I will take care of the plans and the means to get you in a place to walk out my mission for your life. Fear not, for My hand is on you and will protect you."

Getting Rid of the Parasites (Sin) in My Life

Our accountability group met, and we had a great conversation. I shared about the ten parasites that were no longer a part of my life, and then I shared what I had replaced them with: journaling, daily devotions, daily prayers, reading godly books, attending Life Groups, watching TV ministers, listening to Christian radio, and meeting with Pastor Doug. I knew I was a much better person for making these changes, and I purposed to never turn back to the old Steve Kirk. I was moving ahead with God and hoping and praying that Lynn was moving forward too. I also prayed that we were both being obedient to God's Word and Spirit each day of our lives.

I also shared with the group that I felt God had allowed Lynn and me to walk through our present situation for a reason, for something much bigger than just our marriage. This difficult time was proving to be a real cleansing time for me, and I was asking the Lord to please continue, never stop, and work in His perfect timing. I wanted both Lynn and me to be cleansed and whole, committed to each other and, more importantly, to God and His kingdom.

Words from God

"My son, why are you downcast, worried, and concerned? Did I not tell you I have a plan for you? I have been, I am, and I will continue to hold Lynn in My hand. There have been breakthroughs this week, and she is coming to a place of forgiveness, release, and acceptance of you and My plan.

"Fear not, My son, for I am working in Lynn's heart, mind, and emotions. I will lift her up to a higher place. Put your faith and trust in Me and My plan. Believe, receive, and accept My calling on your life. Praise Me, praise My plan, and praise who I am this day."

Five Months of Separation: Is It Almost Over?

"Today makes five months since Lynn left home. At times it has seemed like a lifetime apart. I have believed time and time again that God is saying this separation is almost over. I have believed there is to be a ministry in the future. I have continued to pray for His perfect will and perfect timing.

"Last night, however, I gave up. I can do no more, plan no more, write no more, and love no more than I have already done. How much longer will I cry and hear in answer, 'It is coming to a close and the end is near'? Is this my own spirit, or is it God's Spirit? I believe it is God's Spirit, but I am unsure. I need confirmation, Lord, from another! I trust You completely, but I do not trust myself, and I need wise counsel to come into my life today.

"It's hard, extremely hard, when the pursuit of oneness is basically one-sided. Lynn may not be interested at all in recapturing the unity we once had. Even if there is some desire on her part, there may still be issues between us that are nowhere close to being resolved. But if I'll continue to keep a passion for oneness forefront in my mind and heart, our relationship over time will begin to reflect the inescapable one-flesh design that is imprinted on its DNA. I don't have to go looking for it—it's already there!"

"But the eyes of the LORD are on those who fear him, on those whose hope is in his unfailing love, to deliver them from death and keep them alive in famine. We wait in hope for the LORD; he is our help and our shield. In him our hearts rejoice, for we trust in his holy name. May your unfailing love rest upon us, O LORD, even as we put our hope in you."
—Psalm 33:18–22

"I must not give up because weeks or months pass with no response. I must not interpret delay as defeat. I cannot afford to assume that what I am doing is unfruitful. Most often, love or respect is working on our spouse more than we realize.

"Something is transpiring in Lynn' soul. I must have confidence that God is working. I will not give up trusting God to work this out. I will keep showing Lynn unconditional love and respect. I am holding fast, and help is on the way. My help is from God!"

Words from God

"It is time, My son, to listen closely to the words I am about to speak. Be prepared for the days ahead, for they are dark and painful. You will go through the fire, but it will purify, cleanse, and set you free. The fire is painful, hurtful, and brings a man to his knees; however, I need you on your knees searching for Me, knowing Me, and walking after Me every moment of your life. I will be with you each step of the way, and this time will end in greater blessing than you have ever seen.

"Fear not, for My hand is upon you, and I am guiding you into a deeper walk with Me. The fire you are about to experience will be caused by your sins of the past bubbling up and overflowing into Lynn's life. She is following a way that I have not chosen for her at this time. The hurt and the pain will surface, thrusting forth from her with a mighty force.

"Be prepared for this trial. Face it and consume it with My love and forgiveness, not with your pain and suffering. The outcome of Lynn's decisions will devastate your flesh, but do not let it touch your spirit. With the same love and forgiveness I have shown you, love her, accept her, and forgive her of the sins she has committed against you. Then and only then will this season in your life end. Fear not, for I am with you always and will not leave you, even in your darkest moments."

No More Going Through the Motions

"Do not be moved, Steve Kirk, no matter what comes your way. Regardless of what happens, stay strong and stand firm for God and His ways.

"Lord, I do not want to just go through the motions for even one more day of my life. I want Your all-consuming passion burning deep inside of me, and I want to walk after You all my days. Lord, pour forth Your love, compassion, and Spirit on my soul today. May I have Your wisdom, knowledge, and understanding, and may You bless the work of my hands and my heart."

"Humble yourselves, therefore, under God's mighty hand,
that he may lift you up in due time. Cast all your anxiety on
him because he cares for you." — 1 Peter 5:6–7

The Best Growth Period of My Life

While I certainly never would have chosen this valley I was walking in, it was proving to be the most fruitful growth period of my life. I was learning so many new things about God, Lynn, marriage, and friendship. My cup would overflow in the future as a result of this focused time of growth.

I had long needed a push forward in my spiritual life, and Lynn provided that push. I was praying that Lynn would grow with God during this time and not turn to the things of the world. We both needed to grow as individuals before coming back together in God's timing and will. I wanted to be part of a marriage characterized by deep love between partners and deep love for God, which in turn would spill over to the hurting people of the world.

"Lord, you are my hope, faith, and belief for the future. I put my trust in You, and I will obey Your ways."

Better Understanding of the Owner's Manual

"I must renew my mind daily and saturate it in the Word of God. So many times in the past, I quickly read the Word or spent little time in it. To really know God and His perfect ways in my life, however, I must pour His Word over my thoughts and prayers. By doing this, I will die daily to my own flesh and take up the things God wants me to accomplish. Not only that, but I will be more willing to help others in my daily activities. Helping others first demonstrates the servant-leader style that Christ shows us in the Word. When I accomplish these feats, I am doing exactly what Christ has called me to do: love God and love others!"

It Takes Two Whole People to Live, Love, and Laugh Together in Marriage

I was finally beginning to understand why Lynn was not calling me and why Joanne kept saying Lynn and I had to be two whole people before coming back together. If our marriage was to be truly different from what it had been in the past, we would both have to be whole. Even then, we would have to work to maintain it.

Lynn and I needed to help each other grow stronger and stronger as the days went by. Our love, too, needed to grow in that time frame. There was great hope for our marriage, I believed; we would rise out of the ashes in the coming days, I felt certain. Even if I didn't see anything happening in our relationship right now, I believed God was at work.

"Lord, keep both Lynn and me safe, out of sin, and our eyes on You alone. I believe things are happening in our relationship, even if I don't see them!"

Chapter 9

A Raging Blaze That Both Burns and Heals

"In this you greatly rejoice, though now for a little while you may have had to suffer grief in all kinds of trials. These have come so that your faith—of greater worth than gold, which perishes even though refined by fire—may be proved genuine and may result in praise, glory and honor when Jesus Christ is revealed."
—1 Peter 1:6–7

Words from God

"You shall abide under My shadow. You will walk with Me, and I will walk with you. I will pour out My Spirit on you. You will dream dreams and see visions.

"My son, I am well pleased with your walk with Me. I will show you holiness. I will test your obedience and trustworthiness in the days ahead. Walk after Me, follow Me, and seek Me while I can be found. Listen to My words and follow after My ways, and then you will find freedom for your soul.

"Lean on Me, My son. Though the days ahead are dark, I will bring light. Victory will come out of the darkness. Trust Me, seek Me, and lean on Me."

"When I am the right person before God, I can do whatever task He sends in whatever place He puts me. In doing this, I discover and affirm His calling on my life."

"But as for you, be strong and do not give up, for your work
will be rewarded." — 2 Chronicles 15:7

Life Group and Separation Elsewhere

"I went to Life Group last night and had a good time. I talked to Tim, who is also going through a separation right now. He commented that he and I were going through the same thing, but after talking to Tim for fifteen minutes, it became apparent to me that we are not alike at all, though we both are separated. He has given up, and I haven't. I will fight to the end with love in my heart for Lynn.

"God, You have joined Lynn and me together. I know that, believe that, and will not stop loving Lynn, my partner. My prayer for Tim is that he would not give up, but fight on, change for the better, and love the Lord his God forever."

Note to the reader: Tim and his wife Carrie went all the way to signing divorce papers and sending them to the judge to make their divorce final. At the last moment, Carrie called Tim and wanted to talk. After many meetings and dates, Tim and Carrie reunited and now live together with their three daughters. I am very happy they got back together and now live well with the Lord's guidance.

The Desire to Be Holy in God's Sight

"Lord, I want to be holy, pure, and blameless in Your sight. I want to follow You all my days. I will seek You, worship You, and honor You every day, regardless of what life brings. You are my true source of happiness."

"But you, man of God, flee from all this, and pursue righteousness, godliness, faith, love, endurance, and gentleness." — 1 Timothy 6:11–12

"Therefore, I urge you brothers, in view of God's mercy, to offer your bodies as living sacrifices, holy and pleasing to God—this is your spiritual act of worship. Do not conform any longer to the pattern of this world, but be transformed by the renewing of your mind. Then you will be able to test and approve what God's will is—his good, pleasing and perfect will."—Romans 12:1–2

"I need to continue to build my life in the Lord. I need to continue to seek Him and learn from Him daily. When I open my mouth today, I want blessing, not cursing, to come out. I want to be a positive person who builds and renews people as I walk through this life."

"Be completely humble and gentle; be patient, bearing with one another in love. Make every effort to keep the unity of the Spirit through the bond of peace."—Ephesians 4:2–3

"I need to take time every morning and night to search God's heart. To the best of my ability, I must do what I believe God wants me to do and trust Him to take care of my critics. I must refuse to let people talk me out of what I know in my heart God is telling me to do.

"I must keep my heart pure and stay true to the person God has made me to be. God made me like I am, totally unique, for a specific purpose. I have a specific, God-given purpose for my life. I need God to show me what's close to His heart and implement it in my daily life. I need to be confident in who I am. I am God's masterpiece."

Prayer and Leaning on God for All Knowledge

In *The Love Dare*, as I read about a husband and wife who prayed together, I decided Lynn and I must do the same when we got back together as a couple. By putting God first in our lives, then Kayla, family, and the rest of the word, I felt sure we could look forward to a bright future together.

When our accountability group met again, a friend named Steve mentioned that we generally have only a few pieces of the puzzle of our life. That was certainly true of me, and with the few pieces I had, my view of my marriage and future was probably 99 percent wrong!

"God, You know what is happening in Lynn's life and what will happen concerning our marriage. Please move in Your timing and Your perfect plan! I must have patience and let this whole plan play out as it will."

Kayla Is a Blessing to Me and the World

Kayla was home for spring break, just when I so needed to spend time with her. She had grown into a wonderful young lady with her eyes set on the right things in life. I consistently prayed for the Lord to touch her heart and develop a passion for the things of God in her life.

"Thank You, God, for giving Lynn and me such a major blessing in our lives as our daughter. I cannot wait to see how many people's lives she touches in a positive way in the coming years. I hope and pray that she sees this time apart for Lynn and me is making both of us stronger in our spiritual walk and maturing our faith in You.

"I do not know about Lynn, but as for me, I want to share the goodness of God with Kayla throughout this visit and the rest of her life. I do that whenever there is an opportunity. I do not want to push Jesus down anyone's throat; however, at the same time, I need to live out my faith for Him and let others see it. I know God will never forget anything we do in His service with a clean heart and mind. I have faith that one day Lynn, Kayla, and I will be a family again, serving Him together. What a glorious day that will be!"

Growing Through the Fire of Separation

When Lynn left our home on September 27, 2008, I thought my life was over. It took the wind right out of my sails. I broke down and cried out to God, and I prayed like I had never prayed before. Although it wasn't easy to get back up and walk on, I did and somehow survived. In the midst of my greatest trial, God, in His mercy and grace, met me with His promised peace that surpasses all comprehension (see Philippians 4:7) and kept me on my feet.

Five months later, I was beginning to realize that I had grown into a new person, a better person than what I had ever been. I was proud of my growth as a person, a father, and a godly man. However, based upon the lack of closeness between Lynn and me over this time, I could not say what kind of husband I would be. Nevertheless, because of all the other changes taking place in my life, I felt sure I could succeed and enjoy marriage with Lynn again, if that was God's will and Lynn's desire.

I was now at a point where I knew I had to put my desire for Lynn and our marriage into proper perspective. It had to be second to my relationship with God—now and always. For far too long, I had put Lynn, Kayla, and the things of this world before God. From this point on, I wanted to walk according to God's Word, with no person, idol, or sin having priority over Him.

"I take a stand today to put my thoughts, actions, and plans in this order: God, Lynn, Kayla, family, friends, and the world. Bless my hands, Lord God, as I take this stand for You and Your kingdom. I worship You as the Lord my God this day and every day going forward.

"Help me, Lord, to show respect and love to others, always mindful of the fact that each of us is created in Your image. I need Your love to shine through my life and bring praise and honor to You. I hope in You for all things!"

"Not only so; but we also rejoice in our sufferings, because we know that suffering produces perseverance, perseverance, character; and character, hope. And hope does not disappoint us, because God has poured out his love into our hearts by the Holy Spirit, whom he has given us." —Romans 5:3–5

"So do not throw away your confidence; it will be richly rewarded." —Hebrews 10:35

The God of the Universe Is in My Life

I pressed on in life, secure in the knowledge that the Creator of the universe was directing my path. God was in complete control, so now was not the time to get discouraged or give up. No, it was time for me to get my second wind and move forward in what God was doing and what He wanted me to be doing on His behalf.

God was breathing new life into my dreams, but it always takes work to see God's plans come to pass. I was willing to do whatever was necessary to have my marriage healed and whole. For weeks I had been reading and praying the prayers from the book *The Power of a Praying Husband*, and I was committed to praying them for as long as Lynn and I were married. A spiritual battle against our marriage and our future was raging, a battle with the forces of darkness and the world. The battle was not against Lynn, but against the rulers, the authorities, the powers of this dark world, and the spiritual forces of evil in the heavenly realms. This awareness strengthened the hope in my heart that was feeding my faith.

"We live by faith; not by sight."—2 Corinthians 5:7

"I need God's wisdom in my life like never before. I need Him to pour forth His wisdom anew on my mind today. I need Him to grant me a double portion so I can choose wisely the steps I should take today and every day going into the future."

"If any of you lacks wisdom, he should ask God, who gives generously to all without finding fault, and it will be given to him."—James 1:5

The Fire Also Burns Those Closest to Us

A dark moment descended upon Kayla's visit home. Kayla and I had lunch together on Friday, and then I dropped her at the house and returned to work. Lynn was supposed to be picking Kayla up for the weekend so they could enjoy some time together. At 3:30 p.m., however, Lynn called to tell Kayla that she was going to the city for the weekend with a girlfriend and would see Kayla on the following Thursday. At 4:30 p.m. Kayla called me, crying, and shared what had happened.

For the second time in this journey, I felt as though my flesh was being torn from my body. But this time the pain was not for me, but for my precious daughter. I went home, and Kayla and I cried together for two hours. I slipped away for a moment to call Pastor Doug, and he gave me some wise counsel: support Kayla, he said, but don't make Lynn look bad in her eyes. Heeding his words, I decided to make the most of our time together.

Since then, I have often wondered if Lynn truly understood the pain that Kayla suffered from her decision that day. But then again, I have often wondered what Kayla felt about some of the decisions I made over the years. Regardless, Lynn and I did later talk about what had happened, but Lynn felt strongly she had made the right decision, which was made with her counselor's encouragement.

Spending Time with My Wonderful Daughter

Despite the circumstances, I had a great time with Kayla. The next morning I prepared a breakfast of eggs and sausage—the first time ever I had made breakfast! I couldn't help but wonder why it took Lynn's leaving for me to spread my wings and become a man of the twenty-first century. Why hadn't I ever made breakfast for my family? Why hadn't we spent more time playing games and doing things as a family? It was pointless to ask such questions now; all I could do was to forget my past mistakes and move forward to a different future.

After breakfast Kayla and I went to church, then out to lunch, and then bowling together. Returning home, we shot five games of pool, and then I made homemade chili for the two of us.

I loved my daughter with all my heart. I wanted nothing more than to take care of this bright young lady with such a promising future. In our time together, Kayla shared that she had issues with her mother, and I hoped and prayed they could work through them while Kayla was home and that love would reach deep into the hearts of all three of us.

"Our fathers disciplined us for a little while as they thought best; but God disciplines us for our good, that we may share in his holiness. No discipline seems pleasant at the time, but painful. Later on, however, it produces a harvest of righteousness and peace for those who have been trained by it." — Hebrews 12:10–11

Meeting with Joanne

As might be expected, I wanted to discuss with Joanne Lynn's decision to leave Kayla behind for the weekend. She urged me to stay out of the issue and let Kayla and Lynn handle it. Pastor Doug had advised the same thing, and deep in my heart, I knew I should stay out of it because it did not involve me. Joanne did suggest that I encourage Kayla to see a counselor so she could share her feelings with a third party.

When I shared with Joanne that I felt like an eager dog on a chain that jumped and reacted whenever Lynn wanted to talk or get together, she responded firmly, "You are not a dog on a chain, and you do not need to feel that way. Lynn is gaining control of the situation, not controlling you." For the third time, Joanne also voiced her opinion that I should tell Lynn she needed to begin to financially support herself. She usually brought this up in the context of the unhealthy parent-child relationship Lynn and I had developed as a couple. As long as the issue was not discussed, it raised the question of whether we were still together simply because of the financial support I could offer, which only promoted the continuation of a broken marriage.

"So we say with confidence, 'The Lord is my helper, I will not be afraid. What can man do to me?' " — Hebrews 13:6

"I know what it is to be in need, and I know what it is to have plenty. I have learned the secret of being content in any and every situation, whether well fed or hungry, whether living in plenty or in want. I can do everything through him who gives me strength." — Philippians 4:12–13

God the Father Is the Only Indispensable Person in My Life

"The key to my contentment in this situation is realizing that God the Father has given me everything I need to remain victorious. My ability to remain victorious comes from Jesus' power flowing in and through me. This ability does not come to me naturally; it comes by learning through my reliance on Jesus.

"Though Lynn and I have certainly needed each other over the years and we are still married, she—nor anyone else for that matter—can be considered indispensable in my life. Only God is indispensable. This separation has brought me great despair and turmoil, and it has rightly been pointed out to me that I have at times put Lynn on the throne that should be occupied by God alone. I should never see Lynn as the only source of my completeness in this world. By doing so, I limit my emotional and spiritual freedom and the completeness that comes only from God Himself.

"I really need to put God first and give Him all my focus! I need to stay patient and let God have His way. I trust You, God, and lean on You, Jesus, and I need to hear from Your Holy Spirit."

Willing to Follow God with Every Fiber of My Being

"Even in my darkest hour, the Lord will bless me with His power; His loving grace will surely abound, and in His sweet care I shall be found.

"I feel at peace this morning, knowing God is in control and I am not. God has a plan for my life, and I am willing to walk in that plan. Yes, for the first time in my life, I am willing to follow God 100 percent in all things.

"Speak to me, Lord, and I will trust and obey Your direction this day."

"Praise be to the God and Father of our Lord Jesus Christ, the Father of compassion and the God of all comfort, who comforts us in all our troubles, so that we can comfort those

in any trouble with the comfort we ourselves have received
from God."—2 Corinthians 1:3–4

"I truly believe God has a plan and purpose for me to share His good news with others in this world. I believe my message will deal with relationships, and I believe this ministry will be blessed by the hand of God.

"God, prepare me for today, tomorrow, and the future. I open myself to You and Your ways, even if that includes more pruning and purging in my life. I know that it's the only way I can live in this world and eventually in heaven. Fill me with Your Spirit and ways this day and every day. I love You and thank You for Your hand of mercy, grace, and love in my life."

Meeting with Doug

In my next meeting with Doug, he remarked, "I have never seen a man work so hard to change behaviors that were not right." He added, "I have never seen a man put so many positive, godly behaviors in place so quickly and stick to them."

Doug felt only positive results would eventually result from this time. He likened the process to digging deep into a wound to bring forth total healing. He observed, "Some couples merely put a Band-Aid on their problems and just suffer through a painful marriage. If you and Lynn make it to full recovery, great things will happen in your marriage long-term."

He felt Kayla needed to share her anger and feelings with her mother without my intervention. "While Kayla is in town," he added, "she can share with her mother all the changes she has seen in your life."

I knew one thing for sure: I had to go higher in the Lord and then stay there consistently. If I continually reflected on this revelation and communed with God regularly, I would eventually become more and more like Jesus. And that was exactly what I wanted—to be like Jesus and have the mind of Christ.

"For the eyes of the Lord range throughout the earth to strengthen those whose hearts are fully committed to him."—2 Chronicles 16:9

Vision of a Field

I received a picture of a field and then seeds falling from heaven, followed by a mist. The seeds began to germinate and grow into plants, but they needed to be fertilized. In the vision, I sensed that I should start speaking out words, so I spoke *love, compassion, joy, happiness,* and *unity.* Each spoken word broke apart in the air and fell onto the plants as fertilizer. The plants grew green and very tall.

I had the impression that the field was Lynn's heart, and the words spoken were falling on her heart to fertilize and facilitate her complete growth in the love of Christ and the love of people. No longer would dry, barren, dusty ground occupy her heart, but green, fruitful land that would provide food to her and others, including me, in the days to come.

"Trials can make life seem not worth living. Focusing on me can lead to despair. But putting my total trust in God gives me an entirely different perspective. As long as I live in this world, I can be certain that my all-sufficient God will sustain me. I will always have a definite purpose for my life."

"Indeed, in our hearts we felt the sentence of death. But this happened that we might not rely on ourselves but on God, who raises the dead."—2 Corinthians 1:9

Cleaning Out My Temple

I wanted to be a man whose temple was clean so that the Lord could reside there freely. I wanted to be a man who walked after the Lord daily, filled with compassion, love, mercy, forgiveness, faith, patience, and purity. I wanted all my steps to be guided by the Lord, and my deepest desire was to walk pure and holy all my remaining days, excelling in the things of God and building His kingdom.

I did not want to be a competitive, forceful, hard-hearted man filled with pain. As I cried out to God, "Why am I here at this place in my life?" I heard nothing. But then I opened my Bible, and God spoke to me through the story of Joseph in the Old Testament. As I read the biblical record, it became quite clear that Joseph experienced God's presence the most when he faced the worst, most difficult times of his life. When his brothers sold him into slavery, when Potiphar's wife claimed he had raped her, and even when he was forgotten in prison, the Lord was still with him.

Though my life made absolutely no sense to me, it made complete sense to God. Joseph had to go through his hard circumstances in order to forge steel into his soul. Without them he would not have been ready for the great task God had reserved for him. I believed something similar was going on in my own life.

In September of 2008, I couldn't even get out of my own way. I was sinning, and it was growing worse by the day. Yet through the pain, purging, and pruning, I had been cleansed in so many areas and now had a deeper love for the Lord, Lynn, and Kayla. I knew God was preparing a ministry for me and had a plan for my life bigger than what it had been up to this point, but I also knew I had to stay pure and holy in God's eyes if that ministry was to come to pass. If I was going to treat Lynn, Kayla, family, and friends right every day going forward, I had to walk as a true man of God.

"Lord, let Your will and perfect plan continue to unfold in my life! You always have a plan, though it might not be the plan I want or play out the way I want it to. But Your plan will be fulfilled if I will just follow after Your ways throughout my life."

God Has Not and Never Will Forget Me

"Quick points for me to remember: Stay in the will of God. I am in God's hands. God will remember me; He has not forgotten me. God is going to supernaturally make changes happen. I am not alone and never will be, because I am unforgettable to the Lord. I will not give up on Lynn or our marriage. God has a destiny for me in life. It is not what I am going through that is important—it's what I'm going to!"

Lynn Takes Kayla to the Airport

When it came time for Kayla to return to Florida, I was sad to see her go. But it was her life, of course, and she seemed happiest in Florida with her new friends and boyfriend.

During her visit, there had been five whole days when I didn't see her, which made me sad. There were so many downsides to this separation, and this was certainly one of them. However, as Kayla pointed out, if Lynn and I had been together, she and I probably wouldn't have spent nearly as much time together as we did. That was an interesting comment, and it probably would have been true in the past. But I knew it could never be that way in the future.

"It was good seeing Lynn when she stopped by to pick up Kayla. She is so beautiful and looked quite relaxed. She wants to call this evening or within the next few days to ask me some questions. I want to be open and answer them truthfully.

"Lord, I speak blessings of healing over Lynn, and bless me with healing and the fulfillment of Your plan. Make Lynn and me completely one for the first time in our marriage."

Someone once said, "A problem is an opportunity to step into a new dimension of accomplishment." Sometimes God customizes a problem so that we can fulfill the purpose for which we were created. The problem is merely a stepping stone to our divine destiny.

Thinking on this, I purposed to view my separation as a mere obstacle on the path to victory. What the devil meant for evil, God meant for good! I could never allow these problems to separate me from God's promises on the road to His supernatural plan and provision for my life. The separation in my marriage might end badly, but God would never leave me or forsake me in this life or the life to come.

"But blessed is the man who trusts in the LORD, whose confidence is in him."—Jeremiah 17:7

"Dear friend, I pray that you may enjoy good health and that all may go well with you, even as your soul is getting along well." — 3 John 2

"I must remember that no matter how nice I am, how much time and energy I give, Lynn has her own issues to deal with and resolve. Joanne has been saying this for weeks; I am slowly getting it deep down in my soul. I need to take all the pressure off myself and let God deal with Lynn. I totally and completely surrender Lynn to God. With that said, I, too, need a deeper walk with Him."

Checklist to a Deeper Walk with God

Here are some things that helped me deepen my walk with God, and you may find them helpful too:

1. Reading the Word of God (Josh. 1:8)
2. Obeying the conditions of the promise
3. Proclaiming God's promises in faith
4. Repenting of all sin in my life (Isa. 55:7)
5. Forgiving everyone that may have offended me (Matt. 6:14–15)
6. Tithing (Prov. 3:9)
7. Seeking God daily for my needs (1 Tim. 5:5)
8. Trusting in God to see me through all things (Ps. 78:7)
9. Praising God on the mountaintop and also in the valley (Ex. 15:2)
10. Letting God control my life (Ps. 47:2–4)

"When I am aligned with God's Word, then I will know that the source of the separation is not coming from within any longer, but from somewhere else. I put my trust in God, in His Word, and in His Spirit, and I will wait for His movement in my marriage. I know He has a plan and will free me from the pain and failure I am experiencing. Knowing that I am in God's will means better days are ahead.

"It is great to have freedom and know that God cares for me and will watch over me if I serve Him and seek Him. This separation did

not take God by surprise. It did me, but nothing can ever surprise Him. He is never worried about my marriage or anything else, and He has already provided a way for me to overcome the pain, hurt, and feelings of not measuring up."

Answering Questions That Pained Lynn

"Lynn and I had a conversation last night that lasted two hours. I answered all the questions she and Gwen had put together about what I was thinking when I did and said certain things to her over the years. The questions dealt with the house we didn't buy, the looks of other women, the way I had looked at a friend from years ago, and Lynn's looks and decisions. I answered them truthfully and to the best of my ability. I think it was a good conversation, and Lynn seemed understanding and open to my explanation that much of it really had nothing to do with her but was the result of my own immaturity and unfair treatment of her throughout the years.

"At the end of the conversation, I also shared that I had made a birthday cake for her, and if she wanted us to do something together, I was open to celebrating her day with her. I get the feeling nothing will happen, but I need to keep the door open. Baby steps continue going forward, but they are steps in the right direction—at least I hope they are!"

Actions to Shorten a Stay in Any Problem

Here's another list I came up with. This one dealt with how I might shorten the length of time I had to spend in my problem, and hopefully it will help you too:

1. Acknowledge the problem.
2. Take responsibility for your actions.
3. Be willing to work through it.
4. When you are wrong, admit it.
5. Forgive.
6. Control your tongue.
7. Take your eyes off yourself and put them on God.

"Only when I take responsibility for who I am, what I have become, and the decisions I have made will I reach my divine destiny. I want to reach my destiny, and I am willing to let God use anything in His power to accomplish what He wants when He wants it. For many years, I wanted my own will and desired to plot my own destiny. That included the way I presented myself to other people, including Lynn.

"But this was wrong; life is about the love of God and the love of other people, starting with Lynn—not about me and my plans. I have been wrong, and I have admitted it to Lynn many times over the months. I believe I am now walking in the true nature of the Lord, and I know the outcome will be wonderful at the end of my days."

" 'For I know the plans I have for you,' declares the LORD, 'plans to prosper you and not to harm you, plans to give you hope and a future.' "—Jeremiah 29:11

Accountability Group Meets and Preparing for Lynn's Birthday

I met with my accountability group, and we prayed for our families, places of work, and other people. It was good to get together with other people and focus on God.

The rest of the day also went well as I prepared for Lynn's birthday. I bought roses, a card, and balloons, and I left the cake out for her. Why hadn't I done fun stuff like that before now? Well, regardless of the excuse, I hadn't. All I could do now was pledge to myself that I would never again forget the love I felt and the joy of expressing it. I hoped Lynn would enjoy all the things I had done for her birthday, including the cake. But even if she didn't, I had done it because I loved her and missed her smiling face.

The Movement Towards a Christlike Spirit

I understood a large reason for this valley was to transform me into a more Christlike person. God was taking out the fleshly and immature part of my nature, stripping me of my selfish, controlling, perfectionist ways. I needed to learn how to totally depend on Him and His nature rather than on myself. The purging process was painful, as though my flesh was being pulled from my body, but oh, it was so freeing to rest in God and His control! I was slowly becoming a man looking to fulfill Christ's calling rather than his own selfish desires.

Words from God

"Let Me come into your life, My son, and release you of your burdens. Give your burdens to Me, and I will carry them and release you from the pain you feel. I am the God who puts all things in their rightful places. I am the God who releases love and mercy on all mankind. I am the God who heals you of pains and hurts.

"Walk after Me, My son. Follow My ways, seek My directions, and know My will for your life. The time is at hand for you to walk a new way. I am setting up circumstances for you to minister to My body. Are you ready to travel the road for Me? Are you ready to be guided by My hand into the future?

"Be wise in the days ahead as I pour Myself into your life. Know that I am the God who sets all things into place. You are finding your place, and I am well pleased, Steve. Come to Me, and draw your strength from Me. Blessings are coming your way, so be open to them and realize they are truly from My hand to yours.

"Great is My name to be praised this day!"

"Ears to hear, and eyes to see—the Lord has made them both."—Proverbs 20:12

"A man's steps are directed by the Lord. How then can anyone understand his own way?"—Proverbs 20:24

Lynn Comes by the House When I am Not at Home

Lynn came by the house while I was not there and picked up all the things I had gotten for her birthday. I didn't know if she would accept all of them, but I was delighted when she did, along with several books I had left for her with a note.

Furthermore, she left a note for me that read: "Thank you for the dinner certificate, the roses, the card, and the bottle caps (candy). I really wasn't expecting anything and am at a loss for words. You were very kind to think of me and put all that effort into your plans. I hope your testing period goes well and you become an orange belt. I am proud of you and know you are proud of yourself, as you should be. The balloons were a nice touch too—probably one of the nicer surprises I have had over the years. Again, thank you for your kindness and all the trouble you went to for me."

"When I get notes expressing feelings like that, I grow hopeful. I don't know, though, if maybe I am just fooling myself, and at times, I think I really am. What should I do, Lord?

" 'Never give up, for that is just the place and time that the tide will turn' seemed to be the Lord's answer. The darkest hour does come right before the dawn. So Lord, have I seen my darkest hour yet?"

Lynn's Birthday and Another Dark Moment

Today was Lynn's birthday and also the day I had invited her to come watch me test for my orange belt in tae kwon do. I eagerly hoped that she would come and that afterwards we would do something together for her birthday. Well, Lynn did not come, but she did send me three text messages apologizing for her behavior. It made me sad, though, that she wasn't there to share this moment in my life. I did pass my test, but the joy of the achievement was gone.

For the first time in more than twenty-five years, Lynn and I did not celebrate her birthday together. This was the first big milestone in our married life that Lynn missed. Was this my darkest hour? Was I fooling myself into believing love was still there, when in reality it had been gone for months, if not years?

The pain and darkness ebbed and flowed all that dark day. I struggled to cling to God and pray my way through with a belief in a brighter future.

I Must Not Lose Focus on God and His Plan

"I must invest my time in thinking about what God is doing or will be doing. I must stay positive in all my actions. Every day is a gift from God, so act like it, Steve!

"I must continue to have faith in God. At times I confuse myself and place my faith in Lynn and her ability and willingness to come back to our marriage and home. I must continue to place my faith in God, because He is God and I am not—nor is Lynn in my eyes."

"Now faith is being sure of what we hope for and certain of what we do not see."—Hebrews 11:1

" 'Have faith in God,' Jesus answered. 'I tell you the truth, if anyone says to this mountain, "Go throw yourself into the sea," and does not doubt in his heart but believes that what he says will happen, it will be done for him. Therefore I tell you, whatever you ask for in prayer, believe that you have received it, and it will be yours.' "—Mark 11:22–24

"Lord God, I need Your supernatural blessing on my marriage this week. I believe a breakthrough is coming, and I seek You for that major breakthrough. Bless Lynn, bless me, and bless our marriage this day and every day going forward."

I Will Never Give Up Faith in God

"This day was long! I worked out and listened to five ministers, all good. Then I went to church and heard about Mary's view of Christ, and then I returned home and took a long walk with Angel. Next I was off to Place of Hope to serve food to the homeless. When I got home, I spent two hours doing laundry and ironing shirts.

"Even while doing all this, I couldn't help thinking about my life and where it is going. Will it be with Lynn or another? What is the timing? Why am I here in this place? God, I believe You have given me Your direction, but how long before I see a change in my circumstances?

"God, I believe You and Your Word! I need a supernatural miracle from Your hand. I know I have done everything in my human nature, and I know You are working on my behalf. One moment I see victory, but in the next moment I see defeat and want to give up. Then I remember the covenant both Lynn and I spoke on July 9, 1983, and believe the fire of love will return to both of us at the same level. I also believe this fight is for others who will be blessed when we start our ministry in the future.

"After all this, I say to myself, to Satan, and to You, Lord God, that I will fight on and never give up! Lord, give me strength, and be with Lynn and me on this journey. Let release happen, but in the meantime, I could sure use Your peace in my life!"

"Thus far the LORD has helped us."— 1 Samuel 7:12

"I will continue to put You first in my life, God. I will not go back to the ways of the past. The enemy used September 27 for evil, but You will use this separation for a turning point in my life and victory for Your kingdom. The kingdom of heaven advances with people who serve You; therefore, I will serve You with all my heart, mind, soul, and body."

Count Your Blessings and Name Them One by One

When I looked at my life, I saw so many wonderful things to be thankful for. I had a great relationship with Kayla and the rest of my family, a good job, money to pay my bills, and my health. I had also been blessed with a long marriage to Lynn, who had been a loving wife and mother throughout the years. Lynn's decision to leave and the results that followed were like a small black dot on a large white sheet of paper. The little black dot had no right to capture all my attention. So now I was counting my blessings and naming them one by one. So many blessings and so little issues had visited my life throughout the years. Truly, I had a lot to be thankful for.

"My blessings, successes, and joys are wonderful memories I will hold onto now and into the future. Rejoice and be glad, oh my soul! Good things are about to happen—to me!"

Meeting with Joanne

I had a meeting with Joanne. She advised me, whenever I felt angry, controlling, or embarrassed, to step back, relax, and evaluate what others in the situation might want or need. Quite possibly, I might be misreading the situation and need to reevaluate the moment. When something caused me pain, she suggested I stop, walk around, reread the situation, and just relax in the moment. Own my own feelings, not others', she recommended. Their feelings were their feelings—not mine.

Joanne also pointed out that I seemed to throw up walls quickly. She urged me to resist that tendency by first getting the facts in a given situation and letting them soak in. Last of all, she urged me to get to know my mother better and develop a right relationship with her.

Little by little, I was learning I could control neither people nor circumstances. Life's events happen. It is our responsibility to choose our responses and our attitudes.

Words from God

"There are clouds on the horizon, but they will break up and the Son will shine. Prepare yourself for the great days ahead—days of love and mercy, days of peace in your household. Put away the things that are not pleasing to Me. Go forth with boldness and strength as you fight the good fight.

"The days ahead will be filled with My glory. I am releasing My glory on your head even now. You will dream dreams, and you will see visions. Write them down, share them with the body, and learn from them, for they have a purpose. Great days are ahead, but so are terrible ones.

"Every day you have a choice to serve Me or serve the world. Choose wisely, My son, each day. The days ahead are filled with blessings from My hand if you will follow My ways."

"If you falter in times of trouble, how small is your
strength!"—Proverbs 24:10

"I waited patiently for the LORD; he turned to me, and heard
my cry. He lifted me out of the slimy pit, out of the mud and
mire; he set my feet on a rock, and gave me a firm place to
stand. He put a new song in my mouth, a hymn of praise to
our God. Many will see and fear and put their trust in the
LORD. Blessed is the man who makes the LORD his trust, who
does not look to the proud, to those who turn aside to false
gods."—Psalm 40:1–4

*"God has something specific in mind for me! He has a divine
design for my life, something unique, fantastic, and special that is
above and beyond my ability to think or imagine. His thoughts and
actions are far above my thoughts and actions. They are purer and
more wonderful than anything I have ever thought they could be."*

Words from God

"You can do nothing more than you have already done. It is not
up to you and what you do. The situation can be changed only by Me
and Lynn. Keep doing everything you are doing! Keep searching
My Word, keep seeking Me and My plan, keep desiring the pure
ways of My true essence. Lean on Me, trust Me, walk after Me, and
take every thought captive on this journey called life.

"I have blessed you, I am blessing you, and I will bless you into
the future. Do not turn to your foolish thoughts and actions. As I
have said before, do not look at the outward signs; trust Me! Know
that you are the temple of the Holy Spirit; keep your temple clean
and in order.

"The times of testing will come in a different way in the coming
days, so prepare yourself in the Word. Obey My voice and you will
walk safely through the fire."

Letting Go and Letting God

"No matter what happens to me today, Jesus is walking beside me, strengthening me, loving me, and filling me with faith, hope, and love. I will be obedient to Him regardless of what the future holds. He is the God of all and, most importantly, the God who loves me and cares about me in every way.

"I need a miracle from God to bring healing to my wounded marriage that appears to be falling apart. I know God is an awesome God, and absolutely nothing is impossible with Him. Still, letting God have total control is scary to my human senses. Yes, He can take me to places higher than I could ever go, but He can also take me to places lower than I would ever want to go.

"He can cause me to look in the mirror and see who Steve Kirk really is, and that can be nerve-racking and humbling, as it opens my flesh and exposes the worldliness in me. However, he can also pour in His character and ooze His Christlike nature into me, thus making me a better person, husband, father, and friend who can impact the world for good. At the end of my days, I want to be so Christlike that when people look at me, they do not see me, but the nature of the Savior and Redeemer of the world. I desire to live for an audience of one."

God Must Be First in My Life

My friend Dave said something that really hit me between the eyes. He prayed that my focus would be on the heart of God more than on Lynn. During this journey, there had been times—actually many times—when I was more focused on Lynn than on God Himself. I knew that had to change. Though praying, reading the Bible, and going to Life Group were activities primarily centered on God and my relationships with others, at times I did them more for Lynn and me. That had to stop; God had to be first in all I did.

"Lord, please pour Your Spirit on me and let me feel Your love like never before. I want to serve You first and think of You first in

all that I do. I want to walk pure, holy, and blameless this day and every day from now on.

"As I read about the people of faith in Hebrews 11, I think about each one of them and their journey to holiness. Each one endured horrible, painful experiences as God worked to infuse His nature into their worldly bodies. I believe each one would say in hindsight that it was a very small price to pay for the sake of the kingdom and the Savior.

"My journey has been painful and unbearable at times, but each pain and character- building moment is worth it for His glory. It has been said, 'We will not change until the pain of our circumstances exceeds the pain of change,' and I have found that all too true."

"No discipline seems pleasant at the time, but painful. Later on, however, it produces a harvest of righteousness and peace for those who have been trained by it."—Hebrews 12:11

My Ways Are Not Working, but God's Ways Will!

Throughout the years, I had been far too impatient, and consequently, I had often missed God's very best for my life. I often tried to do things in my own timing and my own way, but God wanted to do things in His timing and His way.

Still, in my present situation, I struggled with God, sometimes wondering who would win long-term. Because of my past behavior, I had gone around this mountain more than once, and it was harder each time. But my skills and abilities, including the ability to wait patiently on the Lord, were being forged by God's right hand. His freedom would come as my character changed, I slowly realized. In the past, I had been unwilling to relinquish certain behaviors because I thought they were working in a positive-enough manner that did not require change; however, now I knew these behaviors must change and change now.

In 2006, when I lost a job I loved at a great company, I wrote in my journal that if things didn't change concerning my behaviors, worse things would happen in the future. At that time, I changed some of my questionable behaviors, but not all of them, and now here

I was—right in the middle of another painful relationship failure. I did not want to walk this path again in the future, so I determined to change all behavioral issues and give up my selfish, controlling, perfectionist nature that lacked patience with other people. I wanted to go forward with God's character, and my old nature included none of it. Interestingly, I was always ready to learn, but not always ready to be taught.

"I will lead the blind by ways they have not known, along unfamiliar paths I will guide them; I will turn darkness into light before them and make the rough places smooth. These are the things I will do; I will not forsake them."
—Isaiah 42:16

"He has showed you, O man, what is good. And what does the LORD require of you? To act justly and to love mercy and to walk humbly with your God."—Micah 6:8

Chapter 10

A New Fire Begins: The Blazing Energy of God's Glory

"The LORD will guide you always; he will satisfy your needs in a sun-scorched land and will strengthen your frame. You will be like a well-watered garden, like a spring whose waters never fail."—Isaiah 58:11

Stop the Fighting Against God and His ways

God can safely guide us through any issue, but sometimes we struggle against Him and His will. Even though He assures us, "This might hurt a bit, but you're going to feel a whole lot better when it's over," we still resist.

"I am starting to face the reality that Lynn might tell me she wants a divorce and does not want me in her life any longer. I still hold out hope in the impossible, the reconciliation of our marriage, but I know it is in God's hands and Lynn's free will.

"This feeling of the unknown is killing me or, better yet, killing my flesh and changing me. I will continue to allow my faith in God and His kingdom to grow through this situation. I know God hates divorce, so He is not going to bring about divorce in order to implement His plan in my life. However, God can use a divorce that someone else brings about for my growth. I do not want to fight against the growth that God has in this, but I will continue to pray and hope for reconciliation."

"And without faith it is impossible to please God, because anyone who comes to him must believe that he exists and that he rewards those who earnestly seek him."—Hebrews 11:6

"I must take my controlling nature completely out of the picture by taking God at His Word. Based upon who He is and what He did and does, I believe I am in great hands. I must continue to develop my faith in the Lord and His ways."

Resolving Relationship Issues

I made a trip back to Wisconsin to visit my mother, two friends, and my brother. I had certain issues to resolve in these relationships, and I wanted to leave behind any past hurts I had caused to these dear people in my life.

I shared with my mother that I wanted and needed a mother-son relationship that was open to sharing between the two of us. Then I met with my friends, and we shared past feelings and worked through them. Last, I talked to my brother and sister-in-law about past hurts in our relationship, both theirs and mine.

In the three days I spent with my brother-in-law Ed, my sister Kim, and their son Eddie, I shared many of the things I was feeling, seeing, and hoping for in the future. They let me talk, but it seemed as though they were trying to prepare me for a future without Lynn. I gave their words great weight because I looked up to Ed and knew he had been through a divorce that took him by surprise many years ago before he met Kim. But now, with Kim, Ed had a great marriage, and I learned a lot through watching them and seeing the growth in their relationship. Still, I hoped for the best with Lynn.

Besides wanting to resolve relationship issues, I had also gone back to Wisconsin to give Lynn the opportunity to move back into the house. She had not taken any money out of our bank account for future rent; in fact, we had not even talked about rent money. Was she ready to move back home? Oh, I hoped so and looked forward to returning to Minnesota and opening the garage door to find Lynn's car there and her furniture in the house.

Is Today the Day?

On the day of my return home, I jumped out of bed early and left for Minnesota a few hours earlier than planned. I eagerly anticipated having my house become a home again if Lynn was there. Though I had enjoyed a great visit in Wisconsin, Minnesota was now my home and my future.

The moment finally arrived when I opened the garage door at my home. Lynn's car was not there. Reeling from the pain of not seeing what I had so desperately hoped for, I slowly walked into the house. At just that moment, the phone began to ring; it was our bank informing me that Lynn had withdrawn a sizable amount from our account. That was how I learned that Lynn had unilaterally decided, without consulting me in the matter, to start paying her rent by the month. I provided the bank with Lynn's phone number so they could call her directly, since she and I were obviously not talking.

"This unknown—yet still hopeful—period in my life is changing me at a tremendous rate. Maybe that is why I am willing to continue to hold out hope for the future. I know God is using this time to grow me and give me hope.

"Nevertheless, I now understand why Ed shared what he did. Lynn and I haven't talked, we are not counseling, we haven't gone out on a date since September, and we have not even hugged in months. With that said, I believe God has told me to love Lynn unconditionally during this time. Going forward, I will do that, and nothing but. I also believe God told me He has more work to do in my own life."

Embracing the Plan Right Where I Am

I did not know the future, but I did know there were certain things I could do to embrace where I was right at that moment in time. I wrote them down, and you, too, might find them helpful:

- I need to relax and accept where I am.
- I am going to relax and enjoy life.

- When I am really in God's rest, I walk in the knowledge that He has me in the palm of His hand.
- This trial is for my good.
- This trial is refining me to do fresh work.
- Faith will carry me through all the problems.
- God is a gentleman. I am too when I back off from Lynn.
- There are three reasons I should embrace God's present plan:
  * It will give me protection from danger.
  * Now might not be the right time for His plan to come to pass
  * Something better is coming.

"I trust You, Lord God, with my life, my wife, and my whole being. Help me, mold me, purge me, and prune me to Your liking. Bless this time in my life. I will never again back down from Your plan."

God's Cleansing and Purging Continue

"My dear brothers, take note of this: Everyone should be quick to listen, slow to speak and slow to become angry." — James 1:19

"The LORD is near to all who call on him, to all who call on him in truth. He fulfills the desires of those who fear him; he hears their cry and saves them." — Psalm 145:18–19

"In a large house there are articles not only of gold and silver, but also of wood and clay; some are for noble purposes and some for ignoble. If a man cleanses himself from the latter, he will be an instrument for noble purposes, made holy, useful to the Master and prepared to do any good work." — 2 Timothy 2:20–21

"The cleansing process continues as I fight through the darkness and pain. I believe there is a major spiritual component to this separation, and I have been praying against it for months now. My sinfulness and Lynn's sinfulness may have opened doors and allowed

the evil one entrance that he would never have had in a godly relationship. I am in spiritual warfare to shut the doors to the evil one and return completely to the Lord and His ways.

"Over the years, there was a slow fade in my relationship with Lynn. That must be turned back, and a holy lifestyle in me and in my marriage must return."

"For though we live in the world, we do not wage war as the world does. The weapons we fight with are not the weapons of the world. On the contrary, they have divine power to demolish strongholds. We demolish arguments and every pretension that sets itself up against the knowledge of God, and we take captive every thought to make it obedient to Christ. And we will be ready to punish every act of disobedience, once your obedience is complete."
—2 Corinthians 10:3–6

Great Things Can and Will Happen by Staying Close to God's Calling

"Satan will pull out all stops to prevent victory in my marriage. I will fight the good fight—a fight I should have been fighting for years. My marriage and every marriage should be fought for. It is painful to see the love of the past and mutual enjoyment eroded by the slow fade and lack of attention of the partners in a marriage.

"If my marriage to Lynn recovers, it will never be the same. It will be better, with more love, respect, care, and kindness, more of God and His Spirit. If given a chance, our marriage and love can grow to the point where it will blow people away. It can open doors to share with others who are going through bad times and those who are considering divorce as an option. The bottom line is that goodness will come out of this tribulation, because God can use the bad things that Satan intended for evil to bring about great things for His kingdom.

"I know God's hand is in everything in my life when I put Him first and obey Him. I am leaving everything in my life in His hands."

Will God Be Happy with 80 Percent? I Think Not!

"I feel good, if not great, about the man I am becoming. I believe the Lord is molding me and shaping me to be a better servant, leader, man of God, father, and husband. Much better days are ahead because I am searching for who I am in the Lord and what He wants me to do. Lord, I lean on You today! There is no other way I want to lean, other than on You and Your ways.

"Every honest man knows the struggle and pain of selective obedience. I know that now and will not go back to this kind of poor behavior. In the past, I deceived myself into believing it was okay to follow the Lord only 80 percent, rather than giving Him the 100 percent He deserves. But God wants me to be a person He can trust wholly, a man who will obey His Word and His plan. I will follow the Lord wholeheartedly; I will not back off. I will push forward, listen, and then obey the Lord and His ways."

"But man who looks intently into the perfect law that gives
freedom, and continues to do this, not forgetting what he has
heard, but doing it—he will be blessed in what he does."
—James 1:25

"I believe the Lord has shown me that Lynn was overwhelmed by my kindness two weeks ago and is trying to work through her own issues right now. This is not my fight, problem, or issue. I will let God be God and work on her heart.

"I must know and believe I am in God's perfect will—right now, right where I am, in this present time and place. Simply put, this separation has me in God's perfect will for my life, and I embrace that my steps have been ordered by the Lord. The truth is, it's possible for me to be in God's perfect will even though I am going through this separation. Nevertheless, I am still troubled and feel pushed down by others, even though I know I am walking in the center of God's will."

"Give thanks in all circumstances, for this is God's will for you in Christ Jesus. Do not put out the Spirit's fire; do not treat prophecies with contempt. Test everything. Hold on to the good. Avoid every kind of evil. May God himself, the God of peace, sanctify you through and through. May your whole spirit, soul and body be kept blameless at the coming of our Lord Jesus Christ. The one who calls you is faithful and he will do it." — 1 Thessalonians 5:18–24

"For our light and momentary troubles are achieving for us an eternal glory that far outweighs them all. So we fix our eyes not on what is seen, but on what is unseen. For what is seen is temporary, but what is unseen is eternal."
—2 Corinthians 4:17–18

More of God and Less of Me—That Is the Plan Now and Going Forward

"I am starting to find the way to love God and put Him first in my life. I desire to serve the Lord with all my heart, mind, soul, and body. I will humbly serve and be purged and pruned by Him to be the man He wants and needs. I will serve Him all the days of my life. I need and want to continue to reach out and be a godly man. Lord, keep filling me with Your Spirit, words, and direction for my life.

"I must stay away from becoming isolated again, like I was for the past two years. I need other godly men and women in my life."

"Flee the evil desires of youth, and pursue righteousness, faith, love and peace, along with those who call on the Lord out of a pure heart." — 2 Timothy 2:22

"As I walk forward, I realize I must be obedient in the Word and in prayer, but I must also continue to experience the Holy Spirit in my life. I believe I take the Holy Spirit for granted at times and focus more on the Father and Jesus.

"The Holy Spirit is an active member of the Godhead that I must have working through my life daily. He is my counselor, comforter, helper, and the Spirit of truth. He is the Spirit that I allowed into my life when I accepted Christ as Lord and Savior back on December 20, 1982.

"Last of all, the Holy Spirit is my daily guide on both small and large items in my life, including the direction I should travel. By surrendering to His leading, I feed the Holy Spirit's ability to win battles in my life. By feeding on the Word of God, which was divinely inspired by the Holy Spirit, I further allow Him to fill me. Finally, when I blow it and sin but confess to the Father, I cleanse myself and allow my body to become the temple of the Holy Spirit.

"With the Holy Spirit in me and working through me, I have the power of the universe dwelling in me and empowering me. I am not defeated, because He loves me and is working through me."

" 'Because he loves me,' says the LORD, 'I will rescue him; I will protect him, for he acknowledges my name. He will call upon me, and I will answer him; I will be with him in trouble, I will deliver him and honor him.' "—Psalm 91:14–15

"I need to start praying 24/7 in both good times and bad. I should always be seeking, knowing, understanding, and following in the example that Jesus set for me. In prayer I free myself to be guided by God, and in prayer God and His angels come to my rescue."

God's Laws, Rules, and Boundaries Help Us Be Better and Give Us Freedom and Peace

"I have come to realize that I need a ruthless pursuit in removing sin from my life. Similar to God's call to the Israelite nation in the Old Testament, I need to root out all forms of sin, including those things that might not be sin but are questionable. I need clean hands and a clean heart to fully set my course on that to which God has called me.

"I am to a point where I understand true freedom in Christ requires restraint and purity. Christ doesn't establish boundaries just to see if I can follow the rules and be a 'good boy.' He gives me boundaries to keep me safe from moral and spiritual failure and out of the hands of the evil one. They are there to keep the door closed on Satan and his demons and on my own dark heart. They are there to help me experience the truly abundant life Jesus Christ came to give all of us."

I Can Be a Great Husband, and I Will Be in the Future

"As I walk in the Word and serve Christ, I need to continue to look for ways that I can be a better husband. I know God has me on a quest to be a great man of God obedient to Him. But it doesn't stop there; I must also be a great husband to Lynn and serve her as Christ serves the church.

"I can be a better husband if I will be God-minded, compassionate, loving, tenderhearted, and courteous. I need to care enough about Lynn that I stop doing things that hurt or upset her. I can do great things for the Lord if I am willing to do little things for others. Truthfully, I would rather do big things for the Lord and others, but I will start small and work from there."

"Remember this: Whoever sows sparingly will also reap sparingly, and whoever sows generously will also reap generously."—2 Corinthians 9:6

"Let your eyes look straight ahead, fix your gaze directly before you. Make level paths for your feet and take only ways that are firm. Do not swerve to the right or the left; keep your foot from evil."—Proverbs 4:25–27

The God of the Universe Is with Me

"I woke up this morning with the words 'You are not alone; I am with you' in my head. God, Jesus, and the Holy Spirit are with me! That is awesome to hear, know, and apply to my life. The Creator of the universe is with me and loves me. God directs my path, and His promises lie ahead of me, so walk on, Steve Kirk. Walk on in faith, knowing that God is with you each step of the way. Do not turn to the right or to the left, and remember, He is always in your sight if you allow Him to be in your nature and spiritual walk."

"For his anger lasts only a moment, but his favor lasts a lifetime; weeping may remain for a night, but rejoicing comes in the morning."—Psalm 30:5

"For a man's ways are in full view of the LORD, and he examines all his paths."—Proverbs 5:21

Words from God

"I am walking with you, Steve Kirk. My hand is upon you, and you are in the palm of my hand. Keep doing the things you are doing. I am well pleased. Keep seeking My face, keep praying, and keep searching for My hidden treasures. Do not give up, do not back down, do not faint in doing good."

"Without God's help, my marriage is sunk! I have nothing left but You, Lord God, but that is enough for a great victory to happen. When all I have is You, I have all I need."

Meeting with Joanne

During this session, Joanne encouraged me to continue focusing on myself and what I was doing in life. I needed to continue those things that were benefiting my growth. This included reading the Word and other good books, ministering to the homeless, attending church, exercising, and playing golf.

Joanne warned me of what to look out for when Kayla came back to Minnesota for the summer. There would be some new roadblocks and speed bumps to maneuver as I dealt with Mother's Day, Lynn's school, and Kayla's days with Lynn. Even if Lynn did return home, there would be times when she would revert back to her old nature of not making decisions and times when I would be tempted to revert to my old nature of taking control. Joanne strongly urged me not to let this happen, but to stop and act in accordance with the new changes in my heart. *"Do not* go back to the old ways," she solemnly emphasized.

I Need to Change

"My circumstances will not change until I change. I am changing with the help of God, Kayla, Doug, Joanne, and many others. God has a plan and purpose for everything that comes into my life. I am making a decision to turn this separation over to God, and I am ceasing my worry about it. I am not going to allow the separation to dominate my thoughts any longer, but instead, I am moving to a place of peace and rest in God.

"I will not talk to Lynn about the next step until she is totally done with school for the spring. She has enough going on without the pressure of dealing head-on with her thoughts and feelings about the next step. I believe God has me right where I am for Lynn's sake as well as my own."

I Do Not Fear the Change God Wants to Perform in My Life

I put the process of change entirely in the Lord's hands, trusting that His timing and methods were perfect. I knew He held everything in His hands, and I continued to release my future to Him. I was fully aware that the restoration of my marriage would likely take a long time and required a miraculous touch from the righteous right hand of God.

"Let us not become weary in doing good, for at the proper
time we will reap a harvest if we do not give up."
—Galatians 6:9

"As for God, his way is perfect; the word of the Lord is flawless. He is a shield for all who take refuge in him."
—2 Samuel 22:31

The Lord Will Always Be First in My Life

"I have perfect peace today and sense God's love and ways at work in my life. He is my life and my guide to better times ahead.

There are glorious days ahead for Lynn and me, and I will not lose focus during this time of growth. I will never go to the place of serving myself and sinning against God, Lynn, Kayla, and my own flesh. With the Lord first in my life, the past is the past and I will move forward, regardless of what comes my way!"

The Birthing Process Paralleled with Deliverance

The following excerpt is from Stormie Omartian's book *The Power of a Praying Husband*:

The most startling thing I discovered about being pregnant was that from the moment I conceived, a process was set in motion. And there was no way I could stop it, outside of doing something that would terminate it. It was entirely out of my control. The process was going to go on with or without my cooperation. That sense of being completely out of control of your body is a strong feeling. Sometimes that's exactly the way the deliverance process feels. It's going on whether you want it to or not. But that's because you have submitted your life to the Lord, and He wants you to be free. When God decides you are ready to go through it, He plants the seed, and it becomes a force that grows until you give birth to freedom. And just as with the delivery of a baby, there's a certain amount of pain that is a part of the deliverance process. But when it's over, you're glad you went through it.

Emotional hurts and bondage usually come off in layers, just the way they got there in the first place. That's why even though your wife may have achieved a breakthrough in a certain area, the whole thing may come back with even greater force.

It may appear to be the same old thing all over again, only worse this time. If that happens, don't be intimidated or disappointed by it. Don't think that things are getting worse instead of better. It just means that there are new layers of hurt or bondage that are coming to the surface for healing and God is leading your wife into a deeper level of deliverance. Often the deepest layers are the most painful. Just cling to God in the midst of the storm, and He will bring you through it safely. Just as with giving birth to a baby, the worst pain comes right before the greatest deliverance of our lives. Things are the most difficult right before the biggest blessing is about to come forth. But God's timing is perfect.

The same is true with deliverance; we have to provide the best conditions we can, give it time, and try not to do anything to terminate it once the process has been set in motion.

"Lynn and I are in the seventh month of separation, and it does indeed feel like a birthing process. The fire is intense, and at times it seems unbearable. But I see the layers coming off, and our conversations have helped give closure to many issues we had between us. I am starting to feel like the birth, or decision, is coming forward in the next few weeks. It is still 50-50 whether Lynn will come back to the marriage.

"I believe everything from the past that Lynn and I needed to face has come to the surface, and we have talked through those things. I would really like to know the future, but I know only God has that prerogative, and that's the way it should be. He is my future! When I know Him, He guides me into the future He has for me."

I Will Not Quit the Marriage

"Maybe what I thought was death pains was in reality birth pains. Sometimes it looks as if our dreams are dying and on their final breath when in reality they are closer to coming to pass than ever before. I admit, I am discouraged and feel like my marriage is dying, but I will not give up the fight for a future with Lynn.

"It is always too soon to quit a marriage—my and Lynn's marriage. We have been through close to seven months of what has felt like pain and torture. I have lost forty pounds and hundreds of hours of sleep. I have experienced loneliness at a level I never knew before, and I have suffered feelings of total hurt and pain from the one I love the most.

"With all that said, I will not stop now, and I will push harder to be a better man and a better husband long-term. I will be patient with Lynn and persevere to the end. I cannot give up, and I cannot cave in to just moving on in life, regardless of Lynn's decision with anyone else. I will not walk away—ever."

Prayer Always Changes Things

"I have committed to praying for Lynn every day, and I have been doing that for months now. However, my prayers are more focused now that I have read The Power of a Praying Husband. *I have never sensed the power of my prayers for Lynn like I have this past week. I know they are reaching heaven, and I know God is moving on behalf of our marriage.*

"Victory will take place in God's perfect timing. I have faith it will take place, and I stand on God's work. Love will be restored, love will be rekindled, and love will come back into our relationship this day. The silence is rebuilding love and respect between Lynn and me. I know God is working. God has a plan, and God's plan will come about this day!

"I need to live a righteous life and always walk after the Lord. Why? Because this is my calling and God's plan for me. I will follow the Lord all the days of my life, regardless of what the world throws at me. God is bigger and better than me, and His plans are bigger and better as well. I will always do well, and the Lord will always do good for me.

"Today is Good Friday, the day when Jesus made it good for all. I want to reach out to the lost and dying of this world, and I hope that all believers, including Lynn and Kayla, will do the same. Great days are ahead for us who believe in the Lord as our Savior, forgiver, and provider."

Jesus Gave of Himself, So I Will Always Give of Myself

I went to Good Friday service at Westwood, and it was fantastic. If for no other reason than the blessing of that church, I was happy I had stayed in Minnesota. I was determined to praise the Lord going forward, regardless of everything happening in my life. Yes, I did sometimes give in to pity parties and thought the worst, but even then, I fought on and did my best to take those thoughts captive.

There could be no backing down now! Every one of God's visions and dreams goes through a process of birth, death, and resurrection, so why would it be any different for me? Plus, it was Good Friday, and a resurrection was right around the corner! Yes, my marriage seemed to be in its death throes at this point, but I refused to give up. My marriage was on the rocks, and the waves were relentlessly pounding, but I knew I had to carry on.

"Lord, send some encouragement and a new supply of faith. It might take a long time, but victory is achievable. I will continue to pray that You will use Lynn and me together in the future to build Your kingdom and see hundreds and even thousands of relationships healed and set free from Satan's grip. Times will change, times are changing, and the heavens are coming down to earth this day."

Easter Day Arrives

"Jesus has risen! He is sitting at the right hand of the Father, interceding for me, the saints, and all who cry to Him. Thank You, Jesus, that You will never leave me or forsake me—never! I love You and want to serve You with all my heart, mind, soul, and body this day and every day going forward.

"Open Your arms, ears, and eyes towards me and guide me into the path You want me to travel. I want to be in Your perfect will this morning and every sleeping and waking moment of my life. Let the flow of the Holy Spirit be upon my head and heart this morning.

"I pray for Lynn, Kayla, and my other family members as well. Bless them, keep them safe, and let Your face shine upon them this day. I pray that their hearts and minds will be turned to You and that they will also want to serve You with all their being. Lord, pour forth Your love on all mankind this day."

"But where sin increased, grace increased all the more, so that, just as sin reigned in death, so also grace might reign through righteousness to bring eternal life through Jesus Christ our Lord."—Romans 5:20–21

My Marriage Was Planted into the Ground So Others Could Flourish

"I have been planted—not buried—by the Lord. When a seed is placed into the ground, it seems like the same seed early on, but the long-term result yields something totally different. A seed planted bursts forth from the soil and bears flowers; a seed buried only remains in the ground.

"I will be that seed planted into the ground, but I will burst out bearing many flowers for the Lord. This separation in my life is a seed that will produce flowers with a wonderful fragrance for all to smell. The Lord will be there for the completion of this journey I am going through. It has already been a blessing to others. Men and women are turning their hearts and minds back to each other. I personally know of seven couples who have changed their views of their spouses. I hope and pray that Lynn is getting better and is also focused on God's goodness and grace. God is and always will be in control!"

Starting to Forget the Woman I Lived with for More Than Twenty-Five Years

"I relaxed in the Spirit of the Lord this morning. I had a great night's sleep and a wonderful Easter Sunday at church and at Trevor's house with friends. Kayla called, and we had a nice conversation. I also talked to my whole family."

"Lynn seems so far away. I am starting to forget her, the things she liked and things she didn't like. I need the Lord—we need the Lord—to pull us together and let us live as one again. We need the clear Word of God and His will to come to pass in our marriage, and we both need to be faithful during this time apart."

"If anyone is thirsty, let him come to me and drink. Whoever believes in me, as the scripture has said, streams of living water will flow from within him."—John 7:37–38

"Lord, let Your streams of living water flow within me and out of me today. I need to be blessed and also to bless others."

God's Destiny Will Be Fulfilled

I agree with something someone once wrote: "I have never talked to anybody who's done anything of any significance and has not hit days, weeks, and months when they had to plow through all kinds of opposition. It just comes with the territory. A God-breathed vision imparts strength into your very core. Then you can press on in spite of everything." That's what I discovered as I walked through my greatest trial.

"God has a plan and purpose for my life—a destiny. He created me to do something special for His kingdom. My life has a plan and purpose from God's throne room, and I have no doubt of that in my mind.

"I believe this separation has awakened my desire to fulfill my destiny, and I believe it will be completed. I might bear major responsibility for all this happening in my life, but I will not just tuck my tail and never use it as an opportunity to share what God can do in a marriage, even if my own dissolves.

"I will trust God all the way through each day. I will keep my focus on Him every moment of my life."

Two Whole People Are Needed for Success

"I realize now that Lynn made the decision to leave long before September 27. Because I was tied up in my own selfish ways and thoughts, I didn't even realize anything was amiss until only a month before she left. I treated Lynn like a child, and children want to leave home at some point. But changes have been made, prayers are being prayed, and hope in God and Jesus is what I have.

"At some point, children who leave want to come home and have everything be okay again. However, I don't want Lynn back in the house as a child; I want her back as the wife and person she wants to be, and I want to be the husband and person God truly wants me

to be. We will then be two whole people coming together as one in God's perfect timing.

"In this day and time, I find peace. I do not know why, other than it is from God's throne room."

"I consider that our present sufferings are not worth comparing with the glory that will be revealed in us."
—Romans 8:18

"Because you know that the testing of your faith develops perseverance. Perseverance must finish its work so that you may be mature and complete, not lacking anything."
—James 1:3–4

"I know God's will is to save and restore my marriage. He would not go against His Word, and His Word is very clear in how He feels about marriage. I seek Him to give Lynn and me everything we need so that we can come back together whole. I pray that God the Father, Jesus the Son, and the Holy Spirit would give me beauty instead of ashes, the oil of gladness instead of mourning, and the garment of praise instead of a spirit of despair.

"I realize everything I do must flow from my love for God and, most importantly, His love for me."

Words from God

"It is I. I AM is the one who is here, and My love is springing forth in your heart. I am present in your heart, mind, and soul. I am pouring out My love on you and your marriage. I am the Savior of the world and the Savior of marriages. I am the one who has a plan for your life. I am the great Redeemer! I am your very help in time of need. I am your king and your Lord. I am the one who brings about victory! I am the one you should lean on and trust always. I am the one who brings plans to completion."

God's Perfect Will Is for Us to Be Together Doing His Will

"Finally brothers, whatever is true, whatever is noble, whatever is right, whatever is pure, whatever is lovely, whatever is admirable—if anything is excellent or praiseworthy—think about such things. Whatever you have learned or received or heard from me, or seen in me—put it into practice. And the God of peace will be with you."—Philippians 4:8–9

"Lynn and I have been called together and have been on this journey for almost twenty-six years. Neither of us will completely accomplish the great purpose God has for us without the other. God designed the two of us to complete each other, and that's what we have done over the years.

"I must recognize, and always will going forward, that we have been called together. This will help me appreciate Lynn's gifts, talents, abilities, and strengths and recognize as inappropriate my selfish behaviors, need for control, and desire for perfection."

Prayer Makes a Difference in Our Hearts, the World, and the Spiritual Kingdom

When I woke up one particular morning, I didn't feel like praying and had no sense that any of my prayers were accomplishing anything. But oh my, when I started to pray anyway, I felt the power release! Satan wanted to deceive me, but the Holy Spirit had another, far greater plan in mind. I knew my prayers were being heard, and I knew God was changing my heart and mind as well as my situation.

Praying aligns our hearts with God and also helps release our authority. God loves it when we go into action for Him and His kingdom. He also enjoys when we use the tools He has given us to fight the good fight against the evil one. When we start praying with God's given authority, the power of Jesus is released into the spiritual realm where most of the fighting takes place.

I was convinced that God had a calling and destiny for Lynn and me, not only as individuals, but also as a couple doing His will. I had to believe God was greater than Lynn's unforgiveness or hardness of heart. However, the life I was trying to make happen would never be as good as the one God would make happen if I just remained submitted to Him and His will.

"My prayers for my marriage have power, even when I am the only one praying. Can prayers alone save my marriage? I believe they can because God is in their midst. If that is not the case, change me, Lord, wherever it is necessary. I have and will continue to have a repentant heart."

"Be imitators of God, therefore, as dearly loved children and live a life of love, just as Christ loved us and gave himself up for us as a fragrant offering and sacrifice to God."
—Ephesians 5:1–2

"Oh God, I pray that You would protect my eyes, ears, heart, and mind so that I do not sin against You. I love You and want to be obedient to You, Your ways, and Your will for my life. Lead me this day into truth, happiness, and Your protection!"

Words from God

"I have you in the place I have you. Do not question this time set apart for Me and for your own growth. Seek and desire the things that I have planned for you. I am the Alpha and Omega; I am your beginning and end. Desire My purity, and desire My love for you. It is time to open your heart and let me pour in My love and purity. I want to dwell with you, show Myself to you, and give you of My kingdom. Lean on Me, and give of yourself. My directions and plans are unfolding in your life and Lynn's.

"Take heed, stay strong, and prepare for the future journey. It will be a journey with a purpose—My purpose, My plan, and My blessings. Stay close to Me, lean on Me, trust My plan and My ways, and then you shall see the captives set free. My hand is on your life, and My right hand is guiding you and will never pull back from your life.

"Continue to seek My kingdom and My ways. Desire the first-fruits and they shall be given to you. What are they? They are love, respect, kindness, goodness, faithfulness, and joy. The works and fruits of My Holy Spirit are in your life and will continue. Believe and receive what I have set forth in your life and Lynn's.

"I have a plan, I have a purpose, and I am guiding Lynn and you into new ways. But first, cleansing must take place, and purifying must take place. Relying on Me and trusting My Words and My Ways must take place. Do not lose faith as I work out My plan in the coming days. Be strong, grow stronger, and do not grow tired or weary in this journey.

"Believe and receive from My throne room this morning the daily portion I have for you. Open yourself up to Me, and let us see the world change this day. Do not lose heart, do not lose desire, and do not lose strength. The desire of your heart will come to pass, and the plan—My plan—will not fail. Trust in Me, lean on Me, and believe in Me. The journey and plan for your life will not fail."

In response to these words, I asked the Lord what I should do, and I felt He instructed me to wait. When I asked for how long, He said for as long as He needed to guide me on this journey.

Releasing the Past and Jumping into God's Love

"I have a choice to hang on to the past, with its pain, suffering, sin, and anger, or I can apply all the learning I have gained and look to the future and the great things that can be planned and executed. I want my new life and the goodness of God that I have applied in the past seven months. Out of that have come the love of God, the love of family, starting with Lynn and Kayla, and the love of my neighbors."

"O LORD, you have searched me and you know me. You know when I sit and when I rise; you perceive my thoughts from afar. You discern my going out and my lying down; you are familiar with all my ways. Before a word is on my tongue you know it completely, O LORD."—Psalm 139:1–4

Adversity Comes Before the Release

"To get the crown, you must first take the cup. The cup will always be before the crown. The cup prepares us. Trials and tribulations always produce character. Jesus had the cup first. It is all right; the good news will come. Jesus took the cup; Jesus had the death, burial, and resurrection. A new place will come in the same place the cup came."

"Jesus knows every move and plan I have and what is taking place and will take place in the future. I am willing to take from the Lord both the good and the bad because I know He will produce a great amount of fruit if I let Him work His plan through my life. The reality is, the hard times in my life are when the most growth takes place. Since September I have experienced more growth as a person and a follower of Christ than I have in many years. With that said, I want to continue growing, but I want that growth to come as Lynn and I work together as a married couple.

"I have wondered at times how I could get through each day, but I know it is only by the grace of God that it is happening in my life. I will not let the cup of separation get me down and ruin my walk with God. Because of this time, I know I will experience success with other people and relationships in my life."

Carry the Marriage and Have Faith in God

"I woke up this morning feeling defeated, pained, confused, and unworthy. However, I knew it was Satan working to defeat me. I prayed and sought God on behalf of Lynn and our marriage. This is my cup to bear.

"My friend Kent talks about how one year he carried his marriage, and the next year his wife Patty carried their marriage. This year is the year I carry my marriage. God, serve this cup until it fulfills Your purpose, Your perfect timing, and Your perfect will. Let not Lynn or me get ahead or behind Your purpose and blow the outcome and the blessings You have for us in the future."

"His divine power has given us everything we need for life and godliness through our knowledge of him who called us by his own glory and goodness. Through these he has given us his very great and precious promises, so that through them you may participate in the divine nature and escape the corruption in the world caused by evil desires. For this very reason, make every effort to add to your faith goodness; and to goodness, knowledge; and to knowledge, self-control; and to self-control, perseverance; and to perseverance, godliness; and to godliness, brotherly kindness; and to brotherly kindness, love. For if you possess these qualities in increasing measure, they will keep you from being ineffective and unproductive in your knowledge of our Lord Jesus Christ."—2 Peter 1:3–8

My Knees Buckle, but God's Word Gives Me Strength

"I want to be a man of the most high God. I want to serve Him all the days of my life. I want to love Him and follow Him with obedience. Lord, come and fill me with Your presence this morning. May I walk in Your wisdom this day."

"I am still confident of this: I will see the goodness of the LORD in the land of the living. Wait for the LORD; be strong and take heart and wait for the LORD."—Psalm 27:13–14

"But he said to me, 'My grace is sufficient for you, for my power is made perfect in weakness.' Therefore I will boast all the more gladly about my weakness, so that Christ's power may rest on me. That is why, for Christ's sake, I delight in weakness, in insults, in hardships, in persecutions, in difficulties. For when I am weak, then I am strong."
—2 Corinthians 12:9–10

The Anchor Holds

God is good; always remember that God is good. Also, He is in control at all times. He knows what you are going through and has better days ahead. Stay in His perfect will and perfect plan no matter what happens in your life, secure in the knowledge that Jesus is your anchor in the storm of despair.

The storms of life make us realize that Jesus is truly our anchor. Without Him how could we get through each day? He is not a crutch, and depending on Him does not mean we are weak. But when storms arrive and our boats are rocking and taking on water, we need an anchor to hold us secure. That is when we need Jesus the most.

"I am anchored to the shores of heaven and to the belief that much better days are ahead. I want to be married because it is the right thing. I believe there is a ministry that God has planned for Lynn and me as a married couple. I still love Lynn, and I love her zest for life.

"No matter what happens, I will always remember Jesus is there. If I put my faith in Him, He will see me through the storm of separation. I believe He is letting this storm go on for this long so He can accomplish everything necessary for long-term success. It might not be the success (marriage to Lynn) that I want, but in the long run, it will be the success I need from Jesus."

"He replied, 'You of little faith, why are you so afraid?' Then he got up and rebuked the winds and the waves, and it was completely calm." — Matthew 8:26

"There is no wisdom, no insight, no plan that can succeed against the Lord." — Proverbs 21:30

God Is Always Working to Accomplish His Will

"I have found that God is in total control. Even when I think that I am in control, I am not, nor is any man. Here are some things that I have learned about God's control in my life: God knows everything

I will face in life. He is always working behind the scenes. God will and is opening doors. God knows whom to influence in my life. God will cause me to be at the right place at the right time.

"I need to turn everything over to God because He is always at work in my life; in fact, He works the most when I see the least. I know God is working in my marriage. Even in my darkest of times, God is still working."

"For it is God who works in you to will and to act according to his good purpose."—Philippians 2:13

Chapter 11

The Words of Divorce Flame Alive

"The husband should fulfill his marital duty to his wife, and likewise the wife to her husband. The wife's body does not belong to her alone but also to her husband. In the same way, the husband's body does not belong to him alone but also to his wife."—1 Corinthians 7:3–4

The Arrows of Divorce Are Flying

The evil one was sending the fiery arrows of divorce in my direction, and I was praying and seeking help from heaven against him and his demons as never before. I knew he was attacking both Lynn and me, just as he attacks all the godly of this world. But like anyone else, I had to stand firm and wield the weapons of our warfare and battle back with major prayer. I knew one thing was certain: the devil is a liar, but he would defeat me if I allowed him to.

"God has everything under control. He will bring me through all the days ahead. He will keep His promises in my life.

"Is anything too hard for the Lord? Of course not! I trust in You, Lord, and believe You can and do change the hearts and minds of men and women. May my heart and mind and Lynn's heart and mind change today as we follow You and Your leading in our marriage. Help us to put You first in all the things we do. I know, God, You can take what has been meant for harm and turn it into something great."

"You intended to harm me, but God intended it for good to accomplish what is now being done, the saving of many lives."—Genesis 50:20

God Will Save the Day in Every Way

"I have faith in God and believe all things are possible with Him. I know I am in the palm of His hand, and I know all things work together for His good. I will bless the Lord and always put Him first in my life.

"God is great and greatly to be praised. I live to serve God and please Him. I want my thoughts, actions, and beliefs to shine forth this day. Bless the work of my hands, Lord!

"God's work done in God's way will never lack God's supply. I may faint and grow weary, but my heavenly Father is all-powerful and all-loving. If I totally abandon myself to God, I will not be abandoned by Him.

"Bless this day, Lord God. Bless this day for Lynn, Kayla, and me."

Words from God

"My son, I am here; I am with you. I will never leave you or forsake you. I see your pain; I feel your pain. Hold on and fight on, for victory is at hand. I will give you the desire of your heart, so have patience and wait for My hand to complete the work I have been doing. I have not been sitting idle; I have been and continue to work on your behalf and Lynn's. It has been a fight through the darkness of sin, but the victory is coming forth.

"I told you it would be days, and I meant it. Lynn is ready, and you are ready. Fear not, for it will take place this week. I have blessed it, planned it, and will see it through. Trust Me, believe in Me, and receive the greatness of the days set before you.

"I know you have fear, doubt, and concerns, but let My Holy Spirit lead you and guide you into all truth in the comings days. Believe in Me, trust Me, and let Me guide you. This is My plan and purpose, and it will be accomplished this week. Hold on, because help is on the way."

"When I am up against the wall, God is there with open arms. God's love still stands when all else has fallen."

"No, in all these things we are more than conquerors through him who loved us."—Romans 8:37

God Is God of My Life, and He Is in Control

"God does have something great for me to accomplish. I will stay in the faith; great things are in store for me! God is in total control of my life because I have given Him that complete control over me. I know that God is working behind the scenes in my life and in Lynn's life. I must not give up, and I will not give up, regardless of the outcome of this separation."

"Be strong and courageous. Do not be afraid or terrified because of them, for the LORD your God goes with you; he will never leave you nor forsake you."—Deuteronomy 31:6

"The LORD himself goes before you and will be with you; he will never leave you nor forsake you. Do not be afraid; do not be discouraged."—Deuteronomy 31:8

"I am anointed, I am talented, and I am blessed by the Lord. My life will be filled with valleys and mountaintop experiences, but the Lord will be with me in each one of them. All my valleys are known by God, and He already has a solution for each one of them. I must use what I have, and then the God of this universe will step in and make it powerful and anointed by His righteous right hand. I will continue to think big and dream big, knowing things are big in God.

"Jesus is the same yesterday, today, and forever. Blessings, not cursing, will be the outcome as I keep my eyes on the Lord. Praise and worship is not an option, but a necessity, in my life. No matter what happens in my marriage, I will serve the Lord, my God and king."

Conversation on Our marriage

I made the decision to talk to Lynn about the status of our marriage after she finished school in the middle of May. I would have preferred to talk sooner, but I did not want to affect her grades by drawing her attention away from school and onto our marriage. At times my thoughts confused me; it seemed I worried more about Lynn and her schooling than I worried about my own future. Things had definitely changed in our marriage while we were apart, and I had become less selfish and controlling. Maybe Lynn was right; since we were on equal footing while we were apart, she could call the shots. I would wait on Lynn and, more importantly, on God and His direction.

Lynn and I had not talked in weeks, and there had been only a few text messages and e-mails. Was I fooling myself into thinking we would be together in the future? Did we really even have a marriage at all? I had been told by several people to give Lynn space to make her decision, but was that really the best thing to do? I didn't know the answers and feared I might never know how far apart we really were.

For so many years, I had assumed Lynn and I had a good, if not great, marriage; nonetheless, here we were in separate spaces and times. My spiritual life had grown. Had hers? My needs and wants had changed. Had hers? My desires and goals had been realigned. Had hers? We had arrived at a place that I did not even know how we had gotten there.

After months of our being apart, I still had so many questions and so few answers. I could not understand how we went from "I love you" one morning in late September to "I need to leave" only twelve hours later. How and why had it happened? I needed to understand when it was that our marriage had started to fall apart in Lynn's eyes.

I did not want to die with God's vision still in me, and I did not want our marriage to die with God's vision still in it. Yet if Lynn decided to go in a different direction from the one God had set for us to accomplish together, it indeed might die. If that happened, I knew I could still become all that God wanted me to become. God was sovereign; He would accomplish what He wanted to accomplish, either with Lynn and me together or in some other way. God's plans would go forward regardless of the status of my marriage.

"If I believe God's perfect will and perfect plan will be accomplished, why do I worry, and why do I fear? I should not do this, and I must stop this behavior. God is God of His plans and His will. God, I put my hope, faith, and belief in You and what You want to happen in my life and Lynn's. I am holding on, and I won't give up. I know my help is on the way!"

Seven Months Later and We Are Only Further Apart

"Today marks seven months apart for Lynn and me. God, on this seventh month, I know You are working in our lives. We are new people with a new plan. Lord God, continue to work in our marriage and on both of our hearts. Let Your perfect will and Your perfect plan come about in our lives.

"Lord, my plan is to walk after You all the days of my life and to bless You each day regardless of any trial the world may bring. I love You with all my heart, mind, soul, and body. I have learned to always pray before planning, to love people more than things, and to please You first, then others."

"Therefore I tell you, do not worry about your life, what you will eat or drink; or about your body, what you will wear. Is not life more important than food, and the body more important than clothes?" — Matthew 6:25

"But seek first his kingdom and his righteousness, and all these things will be given to you as well. Therefore do not worry about tomorrow, for tomorrow will worry about itself. Each day has enough trouble of its own." — Matthew 6:33–34

"I will live in this day and accomplish what I need to accomplish this day. I will be about the Lord's work this day. What is given to me this day, I will take and use for the glory of the Lord."

"Do not boast about tomorrow, for you do not know what a
day may bring forth."—Proverbs 27:1

"I will give you the keys of the kingdom of heaven; whatever
you bind on earth will be bound in heaven, and whatever you
loose on earth will be loosed in heaven."—Matthew 16:19

Seven Months Later and God Has Done a Wonderful Work in My Spirit

*"Through prayer, Jesus has given me the power and authority
in the spirit realm to take charge of this separation, and that is what
I have been doing since day one. I have prayed hundreds of hours
and sought God's intervention in my marriage. By praying, I am
opening the door and welcoming God's healing, transformational,
and restorative attributes into my life.*

*"In Jesus' name, I have authority over the spirits behind this
separation, and I can tell the evil one that my heart and my part of
the marriage are steadfastly fixed on doing what God has directed
me to do both now and into the future. I give no ground to Satan or
his demons. I want to take back the parts that I have allowed them
access to in my life. I say 'no more' to sin, 'no more' to sinful behaviors, and 'no more' to my own selfish thoughts."*

"The LORD is close to the brokenhearted and saves those who
are crushed in spirit."—Psalm 34:18

The Foundation of My Marriage Is Shaking

Arriving home from work late one evening, I had an e-mail
from Lynn asking if she could come over that evening or the next.
I immediately responded that I had just gotten home but she could
come over now, if she still wanted to. Within minutes she answered,
"I'll come this evening." Waiting for her to arrive, I still did not
know, after seven months, if Lynn was about to say she wanted to
come home or if she would ask for a divorce.

When she arrived, she was very pleasant and asked how I had been doing and what I had been up to the last several weeks. I shared that I had been busy trying to overcome the down moments, and she said she had been doing the same thing. Then, just like that, my wife of twenty-six years looked at me and said, "Steve, I want a divorce."

While I would like to say this announcement blew me away, I really cannot. We had been apart for so long, and there was now another person in Lynn's life, though to what extent I did not know. All I could get out was "Okay, what's next?"

Lynn had already talked to Gwen about her decision and thought we should pursue mediation to work through the specifics. Based upon how well we had been working together over the past seven months, this seemed a better option than getting lawyers involved, she explained. I told Lynn that would be fine, and she said she would set it up and let me know the time for the meeting. We then discussed the best way to tell Kayla about it and decided to wait until her school year was finished the next Friday and then tell her together. In shock by the night's events, I didn't have much else to say, and Lynn left within minutes. I had a hard night ahead of me, to say the least.

"Lynn has been a very good wife; in many ways, she could not have been better. But over the years of our marriage, I majored on the minors, and that seems to have been the tipping point. Things I never regarded as major deal-breakers caused cracks I didn't even know were there. I never realized the extent to which I had damaged our marriage until all this came to a head seven months ago.

"Months ago I asked Lynn to tell me face-to-face if she ever came to the point of wanting a divorce. She honored that request tonight. I have heard too many times of people who merely got served papers, and that is cold and uncaring. Lynn has not been cold and uncaring, and I do appreciate that fact."

I Still Believe God Has a Plan for Us Together

"Lord, I know You can still perform miracles, and it will take a mighty one from Your hand to turn my marriage around at this

point. But I believe it is well within Your power, and I believe it is well within Your perfect will and Your perfect plan. Lord, speak to me and let me know the direction and path I should take now and going forward. I am open to You and Your ways this day and every day going forward. Bless the work of my hands, and may they be clean before You."

"Be self-controlled and alert. Your enemy the devil prowls around like a roaring lion looking for someone to devour."—1 Peter 5:8

"In the service of the King, I must be on alert at all times. The call to be effective in battle challenges me to be ready for surprise attacks by the enemy in the spirit realm. I must never let my guard down again so that I may always endure to serve the Lord another day."

"And the God of all grace, who called you to his eternal glory in Christ, after you have suffered a little while, will himself restore you and make you strong, firm and steadfast. To him be the power forever and ever. Amen."—1 Peter 5:10–11

"Have I not commanded you? Be strong and courageous. Do not be terrified; do not be discouraged, for the LORD your God will be with you wherever you go."—Joshua 1:9

Money as the Starting Point

Lynn returned a call I had made to her. We discussed moving the money for Kayla's college fund to the checking account, and Lynn said she would take care of it. We also made plans to talk to Kayla together on the upcoming Tuesday night. I also let Lynn know that I had talked to my family members, and each one was praying for a mighty miracle of God to preserve our marriage.

Wanting to know more about the mediation process, I asked Lynn if the intent of it was to work through personal issues or just for settling financial aspects. Sadly, it was to settle the financial and personal-possession aspects of the marriage, not to resolve remaining issues between us.

Do My Prayers Reflect a Need to Control?

"Lord, I continue my journey in search for Your love and Lynn's. As You know, several people are still praying and seeking Your face for my marriage. I believe it is Your perfect will and Your perfect plan for Lynn and me to remain married. I know what Your Word says, and I believe it.

"God, step in and change Lynn's heart and mind before this goes to the point of divorce. Help us, help me, and help our marriage. I will stand in the gap, and I will stay there as long as necessary. Lord, I will forgive Lynn of anything, just as You have forgiven me of everything. Let her know that, and I will as well.

"Lord, pour forth Your power, and pour forth Your wisdom, knowledge, and understanding on both our hearts and the people who give us counsel. Let us seek wise counsel to know Your plan. Let us surrender to Your perfect will, not insist on what we want."

"But those who hope in the LORD will renew their strength. They will soar on wings like eagles; they will run and not grow weary, they will walk and not be faint." — Isaiah 40:31

"The righteous cry out, and the LORD hears them, he delivers them from all their troubles." — Psalm 34:17

"Let us not become weary in doing good, for at the proper time we will reap a harvest if we do not give up" — Galatians 6:9

Godly Wisdom from the Accountability Group

"Today in our accountability group, we talked about my relationship with Lynn. After that meeting, I wrote her a letter about the love that has been birthed in me. This evening I shared the content face-to-face with her, and she listened. All I can do is plant seed; the

Lord is the one who waters. I hope and pray the Lord uses the spirit in which these words were written to bring about His will. I feel settled, even though I didn't see a major reaction from Lynn.

"This is a different time in our lives, and Lynn is growing and changing, as am I. I hope that growth continues and that we grow together in the coming days. Tomorrow I will fast, pray, and read God's Word to build a bridge in our marriage and to resist the evil one. Lord, bless that day, and may it be a turning point in my life and Lynn's.

"I also spent two hours praying and reading the Word before Lynn arrived at the house. I believe that prayer changes things in the heavens and in our lives. I believe in positive change that brings glory to God and blessings to our marriage."

The Letter Shared with Lynn

Dear Lynn,

Tonight I want to open up to you and share my vision and dream of the husband I want to be in the future. Yes, I know I asked you for a list of things that I do right, but I realize that was somewhat selfish of me. Whether you want to cover them or not is your decision.

In the past weeks, a new love has been birthed within me. It is one of equal and mutual togetherness, of growing and working in unity with my spouse, of listening to my spouse's thoughts, concerns, feelings, pains, and victories.

What I have come to realize is that a big house, cars, money, jobs, and things do not matter as much in a marriage as spouses who love, respect, care for, and cherish each other. I realize I need to be a husband of the twenty-first century, a man who doesn't think his job is done when the day at work is done. I need and want to affectionately take care of a sick spouse, inspire a spouse who has had a bad day and needs to be picked up and encouraged, and work harmoniously with a spouse to complete overwhelming household chores. I want to do all this out of true love and care, while nurturing and showing understanding and patience.

I also want to be a spouse who caresses, touches, and loves his partner without the desire of sex as the outcome. I want to touch and caress as an expression of a great respect, deep connection, and intimate care. I now believe in this more than ever before.

I want to be more spontaneous in my showing of love and respect to my spouse. This means walking through gardens and picking flowers together or taking a ride on a fall day with nowhere special to go, just being relaxed and carefree. It might mean waking up on a Sunday morning and going out to eat instead of working out first and then rushing to church. Heck, it could mean leaving the house a mess but knowing everything will be okay. Buying little things like candy, flowers, or small cards on days that are not holidays, birthdays, or other special days would be another meaningful way to show this new love that has been birthed in my heart.

I want to be a spouse who listens intently to the words spoken and recognizes the ones not spoken, a spouse who relies on the wisdom and sound advice of the one I love and cherish. I know now it is in the best interest of the marriage when the expressions of both spouses are heard, understood, and acted upon. I want to rely on and trust our conversations, and I want to be a builder, uniting in the common causes that are best for our relationship.

I don't want to place emphasis and cast judgment based on appearances, possessions, and activities. It's not outward beauty, the accomplishments of a day, or the material things that matter most. It is a couple's journey together into oneness and happiness that matters most to me now.

Yes, I want to grow old with my spouse, creating memories of the best of times when we were together. I want to learn from the bad times, cherish the good times, and never stop believing that better days are ahead regardless of whether we are healthy, wealthy, or wise.

We talk most of those things we take pleasure in and place high value on in our lives. I will indisputably be a raving fan of my spouse and all she accomplishes in life. Regardless of our position, income, or number of friends, our worth shines forth from our actions, our commitment to acts of selflessness, and the genuine love and care we show to others.

These thoughts and emotions are what truly have been birthed in me, and I so desire to share them with my spouse in the coming days, weeks, and years. These are my feelings of love and desire. I have learned more in eight months than I ever knew or chose to recognize in the past forty-eight years.

I need my soul mate, best friend, and lover to journey with me into what can be a level of marital bliss few have achieved. I believe two people committed to each other and supported by the things I have started can overcome all obstacles in their way. My heart yearns to show the love that has been building within it these past months. It is now and will always be a never-ending flow of love, compassion, care, understanding, and respect for my spouse.

I also want to protect my spouse from any outside harm that might come to our doorstep. Any harm or mistreatment that might rise up from within me, I will correct immediately. As a protector, I must be on the alert, guarding against trouble and protecting the relationship from pain, hurt, or destruction.

These are some of the things I have learned, and you are the spouse that I want to release my love upon like never before. Live with me, breathe with me, unite with me, and we shall overcome the world with love!

Love,

Steve

Push Out Unholy Alliances

I cried before the Lord and sought His face, questioning if all I had thought I heard was truly from Him or from my own flesh. I desperately needed to hear from the Lord Himself and know what He wanted from me. I wanted to know His will for me, my life, my marriage, and Lynn's and my future together.

In my time of prayer, I prayed against any relationships that Lynn might be a part of that were unholy, deceptive, and filled with curses on our marriage. I prayed that these people would come to the saving knowledge of Jesus Christ, that the words they meant for harm would be turned into blessing. I also reminded myself in prayer that the Holy Spirit supersedes the spirit of the evil one.

"Direct my footsteps according to your word; let no sin rule over me. Redeem me from the oppression of men, that I may obey your precepts. Make your face shine upon your servant and teach me your decrees." — Psalm 119:133–135

Like a compass, the Bible always points us in the right direction!

Words from God

"I am here; I am with you, My son. Love Me, reach out to Me, and seek Me in the days ahead. I have a purpose and a plan for your life. Don't stray, seek another, or turn back to the old ways. I know your thoughts; I know your heart. Believe in Me, and reach out to Me as I reach out to you.

"The days ahead are dark, My son. They will once again stretch you and mold you into a different man, a man of Me, if you will let them. Fear Me, fear My plan, fear My purpose, and watch My mighty hand work through your life.

"I am not happy with the course, but I will set a new course that will be blessed by My hand. Know that I will not fail you. There are better days ahead filled with my joy, happiness, harmony, and grace."

Setting a New Course in the Lord

When we move with the Spirit of God, He will never leave us to wander aimlessly in a place of destitution. He will move us in a clear direction within His plan. We all have choices to make, and we all have a free will, but if we choose not to walk in God's plan, He will still accomplish what He set out to accomplish in and through us with whatever means are necessary. At the end of this journey, if God is all we have, then God is all we need.

"Those who oppose him he must gently instruct, in the hope that God will grant them repentance leading them to knowledge of the truth, and that they will come to their senses and escape from the trap of the devil, who has taken them captive to do his will."—2 Timothy 2:25–26

"I may be facing some insurmountable odds right now. I may be overwhelmed by my own doubts. But no matter the odds of this divorce, I must remember that God is much bigger than divorce, the destruction of this world, or Satan himself. I will therefore keep my faith in God, knowing He has a plan and ministry for me and the woman I will join with to defeat Satan's rule.

"I have been broken and poured out over the last several days, and I feel like nothing is going right in my life. But it's exactly in times like that when God is moving behind the scenes and His greatness is about to come forth."

Prayer and Fasting for Unity

"Yesterday was a great day in the Lord. I prayed, read the Word, and fasted for my marriage and for Lynn. There have been several hundred people praying for my marriage off and on since January, and several decided to fast and pray with me yesterday. When you have problems in your life, you find out quickly who your friends are, and I have many more friends than I thought I did.

"My family has been very supportive during this time. Kayla has been a strong tower and someone I can talk to and share my feelings with. However, I must remember she is also hurting, and I must not lay too much on her.

"Lynn is the prodigal wife that must come to her end if she is to return home to our marriage. I know God is working, people are praying, and Lynn has needs to be fulfilled by a man. All these things coming together give me great hope for the future of our marriage, that something good will happen before the papers are signed. Lord

God, I am praying for a mighty miracle from Your hand and in Lynn's heart. Break the walls, break through the pain, and release Your love on Lynn so she might release her love on me and all the world!

"*My brother John arrived yesterday afternoon, which was a real blessing. He is a good man who needs more of You in his life, Lord. I hope and pray that we have a great time together and that I get the chance to share Your love with him. Last time he was here, I was able to share how marriage is better if two partners reach out together and share their deep feelings.*

"*I know John came out both times this year because I am alone without family here in Minnesota. I appreciate the care shown by my family members, mostly John and Sharon. They have reached out to me, and he has twice traveled this distance to see me.*

"*As I enter God's Word this morning and seek Him first, I ask Him to move on my heart and mind and change me from the inside out. I want to be a true man of God, busy building His kingdom and sharing Him with the world. Open the doors of opportunity in the days ahead, Lord, and let love flow through me.*"

Words from God

"Renew your mind, strengthen your spirit, and cleanse your heart. These are the things I require of you, My son. You must gird up your loins to run the race and not faint. The journey is long, but the rewards are great. Power and strength are in My storehouse. Feed on Me and trust in Me, for I will never fail you. If you truly take up My yoke, you will not be ashamed in My kingdom.

"The world is ready for My message that will be spoken by you in the coming days. Relax, feed on Me, and get your nourishment from My Word. Hide it deep in your heart, and never lose hope for the future. Lean on Me, lean on My understanding, and hope for a better tomorrow. There *will* be better tomorrows!"

Blessing and Cursing

One morning I read the story of Balak and Balaam. From it I learned that when God wants something accomplished, it will come about, or else major pain will be the outcome. In the story, God was not pleased with the path Balaam was on, so God put an angel in his way to stop him. Initially only Balaam's donkey saw the angel and thus stepped off the path to avoid it. Balaam, not seeing the angel of the Lord, beat the donkey to get it back onto the path. Similar scenarios were repeated two more times, until Balaam himself saw what the donkey had already seen. The point is, both pain and movement occurred before God revealed Himself.

Balak wanted Balaam to curse the nation of Israel, but God had a better plan and caused blessing to result instead. When God moves, blessings come to His people. Even if the enemy wants to curse, blessings flow. God can and does change the courses of hearts and minds.

"Lord, move like this in my life and Lynn's. If we are walking wrong, change our course. If we are cursing, turn it into blessing. If anyone is cursing our marriage, turn the words into blessing and pull those people completely out of our lives. Bless us with favor this day, and may Your hand bless our marriage now and forever."

God can and does work miracles when we pray to Him. He can change our hearts and others' hearts and perspectives in an instant. He can tear out the roots of sin that lie deep within our lives, and He can resurrect love where it has died. He can make it not only grow again but also flourish like never before. That is what I was hoping for in my marriage.

Big Victories Are Ahead as I Stay Close to God and His Ways

"Words for me to remember today: God's ways are bigger and better than my ways. God is God and I am not. I am not taking matters into my own hands. I need to get ready because my miracle is coming. I will not get discouraged or let Satan steal my joy. The world will see God's joy in my life. No person can stand against our God. God's will and plans will succeed. God blesses us in front of our enemies."

Words from God

"Don't give up; victory will be had in this fight. Long life in purity will be the outcome. My blessings will follow you all your days because you have put Me first in your life. Trust that My actions and plans will bring complete healing for your soul and Lynn's. Believe and trust that My will is going to be completed in this matter."

Meeting with Joanne

Months earlier I had asked Lynn to give me a list of things I did right, but I had never received it. Joanne felt Lynn probably feared putting it together because it would provide me with the opportunity to say, "If I do this, then why don't you love me?" I had to agree that I probably would have done just that and that Lynn probably knew it.

Joanne encouraged me to maintain a kind heart and spirit as well as a positive outlook on life. After all, the only thing I could control 100 percent was my own life—no one or nothing else. I had to live life and enjoy the things I liked, and I had to remember to take care of myself.

God's Peace, Purging, and Pruning Can All Take Place at the Same Time

"I must stay in peace. Jesus was in the storm, but He didn't let the storm get inside of Him. Every day I have the opportunity to apply peace. I cannot let the stresses of life get to me. I must remain calm and relaxed and enjoy life and Kayla. I will not give up on the dream of marriage that God has truly placed in my heart.

"I prayed again this morning for God to purge, prune, and take me completely through the fire. The fire of purging and pruning is taking place and will continue, and God will complete His work. It is very easy for me to whine, complain, and worry, which I have done many times throughout the months. I must get to the point of rising above this to trust in God, rely on Him, and totally sell out to Him. Jesus is my only hope, and I must surrender Lynn and everything else to Him."

"Be still and know that I am God; I will be exalted among the nations, I will be exalted in the earth. The Lord Almighty is with us; the God of Jacob is our fortress." — Psalm 46:10–11

"I will keep listening for God's still, small voice to guide and direct my path. I know He will bring back the joy of my salvation, and I will rejoice in Him daily. I give Him all my problems, issues, and hurts because He can certainly handle them better than I can."

Words from God

"Keep the faith, keep the focus, and keep the fire burning. Do not give up or lose hope for the future of your marriage. Great and better days are ahead of you as you walk in My presence. Love Me, put Me first, and put your marriage in My hands.

"Tough days are ahead, but in the end, they will be My blessing on you. I have a plan for you that will be accomplished by My will. Fear not, for My love will prevail. Keep praying, keep hoping, and keep trusting in Me and My ways."

Top Five Things to do in Marriage

As I thought about all I had gone through, I came up with what I viewed as the top five things to do to keep a marriage strong: (1) pray for each other, (2) validate each other, (3) identify Jesus as the center of the marriage covenant, (4) forgive each other, and (5) walk in humility in life and marriage.

Lynn Shares Her Decision with Kayla

"Tonight, probably right now, Lynn is telling Kayla that she has decided to get a divorce and that it was her decision. She decided to do this herself instead of both of us. It is a sad day that we have arrived at this point. But I believe God is not done in this marriage of Steve and Lynn Kirk. I know He has plans to bless and not curse us.

"I pray for Kayla this evening, Lord. Bless her, Lynn, and me this evening. Rise up, oh Lord, and destroy the plans of the evil one. Let Your glory fall on our flesh and bones."

I Cannot Give Up on Lynn

Because of my disappointment in Lynn, thoughts of not praying for her any longer passed through my mind. But countering that was the strong sense that I must intercede for her more than ever. A battle was raging, and I had to fight and do what I could; then God would do what He wanted in the situation. I had to continue to pray for Kayla as well. She was hurting, as were Lynn and I, and pain filled all our lives. Still, I hung on to my belief that victory in the Lord was coming.

"As believers, the love of Christ is on me, Lynn, and Kayla. Lord, bring that love for each other to a higher place, and bring healing in my marriage. Until then and afterwards, I will follow You all the days of my life. Let freedom reign in our lives this day and every day going forward. I must remember, God is always on time!

"I am waiting for answers to my prayers, and I will not give up. God will show up when the fullness of time is complete. I so look forward to the outcome of His plan in my life. It is starting to look different from what I thought it would be; nevertheless, God's will is going to take place in my life. His timing is always perfect, and this day I will fight the good fight for my family and my God."

God Will Use This Time for His Purposes

"Today is a new day and a new chance to make a difference in the world. I am ready, willing, and able to help other people fulfill their dreams in life. I put God first and will continue to focus on Him and His ways in the days ahead. I want to be a history-maker this day, this hour, and this minute.

"God is going to use this separation and divorce for good purposes, somehow and someway. I will listen to the voice of the Lord and do everything He says, and I will do it when He says to do it.

While I am doing that, I will also stay pure and clean before Him in all my ways. This is a time to live solely on God's promises, pure and simple. I have nothing left in myself. I am totally sold out to Him and His provision. Without Him life would be insurmountable.

"The darkest time of day is right before the dawn. If I can just hang on and fight through the darkest moments of the night, I will see the sun break through and will experience the warmth of victory. I know great days are ahead if I stay close to God and His ways. I do not care what people of the world tell me, how marriages like mine end in heartache. God can and will overcome in my life as I stay faithful to Him and continue to love Lynn."

Not by Might, Not by Power, but by the Spirit of the Lord

"I keep praying for more of the Lord in my life. Yesterday the verse 'Not by might, not by power, but by the Spirit of the Lord' kept going through my head. I know that only God and Lynn can change this situation to see Lynn healed and her love for me return.

"I ask You, Lord, to bless Lynn, bless Kayla, and bless me this day. Let us join together as a family again under the banner of the Lord Jesus Christ. Pour out blessings on our bodies, minds, and spirits this day.

"I know people think I am foolish to believe that Lynn and our marriage will be healed, but I know what the mighty hand of God can do and provide. I trust in God and His ways, and I believe Lynn and I will be together serving Him, seeking Him, and leading others to the promised land that He has provided in marriage. I pray for freedom in every area of our marriage, and I ask God to bless us this day as I turn my eyes to my Lord and Savior."

Words from God

"My blessings are being poured out on Lynn, and my blessings are being poured out on you. Yes, I am your God, and I hear your cries. I will answer your cries because they are part of My will for your life. Great and mighty acts will come out of this time. You will be blessed, Lynn will be blessed, and thousands of people will hear your story and also be blessed.

"My hand is at work, My heart is in motion, and My will is pushing forward. Stand in the gap and keep your focus on Me and My ways. Continue your journey, not looking to the right or to the left. I AM will be with you always, even to the end of the age."

"Now faith is being sure of what we hope for and certain of what we do not see."—Hebrews 11:1

"Jesus replied, 'What is impossible with men is possible with God.' "—Luke 18:27

"Lord, I ask that You calm this storm in my life and bring back peace, love, hope, and joy in Your perfect timing. I believe, I trust, and I will receive from Your hand what You want to give me. I will not fail in life. I am moving out with the Lord and prayer; I will use both in my life to fulfill the destiny that He wants me to complete. My prayers take me places I cannot go in person. It releases the Spirit and angels into the war zone to fight the good fight alongside me as I stand in the gap.

"I hope I am in God's perfect will; I find myself feeling very unsafe at times. I feel extremely uncomfortable right now, but I know God is comfortable and knows the future. I give Him all my fears. I turn my whole life over to Him for Him to move and guide as He sees fit. I want to live by faith and take every step by faith.

"I can do it! Steve, look unto Jesus, the author and finisher of your faith, who for the joy that was set before Him endured the cross, despising the shame, and has sat down at the right hand of the throne of God."

Letter to Lynn for Mother's Day

Dear Lynn,

I hope you and Kayla have a great time today enjoying each other's company and thinking about the days that have gone by so quickly. The other day I started to think about our life with Kayla, and today I want to share my thoughts of your motherhood to our daughter, the one who calls you "Mother" on this great day.

I remember when we found out you were pregnant with Kayla. Because we had gone through so many miscarriages, the joy of the pregnancy was combined with fear of what might happen again. Then days and weeks passed, and we found ourselves in Albany, facing the questions of a risky procedure and the possibility of having a physically or mentally challenged child. We both agreed that terminating the pregnancy was not an option; regardless of what lay ahead, we knew God would give us the strength to raise the child His way.

More months passed and more tests followed, until we arrived at the great day when you finally gave birth to Kayla. Oh, the joy we both felt over our wonderful, healthy baby girl! God blessed you, me, and us as a couple with Kayla, our one and only, perfect child.

The years passed, and we both agreed it was important that you were home with Kayla throughout her years in school. Though we made sacrifices, each and every one was worth it to see the bond between the two of you grow. When Kayla was sick, you were there for her. When she felt pain, you were there for her. When people treated her badly, you were there for her. When she needed medical care, you were there for her. When she needed clothing for school, you were there for her; and when she needed a parent for a field trip, you were there for her. As time progressed and she became involved in sports, you drove her to practices, sat through them all, and attended her games, racking up countless hours as you drove back and forth and waited for her. You gave your time and energy so Kayla could learn to play the flute, even though music would never be her calling. When she needed help with homework, you always tried your best to help her, at times receiving very little thanks in return. But it was a joy to see the two of you bonding in so many ways through so many years.

Yes, I also remember the long months you and Kayla lived without me in New York, waiting for the house to sell. You were a great mother, but you also had to fill my shoes during that time. I know it wasn't easy, with Kayla then in kindergarten, but you found the strength and fortitude to overcome the days, weeks, and months we were apart.

Then ten years later came my travels while Kayla was a teenager. It took patience on your behalf and great skill to manage the most difficult years in a young girl's life. And last of all, there were the months of uncertainty when I lost my job and we knew I had to move to Minnesota without the two of you. Again, hard times, but you rose to the occasion as you have so many other times throughout Kayla's life.

Of course, through all those years, both you and Kayla had to deal with my unbalanced nature and rely on each other when it came to my demands, cleanliness standards, and constant pushing for more, more, and then more. You helped her understand and get through those low days.

People often say Kayla looks like me and acts like me, but the real truth is, she has your beauty, inwardly and outwardly as well. Along with that, she does have my drive in many ways, but the years you molded her are primarily responsible for the great abilities in her life. Because of the role modeling you provided her, she has truly become the remarkable young woman she is today. I so look forward to the impact she will make in this world, and I know her accomplishments will largely be your doing.

Last, but most important of all, you have been a great role model when it comes to serving the Lord and following His lead. The years of reading devotions, taking Kayla to kids' church and rallies, and then seeing that she attended regular services gave God the ability to work within her life. The years of your own studies, your teaching of other women and in cell groups, showed Kayla that she could be a well-balanced woman in this world and make a difference for the Lord. All of your behaviors have helped Kayla succeed and have shown her how to navigate the difficult issues most young people face in their early lives.

With that said, Happy Mother's Day to you, the woman every mother should model herself after and the woman God blessed Kayla with as her one and only mother! I am proud of what you have accomplished, and I am happy I took the time to remember all the great things you have done for your daughter, our child, with the Lord's blessing.

With love,

Steve

I took Proverbs 31 and applied it to Lynn, recording it in my journal:

"A wife of noble character who can find? Lynn is worth far more than rubies.

"Her husband has full confidence in her and lacks nothing of value. Lynn brings him strength, not harm, all the days of her life.

"She gets up while it is still dark; she provides food for her family. Lynn sets about her work vigorously; her arms are strong for her tasks.

"Her lamp does not go out at night. Her husband is respected at the city gate, where he takes his seat among the elders of the land. Lynn speaks with wisdom, and faithful instruction is on her tongue.

"Lynn watches over the affairs of her household and does not eat the bread of idleness. Her child arises and calls her blessed; her husband also, and he praises her: 'Many women do noble things, but you surpass them all.' Charm is deceptive, and beauty is fleeting; but a woman who fears the Lord—and that is Lynn—is to be praised."

Chapter 12

Five- Alarm Fire! Can It Be Put Out Before It's Too Late?

"Oh Wind of God, come bend us, break us,
Till humbly we confess our need;
Then in Thy tenderness remake us,
Revive, restore, for this we plead."
Elizabeth Porter Head

I Am a Good Man Because of What God Did and Does

"Whatever your hand finds to do, do it with your might, for
in the grave, where you are going, there is neither working
nor planning nor knowledge nor wisdom."
—Ecclesiastes 9:10

"*I must do what's expected of me. I must do what's expected
and then even more.*

*As God opens doors in the coming days, I cannot back down; I must
walk through them in obedience. I will not be embarrassed or feel
I am not good enough. With God I can stand strong and know that
I can do all things through Christ who strengthens me. I will walk
through the open doors, and at times I will run so as to ensure that
I will not question the way God desires me to go. I can no longer
play it safe and do what I think people want me to do in life. I need*

to make a difference in the world for Christ. That is my calling, and that is my desire."

"Be strong and very courageous. Be careful to obey all the law my servant Moses gave you; do not turn from it to the right or to the left, that you may be successful wherever you go. Do not let this Book of the Law depart from your mouth; meditate on it day and night, so that you may be careful to do everything written in it. Then you will be prosperous and successful. Have I not commanded you? Be strong and courageous. Do not be terrified; do not be discouraged, for the LORD your God will be with you wherever you go."

—Joshua 1:7–9

Words from God

"I do have you and Lynn in the palm of My hand. I am protecting you from harm that is on the doorstep of your heart. The pain and suffering in this matter are not part of My plan. Release and freedom are coming to your household. Freedom from My throne room is coming!

"Take heart, believe, put your faith and trust in Me, and I will see you through this pain. A testimony and ministry are being birthed out of this period in your life. My plan and purpose will succeed against the evil one's desire to sift both you and Lynn. Victory will take place, not as you see it, but as I see it."

Leaning on the Lord

"I put my faith and trust in the Lord, and I lean on Him for understanding. He will guide me and direct my path into righteousness if I put Him first and look to Him for the way I should go in life, in marriage, and in all relationships. I want and need to know clearly the path I should take and the life I should live for Him. Lord, grant me this day Your blessings on my life, and show me the unclean places in my heart that I need to repent of. Show me the new course I should follow going forward.

"I must remember that my limitations are mostly in my thoughts, sometimes in my spirit, and then other times in my body. To fulfill the calling God has given me, I must break through the old ways of thinking. How I walk with God in the spirit realm is directly connected to my thought life of who I am and whom I serve. I need to take on the mind of Christ and believe that all things are possible with God my king."

"We are hard pressed on every side, but not crushed; perplexed, but not in despair; persecuted, but not abandoned; struck down, but not destroyed. We always carry around in our body the death of Jesus, so that the life of Jesus may also be revealed in our body."—2 Corinthians 4:8–10

"The separation and now the advancement towards divorce seems insurmountable to me. But I am not alone in this effort to see restoration take place in my marriage. The Father, Son, and Holy Spirit are pushing on with me and helping me along the way. I will not quit, and I will not back down—the stakes are too high. The impact Lynn and I can have in ministry is great, and I believe our calling in the future will be to help couples.

"Climbing out of this valley and to the mountaintop continues in my life with prayer, fasting, reading the Word, and seeking wisdom, knowledge, and understanding."

The First Mediation Opens in Prayer

"Last night Lynn and I had our first mediation session. The train has left the station, and only God can prevent the outcome that Lynn wants—divorce. Lynn says she no longer loves me as a husband; again, only Lynn and God can change her heart.

"I look for God to direct and guide my path this day and all my days going forward. Lord, bring peace and love to my house and Lynn's apartment. We need more of Your Holy Spirit and more of Your love in our lives. Also, be with Kayla and help her through this as well. She is a great young lady who needs You more in her life. Please help her and her boyfriend through this time.

"I know You have a great plan ahead for all of us once this time has passed. The fire hurts and burns, but I know this too shall pass. I want You to have complete control of my life."

"However, as it is written: 'No eye has seen, no ear has heard, no mind has conceived what God has prepared for those who love him.' "— 1 Corinthians 2:9

"I am giving this mediation time completely over to Jesus; it is no longer mine to try to control or navigate. I know Jesus can do the impossible for Lynn and me. I believe Jesus can still work a major miracle of restoration, even during this time."

"And without faith it is impossible to please God; because anyone who comes to him must believe that he exists and that he rewards those who earnestly seek him."
—Hebrews 11:6

Our Marriage Is Dying

So many people in my life were aware of what I was going through as Lynn and I headed towards divorce. Many shared encouraging words with me and let me know I was in their prayers, as well as were Lynn and Kayla. I so appreciated all the kindness coming my way.

As I walked through this dark period, my sincere desire was to be a good example. I wanted others to see my total faith in God and His ability to save my marriage. I hoped that Joanne, too, could see God's love working through me as we talked in our sessions. If somehow my example helped others to keep their faith in God or establish faith in Jesus, then all the pain and suffering I had endured would be worth it. I continually reminded myself that a seed planted can bear much fruit. My marriage had been planted into the ground of separation and now divorce. I could only pray it would bear much fruit, both now and in the future.

"Lord, I know You are a miracle-working God. I surrender all my doubts, fears, and hopelessness into Your mighty hands. I entrust this divorce proceeding and my entire life to You. You will not allow me to give up hope in You and Your ways. You know the outcome, and I know You are working on Your future plans for my life. I trust in Your wisdom above my own. I trust in You because You are my God, my king, and my hope for the future."

God Is with Me Every Step of This Journey

"I realize I do not know what the coming days and months hold, but God does! I do know that God is with me every step of the way, and that gives me hope for the future plans He has for me. Knowing God is with me compels me to push forward and be a witness to My hope in Him and His love for me.

"Based upon reading His Word, I know God does not want this divorce. During this time, I have grown closer to Him than maybe ever before, but I still face the reality of divorce at my doorstep. Even if that does happen—and I hope and pray that it doesn't—I know God is going to use this time in my life for His glory and to help many other people through the fire of separation and divorce.

"The evil one and his demons would like to totally destroy my marriage, testimony, and witness, if not my very flesh; but I, for one, will not let that happen in my life. I do not totally grasp everything that brought Lynn and me to this point in time, but I know it can be reversed and hope and love can spring forth again.

"I am fighting through the trial of my lifetime, and I am holding on for dear life. This trial will break free at some point, and then major blessings will take hold. I will not back down in fighting the evil one, and I will not give up on God or my marriage."

"Let my teaching fall like rain and my words descend like dew, like showers on new grass, like abundant rain on tender plants. I will proclaim the name of the LORD. Oh, praise the greatness of our God! He is the Rock, his works are perfect, and all his ways are just. A faithful God who does no wrong, upright and just is he."—Deuteronomy 32:2–4

Words from My In-Laws

I received a thoughtful mail message from my mother-in-law that said, "I want you to know we are feeling bad about everything that is going on right now. I want you to know we are praying that God gives you comfort and peace right now. Please take care of yourself and stay healthy. Please know that we care about you."

"God, I know many people are praying and seeking Your face for Lynn and me. Lord, open the windows of heaven on our marriage. Lord, save the day and pour forth Your love in our lives. Let Your glory and will pour forth in Lynn and in me.

"I want to serve You, Lord. Call Lynn back to our home, relationship, and love so we can separate ourselves from the world and serve You together. We need—I need—a miracle from Your righteous right hand. It will come from You, for You are God and I am not! I seek You and want to serve You all the days of my life."

In the Hands of God

"I am finding it hard not to push and try to fix what is wrong in my marriage. Maybe that is why I am still in this time. I try to do too many things in my own strength and don't let God do it in His own time. I release Lynn into Your hands, Lord, to do as You see fit."

"Our fathers disciplined us for a little while as they thought best; but God disciplines us for our good, that we may share in his holiness. No discipline seems pleasant at the time, but painful. Later on, however, it produces a harvest of righteousness and peace for those who have been trained by it."—Hebrews 12:10–11

"I will serve the Lord my God all the days of my life! I will never turn back to the world or the ways of the world."

"God's voice thunders in marvelous ways; he does great things beyond our understanding."—Job 37:5

"God is truly in control of all things, and I will put my full trust in Him. Lord, mold me as You wish, both now and forever. You can do more with my life than I can. Bless my path, and put me on the path to righteousness."

Is Jesus Enough?

"The question today is, is Jesus enough? I know He is in my life, but I also want Lynn back. Does that mean Jesus is not enough for me? At times I think so and repent, only to still think about Lynn most of the time.

"Lord God, help me go forward in You, always putting You first in my life. I love Lynn and my marriage to her, but let me get to the point of loving You first in all things, including my marriage. I have come to the point where material possessions, money, position, and my own talents do not matter; what matters is my relationship with You and my relationship with others."

Words from God

"Walk in My ways; seek My kingdom and My righteousness. Follow the plans and purposes that I have put into your heart. Seek My face and know My ways. My ways are higher than yours, and My thoughts are also higher.

"Believe in Me for all things, and trust in Me and My power. The time is coming and is even here when all things will be set into place in your life. Trust in Me and lean on Me, and your path will be straight for My kingdom purposes."

I Need to Hear God and Then Obey Him

More than anything else, I wanted to be successful in God's kingdom. I came up with a list of things that I needed to do in order to achieve that goal: (1) I needed to hear God clearly. (2) I needed the ability to believe everything God said to me. (3) I needed the ability to give up worldly security for God's sake. (4) I needed to not lose heart or give up on the journey. (5) I needed to see through to completion whatever God said to me.

In the past, I had often started one mission or another for God and would do great in the beginning. Soon I was doing merely okay, and eventually I would lose heart and let the world take hold again. Other times my attention and interest in the mission would wane, and I would simply pursue something else. If I were to be successful this time, I had to learn to be obedient to God and focus on success in Him, refusing to allow the things of the world to disillusion me on my journey.

"I am totally discouraged right now, but I will not quit. I know the evil one and his demons are fighting against not only my marriage but also other marriages across the nation. I will not quit until there is a breakthrough. I believe God will come in and save the day!

"God knows what He is doing with Lynn and me. And He loves us. I know that we can believe in and depend on Him. When it is time for something to happen, God will make sure it happens. The timing might be slow or fast, but God will be there in the middle of whatever is going on."

My Destiny Is in God's Hands, Not My Own

"My destiny and my future are not tied to Lynn and what she does or doesn't do. I know God will open doors that should be opened and close doors that should be closed. I know He has a ministry in the future for Lynn and me, though Lynn once said, 'Maybe it will be with another woman.' If that is the case, God will bring new people into my life."

Many times I had been advised not to try to convince Lynn to stay with me if she wanted to leave. Nevertheless, I had once begged her to stay and work things out. As a matter of fact, I had asked her numerous times to come home. I had also asked her to allow love for me to come back into her heart. I truly believed we were meant to be together all our lives; however, that did not seem to be our future. If it was not to be, I knew God would move to fulfill the plan that He had for us when we were joined as husband and wife on July 9, 1983.

I knew I needed to stop trying to make things happen in my life. I needed to stop trying to force what I thought was best for me and my marriage. Somehow I had to release myself into God's hands and plans. It seems like such an easy thing, to just let go and let God, but it wasn't that easy for me. Time and time again, I had to consciously focus my thoughts on my need to surrender until it finally got down into my soul.

Despite my trial, and actually as a result of it, many new people had come into my life, people that I now considered friends. As a result of my openness and transparency, my becoming real and letting others know of my pain as well as sharing in theirs, I had more friends and people who cared about me than ever before. I was being equipped, and would continue being equipped, for everything in my future.

Memorial Day with Lynn and Kayla

For Memorial Day, Lynn came to the house and spent the day with Kayla and me. When she accepted my invitation, she made it quite clear that I should not view this as anything more than a day spent together with Kayla. Nonetheless, we had a great day enjoying each other's company. We acted just like a regular family enjoying themselves together—at least that was my opinion of the day.

I made lunch for all of us, and we played cards and games in the yard. In the past, I had never cooked for my family or been very engaged in our times together. I felt bad about that and knew, if given the chance, I would be a totally different person in the future.

"God will make a way / Where there seems to be no way / He works in ways we cannot see / He will make a way for me."—From "God Will Make a Way" by Don Moen

"Consider it pure joy, my brothers, whenever you face trials of many kinds, because you know that the testing of your faith develops perseverance. Perseverance must finish its work so that you may be mature and complete, not lacking anything." —James 1:2–4

The Fire Burns Off Impurities

"I know trials are painful, like being burned by fire. But fire does something more than inflict pain: it burns off the impurities, and what is left is better than the original substance. I know God uses trials to make us more Christlike in nature. I do not like the fire of trials or testing from the evil one; however, if that makes me a better person and more Christlike, I say, 'Lord, be with me, and do what You must to complete Your process in me.' "

Lynn Wants to Move Towards Divorce Quickly

Lynn and I talked, and she expressed her desire for things to progress quickly to divorce. I said I would not stand in her way. We scheduled a meeting for the coming Saturday to talk about our assets and to begin moving towards closure.

I was in shock, much as I had been for the previous eight months. I could not understand how we had come to this point, but it really didn't matter anymore. I had no choice but to pull myself together, pick up the pieces, and walk towards the new life the Lord would give me in the future.

Thinking back over the years, I remembered how in 2001 I had largely turned off the light switch in my relationship with the Lord. Sadly, it took the fire of separation and divorce to turn it back on again. But no matter what happened in my life, I would not turn back to the world or change my new course of walking with God. I wanted Him to flow through me and release me to do His will and work in the world.

"Lord God, I believe in You and what You can do, no matter the circumstances in my life. I know You want the best for me, and You alone know my future. I am slowly learning to live in the moment and in the day. May I continue to search for You each day and

know Your ways. May Your hand of blessing be upon my life this day, hour, and minute."

"Put on the full armor of God so that you can take your stand against the devil's schemes." — Ephesians 6:11

I Want to Be Pure as Snow

"Yet if you devote your heart to him and stretch out your hands to him, if you put away the sin that is in your hand and allow no evil to dwell in your tent, then you will lift up your face without shame; you will stand firm and without fear." — Job 11:13–15

"I continue to tighten up my life and look to ensure that I have placed my life in God's hands. I am not perfect, but things in my life are getting better. I want clean hands and a clean heart in front of both God and man. I didn't always want that, and I let small sins become big sins—sins that at an earlier point I would never have thought of doing. I have cleaned those out of my life now, and going forward I will stay close to God for purification."

Stumbling and Bumbling Through Life, Too Many Wasted Years

"People are the ones who abandon God; He doesn't abandon them. I have learned that I can abandon God though I still go to church, read the Word, do devotions, and try to live a good life. The reality is, I did just that by not giving Him total control of my life in 2000 and 2001. For too many years, I merely stumbled through life, alive but not truly living for Him or living a life I could be totally proud of.

"I have prayed for a life that is alive and thriving, and strange as it may seem, I have found that in the fire I have walked through. Finally, I am no longer going through the motions in my walk with God."

"Faith looks across the storm—it does not doubt or stop to look at clouds and things without. Faith does not question why when all His ways are hard to understand, but trusts and prays."—Anonymous

Meeting with Joanne

I had a meeting with Joanne, and several thoughts came from that meeting. I should take a long time before considering marriage in the future, Joanne recommended. In general, men get their emotional needs met through women, so based upon that fact, I should not immediately start dating. Joanne suggested that when I did start dating, I should date multiple women and let them know what I was doing. There should be no competition between women, and they should also be free to date other men. She told me to work on a list of what I would want in a woman in the future.

Then we talked about the great benefits found in obeying God. First of all, the true nature of God works through us as we obey Him. God will help change take place deep within us if we maintain a clear conscience before Him. When we hear His voice and read of His ways in the Word, goodness will follow us if we obey His set directions. By obeying God, we will live life better and be a magnet to other people, who will want to be around us and communicate with us.

At the end of our session, I wondered why I had failed to whole-heartedly follow God's ways for so much of my life.

Second Mediation with Wayne and Janet

"Surely goodness and love will follow me all the days of my life, and I will dwell in the house of the LORD forever."
—Psalm 23:6

Lynn and I attended the second mediation session, and it was very hard and painful. We gave each other disparaging looks and said painful things, especially me. But at the end of the two hours with Wayne and Janet, Lynn and I talked, cried, and enjoyed a meal together. At the end of the evening, Lynn remarked, "It was a good time," and I felt the same.

As we walked through these painful times, I knew God would somehow turn it to good in the future, but I still had a ways to go with God in the here and now. I wanted the words I spoke to be uplifting and encouraging, but some of the words I spoke that day in mediation were hurtful. I had no excuse for my behavior and vowed to learn to control myself better, no matter how much pain I was feeling.

> "May the favor of the LORD our God rest upon us; establish
> the work of our hands for us—yes, establish the work of our
> hands."—Psalm 90:17

List of Desirable Attributes for a Woman in My Life

Following Joanne's instructions, I went to work on a list of attributes I would like to see in a woman in my life. This is what I came up with:

- A godly woman with the fire of the Lord burning within her
- Often in the Word
- Often in prayer
- Compatible with me, both mentally and physically
- Desirous of mutual love; that is, unconditional love for each other
- A relationship of mutual respect
- Best friend
- Trustworthy
- Honest
- Faithful
- Able to share feelings openly and honestly
- Great listener and communicator
- Sense of humor
- Willing to work together on making our non-strengths, strengths
- Sweet spirit
- Compassionate

- Caring
- Kind
- Open to our having separate interests as well as mutual ones
- Independent spirit
- Willing to debate and not fearful of it
- Intelligent and knowledgeable about many subjects
- Adventurous
- Enjoys fellowship with other women and couples
- Physically active
- Clean and organized

Meeting with Lynn to Discuss Splitting Assets

"Lynn and I had breakfast together, went over tax information and a furniture list, and then discussed how much I could give her monthly for two years. We seem to be past the house, furniture, pictures, etc., and now are down to monthly support.

"Lord, I do not know what to do any longer. Should I give, give, and give some more? How long does this go on? How long does life carry on in this direction? What should I do? What should Lynn do? I keep thinking I should fight on, fight on for the marriage with the sword of the Spirit, which is the Word of God. So I will fight on. I will take back the ground that has been taken from us. It is not too late; victory over Satan will happen, and I believe that in the Lord."

"The Lord blessed the latter part of Job's life more than the
first." — Job 42:12

What Does God Have for the Future?

"This day I find myself wondering what God has in store for my life. I know it is good, and I know great things will take place as I rest in the palm of His hand. I will walk with the Lord all the days of my life in the land of the living. I am open to You, Lord, in every way this day. I seek You and lean on You for Your calling in my life.

"We are having another mediation session this afternoon, our third with Wayne and Janet."

"I have been young, and now am old, yet I have not seen the righteous forsaken."—Psalm 37:25

"As you do not know the path of the wind, or how the body is formed in a mother's womb, so you cannot understand the work of God, the Maker of all things."—Ecclesiastes 11:5

"When times are good, be happy; but when times are bad consider: God has made the one as well as the other. Therefore, a man cannot discover anything about his future."—Ecclesiastes 7:14

"Today Lynn and I are going to meet with Wayne and Janet in mediation. I have the feeling that this will be the last time. We have agreed upon all terms except the support portion. I believe we will agree because I will up the dollar amount and the length to match Lynn's wants and desires.

"I have prepared a prayer of blessing to pray over Lynn at the end of today's mediation if she will allow me."

My Prayer for Lynn

At the end of mediation, Lynn agreed to let me pray the prayer I had prepared. This is what I said:

"The Lord bless you and keep you; the Lord make His face shine upon you and be gracious to you; the Lord turn His face towards you and give you peace. Be strong and courageous. Do not be terrified, and do not be discouraged, for the Lord your God will be with you wherever you go.

"May Lynn's coming and going be blessed by Your hand, Lord God. May her waking hours be blessed by Your Spirit leading her thoughts, motives, actions, and desires. May her schoolwork come easy to her, her time with friends be blessed, and her time with Kayla and family be heartfelt, prosperous, and enlightening.

"May Lynn's sleeping hours be covered by Your protective hand. May she dream dreams and see visions about her life, her calling, and Your perfect will. At the end of her days, let the words spoken about her be words of amazing feats she accomplished, acts of kindness she performed in unity with others, and, most importantly, true words of love from those who had the opportunity to be blessed by knowing the woman she really is.

"May Your words abide in Lynn so that when she prays, You will give her the desires of her heart. May Your light give light to her pathway. May her pathway be so blessed by Your hand that everyone is amazed by her beauty, intelligence, knowledge, wisdom, and the financial flow from Your throne room.

"Lord, I ask that You would restore Lynn's soul, heal her brokenheartedness, and bind up her wounds. Take away all fear, doubt, and discouragement, and give her clarity, joy, peace, faith, hope, and love. Bless her, Lord, with Your faith, hope, and love. Give her the peace that surpasses all understanding, and wrap her with Your faith, hope, and love. Calm her spirit, soothe her soul, and give her peace all the days of her life. Even if one thousand falls at her left side and ten thousand at her right side, let no harm fall upon her. I pray she lives with health and happiness many, many more years. At the end of her life, I pray she has the same strength as in the days of her youthfulness.

"Lynn, let the peace of God rule in your heart, and be thankful all the days of your life. I pray you will be tenderhearted, forgiving, and compassionate, as you have been in the past, and that you will be even more so in the future as new relationships develop in your life.

"Lord, give Lynn the incorruptible beauty of a gentle and quiet spirit, which is very precious this day and every day of her life. May the beauty of her life explode from within her and touch every life she comes into contact with. I pray she has peace with all people throughout the days of her life and that at the end of her days, no one can stand up and say she was an enemy.

"I pray that Lynn will have no fear or anxiety that would prevent her from all the blessings You have in store for her life. May she claim You as her light and her salvation and say, 'Whom shall I fear? The Lord is the strength of my life; of whom shall I be afraid?' Lynn, always remember to wait on the Lord and be of good courage, and He shall strengthen your heart, mind, soul, and body.

"May you be released into the perfect plan God has for you. I pray you will fulfill the destiny that has been planned for you and that you will be blessed by it as well. Remember to always use your gifts and talents to bless others in this life. Let these words be spoken of your life: 'Many daughters have done well, but you excel them all.'

"Lord, I pray that when Lynn passes through deep waters, You will be with her, and when she passes through the rivers, they will not overflow her. When she walks through the fire, she shall not be burned, nor shall the flame scorch her. I pray she will always make You her refuge and abide in the shadow of Your wings until these calamities have passed by her and the ones she loves.

"Let no weapon formed against Lynn prosper in this world or in the spiritual world, Lord. Make darkness as light before her, and make her crooked paths straight. As Lynn walks wisely, deliver her. I pray she would always walk with wisdom and find full deliverance from Your hand. Lord, do not withhold any good thing from Lynn as she follows You and walks a righteous path full of mercy and grace. Let the words of Lynn's mouth and the meditations of her heart always be acceptable in Your sight, Lord, You who are Lynn's strength and redeemer.

"I pray Lynn's life would be blessed by the plans You have for her, plans that are for good and not evil, to give her a future and a hope. Give her confidence that the future is something she never has to fear. I pray she would have contentment, longevity, enjoyment, vitality, riches, and happiness all the days of her life. May she find Your protection, grace, and rest. May she enjoy freedom from fear and walk in confidence in You. May the fruit of her life be seen every year, and may she be fresh and flourishing even into old age.

"Lynn, arise, shine, for your light has come! And the glory of the Lord is risen upon you.

"Lord, bless Lynn in every way possible this day and in the days to come. I have been blessed by knowing her, and as the days of our marriage end, I will always remember her love, kindness, and caring, and the blessing she has been to me. I pray she finds true happiness in this life and the life to come.

"Pour forth and release Yourself onto Lynn in mighty ways, and bless all her days!"

Is This the Final Settlement Meeting?

Lynn and I made plans to meet at a restaurant called G-Allen's. I hoped this wasn't going to be our last meal together, but that was up to the Lord and Lynn. I still wanted to live with her as her husband, but that could happen only if Lynn's love for me returned.

"Lord, bless my marriage, family, and future. If a future with Lynn is not to be, open new doors for me so that I can serve You and have a partner to share my love with and care for. I hope all the things I have learned over the past nine months will never be forgotten. I want to love You first and then love my wife, my daughter, and the rest of my family. Continue to show me the pathway I should walk in this life, and I will follow You all my days.

"This is Your day, Lord God, to lead and guide in the way that You see fit. I am Your son and will follow You all the days of my life. You are my God and king, and I will serve no other in my life. I seek You, and I seek Your ways. May this day be blessed by Your hand, Lord. I want to be obedient in all that You share with me. Fill me with words to be shared with others.

"Lord, I ask that You bless the time that I have with Lynn this day. May our conversation be uplifting and full of Your mercy and grace. I know that great communication is the starting point for learning others' needs, especially Lynn's. Help me to communicate well with Lynn today as we have lunch together to work out the final details. Until the end, Lord, unify our relationship by our showing love to each other and not just talking about it.

"God, come in and save the day in my marriage. Help both Lynn and me to see past money, possessions, and other things. Help us see past hurts, pains, and unforgiveness. I pray that Lynn and I would forgive each other; wash our hearts and minds in Your forgiveness, and let healing come to our marriage.

"I will always believe in You and what You want to accomplish in my life, God. I turn to You, the author and finisher of my faith,

for all direction and purpose. Open hearts and minds today, and let Your mercy and grace fill this place, the church, and Lynn's heart and mind."

Lynn and I met for two hours and talked about future support. We agreed on a sum and duration of time that I could afford. Lynn also brought with her a letter sharing the things that had caused our separation and divorce—it was nineteen pages long. We left in agreement with each other, with Lynn saying she would talk to Janet to draw up the remaining terms to be finalized and signed.

It was great seeing Lynn and talking to her. While I continued to pray for a miracle, it was clear the final days were closing in on our marriage. As much as I hated to admit it, I could see that now. Although Lynn was polite, kind, relaxed, and caring, it was apparent the day was coming.

> "Finally, brothers, whatever is true, whatever is noble, whatever is right, whatever is pure, whatever is lovely, whatever is admirable—if anything is excellent or praiseworthy—think about such things."—Philippians 4:8

Support of My Loving Family

God is good—all the time! Ed, Kim, and Eddie came to visit with Kayla and me for the weekend. We had a great time visiting many sites and enjoying family time at our house. We all went to church on Sunday, and they really liked the worship and the words spoken by Pastor Doug.

Ed and I spent some time talking about the future of my marriage, or rather, my divorce and life without Lynn. Kim and Lynn went to lunch and seemed to have a good time. When Lynn stopped by the house to drop Kim off after lunch, she came in to visit with everyone, including me. I thought again what a nice person she was and how good she looked.

During their visit, Ed and his family unintentionally heard me praying for Lynn and our marriage. That embarrassed me a little, but

I just couldn't give up as long as I believed there was still hope. It also seemed to make a positive impression on Eddie.

I was sad when it was time for Ed and his family to leave. This was the first time we had visited with just our two families. I took comfort in knowing that at least Kayla would still be home after they left.

Trials and Tribulations Come for a Reason

"God refines with trials and tribulations, and that refinement brings heat to my soul and separates the impurities of unforgiveness, anger, and bitterness from the nature of God that He wants to see in me. I do not believe God put this separation and divorce in my life, but I do believe He will use it for His long-term glory if I stay true to Him and His ways."

"In this you greatly rejoice, though now for a little while you may have had to suffer grief in all kinds of trials. These have come so that your faith—of greater worth than gold, which perishes ever though refined by fire—may be proved genuine and may result in praise, glory and honor when Jesus Christ is revealed."—1 Peter 1:6–7

Chapter 13

The Fire Has Seared the Core of Love

"The Son is the radiance of God's glory and the exact representation of his being, sustaining all things by his powerful word. After he had provided purification for sins, he sat down at the right hand of the Majesty in heaven."
—Hebrews 1:3

When Is Enough, Enough?

I had a very tough night with Lynn at the house. Her requests continued to expand, despite the agreement I thought we had reached three times in the past few weeks. I was confused, to say the least, and desperately needed God's direction. The situation was so muddled and seemed to be always changing. *What happens tomorrow or the next day?* I wondered.

During our conversation, we talked about the best way to handle Kayla's college fund. We agreed it would be easier on Kayla if I assumed that responsibility. Then Lynn and I talked to Kayla together. Kayla and I cried because we knew the marriage was over.

I Finally Understand the Marriage Is Over

After Kayla went back upstairs, I asked Lynn if we could spend as much time working on our marriage as we did talking about nickels and dimes. Her response was a laugh and a very loud no. Something died in me when she responded that way. Up until then, I still had faith and held onto hope that our marriage would be restored.

Words from God

"Don't rush, and don't hurry; be patient in this matter. Let this word soak in and get into your spirit. Do not let anything harm you or your walk with Me. Seek My wisdom and know My ways. Fear not, child of the most high God! Watch My mighty hand move now that you have released your control. Let Me control the future. Do not get out ahead of Me and My plan for this time."

Love Is Completely Gone

A change was gradually taking place in my heart for Lynn: the love was slowly dissipating. It was time to move on and accept the fact that the marriage had been over for months, if not on September 27 when she had first left home. Her heart for me had changed; she had shared many times that she did not love me, but now I was finally beginning to accept it.

"Lord, please let Lynn release me to live a life free of her. I need release to move forward. I can no longer see one thing and believe another; it is tearing me apart. I must move forward, knowing it will be without Lynn. Hopefully, I will someday find someone who fills what God wants and who fits the attributes I am looking for in a woman.

"Lord, be with me today as I search for Your plan and purpose. I pray You bless the work of my hands and the attitudes of my heart."

"So do not fear, for I am with you; do not be dismayed, for I am your God. I will strengthen you and help you; I will uphold you with my righteous right hand."—Isaiah 41:10

290

I Understand How David Felt

After Bathsheba gave birth to their son, David pleaded with God for the child's life. He fasted and spent nights in his home, lying prostrate before God and interceding for the child.

Second Samuel 12:16–23 records what happened:

> David pleaded with God for the child. He fasted and went into his house and spent the nights lying on the ground. The elders of his household stood beside him to get him up from the ground, but he refused, and he would not eat any food with them.
>
> David noticed that his servants were whispering among themselves, and he realized the child was dead. "Is the child dead?" he asked.
>
> "Yes," they replied, "he is dead."
>
> Then David got up from the ground. After he had washed, put on lotions and changed his clothes, he went into the house of the LORD and worshiped. Then he went to his own house, and at his request they served him food, and he ate.
>
> His servants asked him, "Why are you acting this way? While the child was alive, you fasted and wept, but now that the child is dead, you get up and eat!"
>
> He answered, "While the child was still alive, I fasted and wept. I thought, 'Who knows? The LORD may be gracious to me and let the child live.' But now that he is dead, why should I fast? Can I bring him back again? I will go to him, but he will not return to me."

As I read this passage, I was struck by its similarities to my marriage. I had prayed, fasted, sought counsel, pleaded and begged with both God and Lynn, and cried many nights for the restoration of my marriage, but that did not happen. With that realization, something broke in me, and now I was off my knees and moving forward in life, knowing I had done my very best to change the path that had been set months ago. But the great news was, I was a changed man and would continue to change for the better in the days ahead.

About this time, I also had a very helpful conversation with a friend, who pointed out that great days lay ahead. I was finally starting to see purpose in my being in central Minnesota. I had made new friends, started a new life, and discovered a new sense of calling. I rejoiced in that knowledge and prayed for God to open His windows and pour forth His blessings with wisdom, understanding, and knowledge.

Thank God for Kayla!

Kayla and I made plans to spend Father's Day together. I was continually blessed by my daughter and thrilled with the wonderful young lady she was becoming. I wanted nothing more than to show her how much I loved her and for her to understand that I desired nothing but the best for her.

I continued to pray for Lynn and the decisions we faced in regards to financial support and the closing out of our marriage. I fervently asked God to guard her heart and mind from Satan and all ways that were not pleasing to Him.

"I personally will not be satisfied with where I am now in You, Lord. I will push forward and walk in Your Spirit, and I need You to lead me like never before. I know You have great plans ahead for me to accomplish. I will be obedient to Your calling and Your ways.

"I truly thought my life would end if my marriage ended, but I know now God has new beginnings ahead in relationships and in the destiny He has planned for my future."

Open Doors Ordained by the Lord

"Those who sow in tears will reap with songs of joy. He who goes out weeping, carrying seed to sow, will return with songs of joy, carrying sheaves with him."—Psalm 126:5–6

"I am starting to realize God will never do anything to harm me. Whatever He does or does not do in my life is in my best interest. I will give myself to Him always. I am still working through why my prayers for my marriage were not answered; however, I realize free will is a major reason. I still have a purpose from the Lord to accomplish, and that will be fulfilled with another woman in the future.

"This is a critical day for Lynn and me to resolve the remaining financial issues between us. Bless our conversation, Lord, and may we both be relaxed and agree on what is fair for both of us. Keep any bitter root from entering our hearts. Your higher calling is what is best for both of us."

Words from God

"Listen to the words I speak today. Use caution, and advance slowly in your quest to lay out the facts. Use care and understanding, and be patient with Lynn. She will understand and take it in, if given in a spirit of love, care, and kindness.

"Relax and accept Lynn's feedback and questions without getting defensive. My Spirit will guide you, and My wisdom will uphold you during this time. Do not take in fire, or you will be burned by it."

The Quest for More, More, and More Continues

"I am confused, torn apart, and pained, and I lack direction and hope this morning. Lord, please help me through this time of confusion. I want to be free in Your will and plan. Show me my steps, and lead the way clearly so I can follow. I seek You and Your ways."

Lynn had rejected my final offer concerning the settlement in regards to support. She planned to obtain a lawyer and start the process of agreement all over again. We had already come to an agreement several times in the past, and each time I had felt the arrangement took care of Lynn and enabled both of us to live a good life apart from each other. I had no choice now but to wait and see what the next step was going to be.

Words from God

"Victory is coming—victory and not defeat! Have faith and hold out hope as I work in your life today. Goodness, gladness, and joy will return to your heart. I have a plan and purpose for your life that I will fulfill as you become more obedient to My will and direction. Be patient, and become a man of understanding. I have come to give you life, and life more abundantly."

God, Please Keep the Bitter Root from Me

I received an e-mail from Lynn concerning decisions on accounts we held together. Lynn's behavior confused and hurt me, and I did not want to have to deal with that kind of pain.

"Lord, please don't let that pain come to my doorstep. I do want to walk as a man of integrity. I never wanted this cross I must bear, but it is here at my doorstep. Lord, perform Your will and have Your plan come about.

"I want to take what I've learned and never repeat the things that pulled apart my marriage. In my next relationship, I want to be more focused on You, the woman, and our love, and I want to overlook the small things that do not matter. I would like our relationship to be focused on love for You, love for each other, and love for other people in the world.

"Release Your Spirit on me this day, and help me move towards the future alone without holding the sin of unforgiveness in my heart."

Satisfaction in the Lord

Life is strange—one minute up, the next minute down. What the future held, I did not know, but I knew it must be filled with God and my love for Him. I would never turn back from Him or His ways. I would pursue Him, seek Him, and focus on Him all my days.

I could be satisfied walking in the Lord and His Spirit. I could be satisfied reading books, relaxing on my porch, and listening to the call of nature all around me. I could be satisfied going to church,

Life groups, and work. But there is more to life than just being satis-fied. God wants us to be thrilled, engaged, excited, and happy doing His will and being a history-maker in this land.

"Today is month nine in the separation and divorce proceed-ings. It's been hard to see this thing birthed from start to finish. I have had no control over the decisions and timing. I feel helpless but now must move on to a different journey. I want to hear God's voice, plan, and call on my life. I seek His plans alone for the decisions made in the days ahead."

"Get rid of all bitterness, rage and anger, brawling and slander, along with every form of malice. Be kind and com-passionate to one another, forgiving each other, just as in Christ God forgave you."—Ephesians 4:31–32

"I know that I have grown in these hard days of the past nine months. It has not been easy to be engaged at work and to continue eating and sleeping as usual, but I have done that so as to carry on into the future. This hard place is a part of my journey with Christ. I cannot escape this place; I must face it with all my might and, most impor-tantly, with God in the midst, fighting with me and helping me through.

"This time will help in my process of becoming perfect in Him. I will not run from this, but I will finish the race and grow for the future. I know that through this I will grow stronger in the Lord and become more compassionate, not just to people who are close to me, but also to strangers in need of a helping hand."

The Love of God Is Key

"I know God has a calling on my life, one that I must fulfill. I will follow His calling and plan. This day and every day going forward, I choose to walk in my destiny. I know I also need a mate who is willing to follow God's plan and be a part of my calling.

Search me, know me, and release Your Spirit in my life, Lord, so that I can serve You and resist sinful thoughts and desires. If I keep the love of God as my motivation, I will not fail You, Lord, for love never fails. When I love others the way Jesus loves me, I will be free."

> " 'For I know the plans I have for you,' declares the LORD, 'plans to prosper you and not to harm you, plans to give you hope and a future. Then you will call upon me and come and pray to me, and I will listen to you. You will seek me and find me when you seek me with all your heart.' "
> —Jeremiah 29:11–13

A Week in Wisconsin with Family and Friends

Kayla and I decided to visit family and friends in Wisconsin and had a great time of bonding as we drove there together. We spent time with Ed, Kim, and Eddie, and I even had the chance to read the Word to Eddie and converse with him about the Lord. It was a much-needed, relaxing trip and greatly helped the healing process move forward.

It was very important to me to keep exercising, talking to people, reading the Word, and doing things to stay active, even though I was out of my usual routine. At times I just wanted to retreat inwards, but that would have destroyed me and inactivated me for the plans ahead.

During the visit, I met a good friend for lunch one day, and he commented, "We have only a few years to make the most of our lives." Believing that to be true, I determined to make the most of each moment I was alive, for the Lord, family, friends, and mankind.

> "The one who sows to please his sinful nature, from that nature will reap destruction; the one who sows to please the Spirit, from the Spirit will reap eternal life. Let us not become weary in doing good, for at the proper time we will reap a harvest if we do not give up." —Galatians 6:8–9

"No turning back is my cry today. No turning back to the world. No turning back to the sins that were habitual in nature. No turning back to going through the motions. No turning back to my own ways of dealing with life. I am turning to God and His nature, His calling,

and His path in life. I am far better off serving Him and His ways than serving my own selfish, controlling, perfectionist ways.

"Today is Independence Day, but it doesn't give me the right to do what I please. It gives me the right to do what pleases my Lord.

"These days I will remember for the rest of my life. The time with Kayla this week has been outstanding. The time with family and friends has renewed my strength. The time in devotion to God has been priceless, and it centers my core to have the right priorities when I go through the day in the Spirit's strength rather than my own.

"While I am still in the midst of a divorce, I turn to God's role in my life and Lynn's. I ask Him to redirect my thinking from the hurts, pains, and heartaches to the greatness of God and the wonderful years Lynn and I had together."

"Yet if you devote your heart to him and stretch out your hands to him, if you put away the sin that is in your hand and allow no evil to dwell in your tent, then you will lift up your face without shame; you will stand firm and without fear."—Job 11:13–15

"I must always remember no one but God holds my destiny. Lynn does not, Kayla does not, my family does not, my workplace does not, and certainly Satan does not. No one and nothing can move me out of the will of God and the plan He has established for my life."

Home to Minnesota

As Kayla and I prepared for the return trip to Minnesota, I looked forward to our talks and time together. Over the past months, we had grown closer and could share most things. But I wanted an opportunity to share more about Christ's love and her need for a deeper relationship with Him, so I asked the Holy Spirit to prepare her heart and to give me attentive ears to hear and the right words to speak.

I was moving forward in life with a great attitude and a right focus on God. I had become passionate about the right relationships and the things of God. My life was filled with love, joy, and happiness even though the process of divorce still surrounded me. Despite that shadow, life was getting better and God's plan was becoming clearer. God had allowed the divorce, but He had not sent it into my life. Mindful of that fact, I was watchful of His message within the storm. Somehow, someway, I knew He would take what was intended to destroy me and turn it around for His glory.

Meeting with Joanne

Joanne's words of advice to me in this session were to take it slow in developing any new relationship. Clearly defined boundaries would need to be established, and I would have to learn how a new person reacted in certain situations. I would have to observe the way the person fought and the way she listened, and I would need to remember that conflict will happen in any relationship. Joanne urged me to stay involved in groups and relationships with other people, to stay whole and keep seeking the path of wholeness. "Allow the energy to open up, and then share it with the world," she advised.

The Compass of God Points True North

"God's Word is a sure foundation whether we are standing on the mountaintop or walking through the deepest valley. God's Word is the compass to point us back to His holy mountain, the place where we should dwell. If things are going right in my life, I must run to God's Word. If things are falling apart in my life, I must run to God's Word. I must never let the Word of God leave my sight as long as I live."

The Marriage Lasted Twenty-Six Years

"Twenty-six years ago Lynn and I stood before God and man to enter into a covenant with each other. Today we are at the end of our marriage, and this pains me; but I know Lynn has free will and has decided on this divorce.

"Lord, I have been seeking Your perfect will and plan for my life and Lynn's. I ask for forgiveness for any of my actions that were not

pleasing to You, Lynn, or Kayla. I can go on only with the knowledge that I have done what I could to make things right.

"As Lynn and I continue to walk down the road of divorce, bless and protect both of us and the people we let into our lives. I want godly people in my life to grow with and also people that I can share the gospel with. I want to be a godly man who never goes back to the vomit of my sins and disobedient behaviors."

Now Is the Time to Reinvent Myself in God's Ways

"As long as I am obedient to God's will and destiny in my life, any failure is not the end of the journey. As a matter of fact, it might enhance and expand the impact to me and others. Life may not work out just the way I planned or wanted, but God has a way better than my own.

"I must be willing to reinvent myself as God reveals more of His will to me. I must let the past go and move on to the newness that God is providing. God would never let one door close if He didn't have a better one poised to open. I think that might be why this entire separation-and- divorce process has taken so long. God has been working first to resolve the matter and then to formulate a better way. What I think of as a setback might truly be a setup for greater things to come."

Words from God

"Seek My face, know My ways, and walk after My judgments. My son, desire the firstfruits in your life. My blessings are on your firstfruits and your joy in them.

"Know that My hand is working on your behalf. I desire a relationship with you through this life. Walk with me and talk to Me, and doors will open as you go forward. I am blessing you, My son, and will continue to bless you in the days ahead. Know that I am the King of Glory and the one who provides. Seek Me, know Me, and trust in Me."

A Cry for Help in the Darkness

"I cry out to the Lord in my distress and find He is the only true stabilizer in my life. The Lord is my rock, my fortress, and my deliverer—my God, my strength, in whom I will trust."

In Need of the Joy of the Lord

Time passes so quickly in life. It seemed like only yesterday I had lived in New York with Lynn and our young daughter. Then came the move to Wisconsin, then the move to Minnesota—so many changes. Just since being in Minnesota, we had moved into our house in May of 2007, taken family vacations, and seen Kayla go off to school in August of 2008. Then, in September of that year, Lynn had moved out.

I thought ahead to my future and wondered what the next year held in store. Would there be happiness, joy, and goodness, or pain, defeat, and harm? Only time would tell, but one thing I knew: the goodness of the Lord would be with me. And no matter what life brought, my desire was to be a man of God searching after His ways.

"We had Life Group last night, and it was good to be with fellow believers. Our God is great all the time as we serve Him and walk after His ways. I want to stay in His perfect will and follow His plan. Help me, Lord, to keep my life in order, and cleanse me from the past so I can have a future serving You and Your kingdom.

"I want to be filled with joy and happiness this morning and throughout the day. I desire to work hard and have a joyful attitude. I want to pursue fun. I want to have joy in my life so believers and nonbelievers alike will want to know what makes me different. I want to share Christ with joy in my heart."

"Rejoice in the Lord always. I will say again: Rejoice!"
—Philippians 4:4

"Joyful people stay in the here and now, not in the past. I am becoming more joyful, and I stay joyful when I stay in the present

moment and not allow myself to relive the days that have brought so much sorrow and pain."

"I know that there is nothing better for men than to be happy and do good while they live. That everyone may eat and drink, and find satisfaction in all his toil—this is the gift of God. I know that everything God does will endure forever; nothing can be added to it and nothing can be taken from it. God does it so that men will revere Him."—Ecclesiastes 3:12–14

The Sins of the Past Will Find Us Out

"I found out yesterday that Lynn has been talking to, chatting with, and now seeing another man for over a year now. She has been blaming me for everything, but now I know she has been apart from me in her mind for a long, long, time. Why can't she just let me go? Why can't I be free of her and the pain she has caused? Help me, God, to find release from this pain. Lord, I hope this day is a major victory in Your destiny for my life!"

Lynn had been very kind the last several times we had spoken by phone. On the day when I found out about the other man, she was in New York with friends. Upon my asking, she confirmed she was with the man from Canada. Since this was the third time this man had come up in our conversation, I asked Lynn to give me the true scope of her relationship with him, and she said she had been involved emotionally for well over a year.

This information, of course, did not erase the fact of the sin in my life and the actions I had taken in our marriage. But it did help me move forward with clean hands and a clean heart, understanding now why Lynn and I had not moved closer together.

Lynn also said this was the first time she had been with the man in person. Sad and heartbroken for Lynn, I mourned the fact that she was now doing things she never would have done before—or at least the person I knew and loved for many years would never have done them. I truly hoped she would find the happiness she was looking for. But as for me, I was discovering true happiness in the Lord, and I wanted this to continue.

People will always let us down. God alone is always there, and He never turns away and leaves us. What joy it brings to know that Jesus loves us and will never leave or forsake us—neither now nor into eternity!

Words from God

"Release is coming, Steve Kirk! Freedom is coming, healing is coming, peace and joy are coming. My release this day will be the release you need in your life.

"Be open, and accept what I have for you. Do not reject the calling because it is new and requires much strength in My Spirit. Be open this day, forget the past, release the past, love Me, seek Me, and know Me. Turn your whole heart to Me, and see the great and mighty works I will do through you. My hand is on you, so fear not. Do not turn away, but seek Me this day."

I Need a Clearer Picture, Lord

"What does the future hold for me, Lord? How can I push forward in You and forget the things of this world? How do I completely forget my past life, marriage, and friendship with a person I thought I knew? I can do this only through You and Your Word and by living according to Your ways.

"Help me, release me, and direct me into new ways, new steps, and new relationships, oh God. I cry out to You loudly, so make Your path clear to me this day and every day going forward!"

The Flames Are Dying Down

This trial was making me stronger in the Lord than I had ever been. I sincerely believed that for the long term, my greatest blessings would come out of this time. I had cried out to God in my lowest valley and in the midst of my deepest despair and heartache. Many times I had asked that this cup be taken from me, but now I realized I had to drink from the cup and move forward in God's victory. With God walking with me through my times of hurt and pain, I could make it through anything and come out more Christlike in the process. I was slowly starting to forget the past and resolve lingering issues as I talked with Pastor Doug, Joanne, Kayla, friends, and family.

"I will fight the good fight. I will endure through the pain that keeps getting uncovered. The flames of this fire are starting to die down, and the sun will shine once again in my life. The blessings will fall if I stay close to God and refuse to let sin burn me by holding unforgiveness towards another."

"Save me, O God, by your name; vindicate me by your might. Hear my prayer, O God; listen to the words of my mouth. Strangers are attacking me; ruthless men seek my life—men without regard for God. Surely God is my help; the Lord is the one who sustains me."—Psalm 54:1–4

"But now, this is what the Lord says—he who created you, O Jacob, he who formed you, O Israel: 'Fear not, for I have redeemed you; I have summoned you by name; you are mine. When you pass through the waters, I will be with you; and when you pass through the rivers, they will not sweep over you. When you walk through the fire, you will not be burned; the flames will not set you ablaze.'"—Isaiah 43:1–4

I Need to Be Sold Out to God 100 Percent of the Time

"Lord God, fill me with Your Word, presence, and Spirit this day. I feel alive in You, and I know I am being directed by Your power and will. Lord, thank you for getting me on the right path again. I want to serve You all the days of my life.

"I have turned my heart and mind towards You, oh Lord. I know this will cause my actions, desires, and thoughts to change according to Your will. I want to be a man totally sold out to You and Your ways. As long as You are leading my life, I am in great hands.

"I know You know all things, including what is best for me to grow in Your kingdom. I ask You to give me what I need to grow and help others this day. I so desire Your direction this day and every day going forward. If I have the God of the universe guiding me today, I cannot fail!"

Happy Birthday . . . or Not

"Today is my birthday! I am now forty-nine years old and looking forward to the next forty-nine years of my life. God is moving in many areas, and I must never let go of His true gospel: Jesus Christ died for my sins, was buried, and rose again for my salvation, declaring me righteous before God the Father. I will be going to heaven someday to spend eternity with Him.

"I know God is honored when my heart beats in the same rhythm as His. He wants me to live right, walk humbly, love kindness, and dwell in harmony with all mankind. Living right means to live on the side of truth and never doubt the Word of God and His calling. When that takes place in my life, His will and ways will prevail."

My birthday started out great, but darkness set in by the time I reached Wisconsin, where I was going for my birthday. On my way to Milwaukee, I received a call from Lynn, who said she was trying unsuccessfully to get into the house. I shared that I had changed the locks upon the recommendation of my lawyer and that I was in Madison and couldn't let her in. She was very unhappy and shared her displeasure with me for over an hour.

Once I arrived in Milwaukee, my mother and I had a disagreement. By six o'clock, I was an emotional wreck! I obviously still had a long way to go before reaching the point where I could easily handle pain, frustration, and heartache.

"I need more counseling and help from You, Lord. God, help me make it through this time. I want to walk with You and talk with You. Clear out the pain, hurt, and bad feelings I have. I know there are better days ahead as I walk according to Your ways.

"I hope that my fiftieth birthday will be better than this one. I hope it will be filled with happiness, enjoyment, and care from family and friends.

"I know the God who created the universe is the God who knows me! I will seek the Lord my God all the days of my life."

Time to Pick Myself Up and Become Holy

"Lord, today is a new day! I will praise Your name all the days of my life. Come to me this day, and bless me and keep me. May Your face shine upon me, and may You never leave me or forsake me.

" 'Be holy for I am holy,' You command. Lord, show me more of Your holiness and more of my sinfulness. Help me to hate sin and love righteousness as You do. Grant me a deeper conviction of sin and a more thorough spirit of repentance, and make me holy as You are holy."

"Come back to your senses as you ought, and stop sinning; for there are some who are ignorant of God—I say this to your shame."—1 Corinthians 15:34

"Love must be sincere. Hate what is evil; cling to what is good."—Romans 12:9

"This week I begin a Bible study on holiness. I want my heart to be open and prepared for the words on the paper. Lord, birth a spirit within me to be holy and set apart for Your kingdom advancement. Purify me, cleanse me, and wash over me with newness and holiness. I want to stay pure and continue on the path of holiness. I want to stay focused on this calling in my life."

"Therefore, prepare your minds for action; be self-controlled; set your hope fully on the grace to be given you when Jesus Christ is revealed. As obedient children, do not conform to the evil desires you had when you lived in ignorance. But just as he who called you is holy, so be holy in all you do; for it is written: 'Be holy, because I am holy.' "—1 Peter 1:13–16

"This is a prayer I will pray daily: 'Lord, I set apart my mind for You today. I set apart my passion. I set apart my eyes. I set apart my ears. I set apart my motives. I set apart my discipline. Today I set apart every limb of my body and each area of my life unto You as Lord over all I am and all I have.' "

"For a man's ways are in full view of the LORD, and he examines all his paths."—Proverbs 5:21

"As I continue down the path of holiness, I must make sure that I pay very close attention to what I look at. I need to look away or turn the channel from any impure thing and fix my eyes only on the goodness of God. The world is full of enticements. I must give them their due place while remembering God's call for purity. If I give in to the world, I fail myself and God. That failure creates opportunities for Satan and his demons, as well as for my flesh, to continue on the pathway to sin.

"I believe that in the past, my sinful nature has caused many issues in my life. There are consequences to sin, even though it feels good for a brief moment. I need to toss out sin and its fleeting pleasures and put on the holiness of God and the long-term benefits of living in obedience.

"Lord, as I pray, seek Your face, read Your Word, read devotions, and meditate, I want to sense Your presence in my life. I want to be in prayer continuously throughout the day to remind me of who You are and what my primary focus in this life is. Each day I walk in the world, I must live clean, do well for people in the kingdom and in the world, and never forget that I am being watched by others, including the evil one."

When I looked back over the past year, I was convinced that the lonely days had actually been some of the best days of my life. I now walked with the Lord far more maturely than ever before. The lonely days had provided the fire to burn out the impurities that had so long been a part of my life. As I dealt with them and purged them from my life, the pain and destruction they had inflicted upon my walk with God and in my relationships with others were erased.

Born Again in the Newness of God and Friendships

As I listened to Third Day's song "Born Again," I realized that a new birth had actually been taking place in my soul. Through this trial of fire, I had come alive, and I anticipated better days ahead once the divorce process was complete.

> "But those who hope in the LORD will renew their strength. They will soar on wings like eagles; they will run and not grow weary, they will walk and not be faint."—Isaiah 40:31

I wanted my strength in life to be Christ-centered, not self-centered as it had been for many, many, many years. My pride needed to be replaced with God's will for my soul. I knew I could live confidently in a Christ-centered life, remembering how I had failed in my quest for a blended life of Christ and me.

Yes, I had always moved quickly at work and in my personal life, but in each segment along the way, failure had been the long-term result. After achieving the role of vice president at work, I failed in that role; and after more than twenty-six years of marriage, I failed in that too. But if Christ was the center of my life, no longer would I need to fail in order to learn life's lessons.

Jesus came not to destroy, but to save. Everything is safe that we commit to Him, and nothing is really safe that is not so committed. If we place our hope in Him, He will supply our needs out of His limitless resources, and He will never run dry of creative ideas to help us.

Package to Lynn's Lawyer's Office

"This day is a big day with the settlement package going to Lynn and her lawyer. It has been almost three months since Lynn first asked for the divorce, six weeks since she retained a lawyer, and three weeks since we talked about our final wants and needs. We need the Lord's hand to be working in this situation.

"Lord, may Your will be done and Your love be present when the settlement package is looked over. May Your peace, love, kindness,

and grace be upon all our souls this day and this week. Bless our walk and the work of our hands, and bless the direction of our hearts."

"Casting all your anxiety on him, because he cares for you."—1 Peter 5:7

Words from God

"This is the day, and this is your hour. My joy and gladness will break forth from your heart this day. Better days are ahead, days filled with joy and laughter. I am with you, and I will guide you into My truth, My love, and My power. Seek Me, seek My face, and seek My Word. Open your heart and be patient as My will comes about in your life. New days, better days are coming, Steve Kirk. My blessings will be upon you as you seek Me."

Seek Christ in All Decisions

Christ patiently waits for us to sacrifice ourselves in each small decision of life. One decision at a time and then one day at a time leads to a closer walk with Him. Each time we obey Him, we gain a closer relationship with Him and are better able to hear His voice and respond as He would like us to.

"I feel a change is in the air this day. God's hand is moving on hearts and minds, and something good is going to happen this day. Lord, release Your power in my life, this state, the country, and the entire world. May I speak forth the truth and keep Your love within my soul."

"Create in me a pure heart, O God, and renew a steadfast spirit within me. Do not cast me from your presence or take your Holy Spirit from me. Restore to me the joy of Your salvation and grant me a willing spirit, to sustain me."—Psalm 51:10–12

"I have purposed to always do what is right, putting away my sinful nature and letting God have His way. Can I do that? Yes,

I have been given the power. Will I do that? With God's help and power, I will do my best to walk as He directs, turning neither to the right nor the left.

"I know my best days are ahead of me. I have had a good life with good relationships, but better, greater, more awesome days are ahead of me as I put the Lord first and develop my ability to love. I see great opportunities and great doors opening, with great love being expressed."

My Changing Relationship with Kayla

Kayla and I made plans to travel to Florida in her car, so she has transportation. It would, of course, alter the life we had shared in the past. With her car and freedom as well as taking on of a job, she would be spending less time in Minnesota. I prayed that as we traveled together, we would enjoy ourselves and form fond memories that would enrich us in the future.

Even before this major change, my life had already changed dramatically over the past year. I never wanted to go back to the way life had been before, because now I was walking on a fresh, new pathway.

"I have to find a new normal for my life. I do not know what tomorrow will bring, but I am very hopeful that goodness and God's will are going to take place. I remember the great things God has done for me. I can trust Him to help me with everything that comes my way."

The Marriage Is Dead, but God Will Not Leave Me in This Place

Weeks earlier I had finally accepted that the divorce was going to happen, but now the pace slowed considerably. For a long time, I had refused to admit that the divorce would actually take place, but I finally realized the marriage was over. Two people must love each other in order to have a real marriage, and that time for Lynn and me had passed. However, I knew the present pain would eventually bring newness of life and personal growth.

Knowing that God is against divorce, I would never have sought one. Yet divorce was my new reality, and I had accepted that fact as far back as June 17. Lynn had been a part of my life for many years, but now she was gone for good. Now I had my own life to live, and I decided to make the most of it. And who was to say it wouldn't be even better than my life in the past?

"When this divorce is over, I will be empty. But that emptiness will not last; great days will take its place, and fullness of life will come again.

"I realize that my marriage to Lynn is a thing of the past, but I can learn from it. I recognize the mistakes that I made, and as much as possible, I have asked both Lynn and God to forgive me. I will always remember my past mistakes and improve on my areas of weakness as I go forward in new relationships. I will also remember the things that I needed but did not have in my marriage to Lynn, and when the time comes, I will let the new person in my life know that.

My new direction in life will be great because the Lord is with me and always will be if I cling to Him daily. My old life is coming to an end. I have been in a place of emptiness for the past eleven months. But now fullness is coming, goodness is coming, and blessings are coming my way!"

Contentment in the Lord, Now and in the Future

"I want to be content in my relationships, my vocation, and the things that God has given me. Too many times in the past, I have wanted more, only to want even more when I received what I had sought. There was no satisfaction in that way of living.

"I know God wants me to enjoy my life now and into the future. But my contentment will come when I release everything to Christ and focus on advancing His kingdom."

"Taste and see that the LORD is good; blessed is the man who takes refuge in him." — Psalm 34:8

"Maybe the best way to view this part of my life is to remember these dark days will break and the sun will shine again. If the sun always shined, I would get too contented and stay in that place. I need to push forward and see the goodness that can come out of dark days. This life will never be perfect; that day will come in the future and can be found only in eternity with our Lord."

One Step at a Time

As I looked back over the past year, I identified many times when I didn't think I could make it. The pain and sleepless nights exacted a toll, and my goal was simply to take one step at a time and to walk towards the light, Jesus Christ. Without Jesus in my life, I do not know how I could have made it.

Jesus is not a crutch; He is our Father, our Savior, our peace, a wonderful counselor, and an ever-present help in time of need. No matter the situation, Jesus is with us, even if it does not always seem like it. With Him by our side, we can learn to release the past, live in the present in a new way, and look forward to a bright future with people who love us.

"I look to be more holy, but I know that can come only through Christ and my relationship with Him. It is not my goal setting, striving, and effort that will achieve it, but only Christ in my life. Jesus is now my source for living—Jesus Christ first, all others and all things a distant second!"

Chapter 14

Lawyers Fan the Flame into a Blazing Fire of Divorce

"Those whom I love I rebuke and discipline. So be earnest, and repent. Here I am! I stand at the door and knock. If anyone hears my voice and opens the door, I will come in and eat with him, and he with me. To him who overcomes, I will give the right to sit with me on my throne, just as I overcame and sat down with my Father on his throne."
—Revelation 3:19–21

"I feel I will hear something from the lawyer today concerning this final stage. Based upon the feelings I have deep in my spirit, I do not believe the return offer will be the final settlement. I do want to be set free so I can live my life to the fullest going forward. Lord, help, direct, and guide our spirits in these final days ahead."

"Now to him who is able to do immeasurably more than all we ask or imagine, according to his power that is at work within us . . . "—Ephesians 3:20

Bitter or Better—One Letter Difference but What a Chasm Between the Two!

My friend Kent talked about the one letter difference between *bitter* and *better*. I did not want to be bitter, but rather to be better in all the situations of my life. As I moved forward, I wanted to be a better person, a better father, a better friend, a better family member, and a better representative for Christ. And one day in the future, I hoped to be a better husband who would be loved and enjoyed by the woman in his life.

Self-Control and God-Control

"At times I lack self-control; I don't follow God's Word or remain clean in my thinking and actions. I truly want to follow God's ways and His will for my life. I need His leading, guiding, and shaping of me into the vessel He wants me to be. I need His forgiveness, blessings, and promise."

"For what I do is not the good I want to do; no, the evil I do not want to do—this I keep on doing. Now if I do what I do not want to do, it is no longer I who do it, but it is sin living in me that does it. So I find this law at work: When I want to do good, evil is right there with me."—Romans 7:19–21

As the days of my marriage drew to a close, I took stock of what I had learned. It was time to move forward, not forgetting the lessons of the past, but using them to build a better future in a new relationship. I also had to learn to forgive myself for my failures. I needed to get to the place where I could rejoice in what God had given me without reliving the events of the past year over and over again in my head.

"I take too many things for granted in my life. I have family, friends, new relationships, health, and happiness. There is something God wants me to do that I could never have done if this time had not happened. I believe doors in ministry will be opened that never would have been opened if this time had not taken place. I will be listening for God's voice for my next step in the journey.

"I must keep myself pure and holy for God! I must follow Christ's example and put on my armor to fight the evil one and the temptations of the world. God, help me fight the good fight today."

Words from God

"A breaking free, a new life, and fresh strength for your bones are coming. I will lift you up and strengthen you for the race you are about to run. Fear not, but forgive, release, and renew a right spirit within you. Draw your strength, your power, and your encouragement from Me.

"This day is My day, and this hour is My hour. Watch and see the great and mighty things that will come about in your life. Fear not what man can do to you; only fear Me and worship Me in spirit and truth. I am coming, I am working on your behalf, and My glory will fall. Watch and see My hand at work as you walk after Me and My ways. This day, this hour, this time, I am going to blow you away with My blessings."

God, Family, Friends, and a New Study

As I matured in my spiritual walk, I realized more clearly that I was an overcomer in Christ. I was delighting myself daily in the Lord and His goodness. I had hundreds of people all across the United States praying for me, as well as the support of friends and family. I was spending at least thirty minutes in the Word each day and gaining a better understanding of God and what He wanted from me. Although I needed to continue expanding my obedience, I was finding it easier to obey God. I was also participating in a Bible study of Romans with people at work, and I was reaching out in the community to do my part to make it a better place to live.

My quest was focused on becoming a better person serving the Lord now and into the future. I wanted to be an overcomer because that is the pathway God wants for all of us. I was learning that if I consistently asked for God's will for my life, it was much easier to obey Him and live as an overcomer. Furthermore, I was discovering that His will was wrapped up in loving Him and loving others.

I also believed God had big plans for my life, just as He does for all His followers. I purposed to keep my eyes open for His plans and to take advantage of every opportunity He put in front of me. God even put a book within my heart, and both Kayla and Lynn encouraged me to write it. And when I was ready to share my story, I did indeed write that book—the one you hold in your hand. My hope is that it will encourage and save people who are headed for divorce.

Every marriage should be considered sacred. Vows are vows for a reason! Folks, bad times come and go in every marriage, but push through them and live the life you committed to live in the presence of God and man. This is not to condemn anyone who has done otherwise, but rather to point out that having a good marriage requires battle against the evil one, the world, and our own selfish behaviors.

"Today is the start of a new month in You, Lord. I want, need, and desire to serve You with all my heart, mind, soul, and spirit. Grant me wisdom, knowledge, and understanding to serve You in a deeper way. Help me this day, and help others to turn themselves over to You. Your blessings pour over my life and into the lives of those around me. Forgive me, cleanse me, and help me be an overcomer in this life."

"Brothers, I do not consider myself yet to have taken hold of it. But one thing I do: Forgetting what is behind and straining towards what is ahead, I press on towards the goal to win the prize for which God has called me heavenward in Christ Jesus."—Philippians 3:13–14

"Forget the former things; do not dwell on the past. See, I am doing a new thing! Now it springs up; do you not perceive it? I am making a way in the desert and streams in the wasteland."—Isaiah 43:18–19

"Blessed is the man who trusts in the LORD, whose confidence is in him. He will be like a tree planted by the water that sends out its roots by the stream. It does not fear when heat comes; it leaves are always green. It has no worries in a year of drought and never fails to bear fruit." —Jeremiah 17:7–8

Learning Patience in a World Where I Want It Now!

"I am a very impatient person who is learning to be more patient. I do not have the ability to control what is going to take place and when. Knowing that He is always with me as I go through life's journey, I am learning to lean on God's ability to grant me patience. This kind of patience means waiting for God's timing without doubting God's love."

"Keep your lives free from the love of money and be content with what you have, because God has said, 'Never will I leave you; never will I forsake you.' " —Hebrews 13:5

Many times in those days, I thought of Joseph and how he must have felt about the circumstances in his life. After all his big dreams, he ended up in a pit by the hands of his brothers. Then he did all the right things and moved up in life, only to be beaten back down by Potiphar's wife and thrown into jail. Even in jail, however, God showed him favor and used him, but he remained forgotten for two long years. Finally, a former prisoner remembered him, and Joseph, using his God-given gifts, prospered in a better position.

Did all those ups and downs cause Joseph to think his life was being wasted or that it was pointless to serve God? Did he feel like God had abandoned him? Did Joseph just sit back and do nothing while his life was in turmoil? I don't think so. I believe he worked for God, sought after God, and was used by God every day of his life. And the same thing can happen for each of us as we serve God in whatever circumstance we face.

"My better days are ahead. There will be days of blessing, days of serving God, days of building relationships and starting new ones. I pray that God blesses the work of my hands and all my relationships.

"God, let me be an impact player for Your kingdom here on earth. Show me Your direction, Your plan, and Your will for my life, and I will walk after You and serve You all my days."

316

Our Accountability Group Meets

"The journeys that we take in life / Though unexpected they may be / If we commit to follow Christ / His work through us the world will see."—Sper

"Steve, Dave, and I met this morning and experienced a major breakthrough in study. We all agreed to stay in the Word each day this coming week. We talked about how the Word must be in us and how we must follow Christ daily. Lord, may we follow You all the days of our lives, regardless of what takes place in the days ahead. I want to hold on to You, my anchor in this sea of life."

"As for man, his days are like grass, he flourishes like a flower of the field; the wind blows over it and it is gone, and its place remembers it no more. But from everlasting to everlasting the LORD's love is with those who fear him, and his righteousness with their children's children."—Psalm 103:15–17

"Let your eyes look straight ahead, fix your gaze directly before you. Make level paths for your feet and take only ways that are firm. Do not swerve to the right or the left; keep your foot from evil."—Proverbs 4:25–27

"There are many days when I try to figure out the right path instead of letting God direct me in it. Yes, I read, pray, and meditate on His Word, but I also try to determine the best route to take instead of letting His Spirit lead me to the best path. My way inevitably leads to a stop sign that I blow right through, and then I crash. God's way may look like a detour, but it leads to a road filled with blessings and protection."

God, Mold Me into a Person You Can Use

"Many times I have cried out to God to answer my prayers the way I wanted them answered. Though God did answer, He did so in the context of the total plan He has for me. His will, plan, and

purpose will be carried out in my life as I yield myself as a vessel to Him. I give Him the ability to work through me by bending my free will to His perfect will.

"I cannot wait to see His perfect plan come together in my life. I have many rough edges for Him to smooth, so at times it might be painful. But His plan will be so much better than anything I could come up with on my own. God's plans and abilities are so much wiser than the prayers, needs, and wants that I ask for from my vantage point."

"For a man's ways are in full view of the LORD, and he examines all his paths."—Proverbs 5:21

"I must keep God's Word always before me, in me, and about me. I will seek Him and His ways daily through the Word and prayer. When I do this, I will know the Lord better, understand His plan better, and pray for His will better because His will and mine will be more nearly the same. That perfect blending must take place."

"My son, keep my words and store up my commands within you. Keep my commands and you will live; guard my teachings as the apple of your eye."—Proverbs 7:1–2

None of us can be perfect, holy, and just by our own doing. No matter our striving and steadfast focus to be clean and free of sin, without Christ and the Holy Spirit working in us, we will fail and fail again. Oh, but with Christ, the Holy Spirit, and the Word in us, we can live as overcomers who fight the fight and win the battle for the name of God and His kingdom!

"As I fight my battles, I will suffer some setbacks. At such times, I must remember that the Lord will bring comfort to me through His Word and through fellow believers, which He has done throughout this whole journey. The Lord will comfort me so I can comfort others and come alongside them in their journeys as well. That is the great thing about the Life Group I am a part of: we help each other and

pray for each other. It's the same in the accountability group; Dave,
Steve, and I help each other in this journey called life."

"But you are a chosen people, a royal priesthood, a holy nation,
a people belonging to God, that you may declare the praises
of him who called you out of darkness into his wonderful
light." — 1 Peter 2:9

"I want to have a spirit of contentment and enjoy life — the life
God gives me to live."

"He who dwells in the shelter of the Most High will rest in
the shadow of the Almighty. I will say of the LORD, 'He is my
refuge and my fortress, my God, in whom I trust.' "
— Psalm 91:1–2

Words from God

"Let go of the past, and cling to Me, My son. Do not carry on
with foolishness, but release your pain and your burdens to Me, and
I will give you the rest you desire.

"Seek My ways and My Spirit; then and only then will you find
what you are looking for. I know your heart, and I will satisfy your
longings. My love is being poured out on you, so have patience and
let My will be done in this life. Come to Me with your burdens, and
I will give you rest."

Looking for Love and Respect

"I know I must be honest and truthful in all my activities and
actions. I need to be pure and have Christ's purity in my life. I have
many questions and many thoughts, though. Am I good enough for
people in this world? Do I help people move forward in their walks
with God? Do I make a difference in lives around me? I seek answers
to my questions and insight into my thoughts.

"I feel pain and hurt this morning. To a large degree, it seems
like the things I have worked for and tried to accomplish haven't

made a difference to many people. I want to be respected and loved. I want to make a difference to the people in my life and be a good father, husband, worker, and follower of Christ. And at some if not all levels, I want completeness."

Paperwork Sitting for Ninety Days and Counting

It had been weeks since the paperwork had been sent to Lynn's lawyer, but still I had heard nothing in response. When Lynn had said "quickly," I didn't think this was the time line she meant. Everything we had agreed upon back in mid-June had been put into the paperwork, except for the longevity of support.

Though this stage of limbo was draining, the thought that I could soon move forward and find a person who wanted to be with me was exciting. But at the same time, it was sad to think that twenty-six years of my life had gone by the wayside. I had to remind myself, however, that there had been many good times over those years, so they really were not wasted. I turned my face forward to the fantastic times ahead in my future.

"Not only so, but we also rejoice in our suffering, because we know that suffering produces perseverance; perseverance, character; and character, hope. And hope does not disappoint us, because God has poured out his love into our hearts by the Holy Spirit, whom he has given us."—Romans 5:3–5

"Righteousness guards the man of integrity, but wickedness overthrows the sinner."—Proverbs 13:6

"I want to be a man with a purpose and a man of complete integrity. I need accountability partners, Life Group members, and other believers in Christ to hold me accountable and keep me moving forward. I believe we all need accountability partners and people close enough to us to provide feedback and hold us to high standards in the mirror of God's Word. Of course, the greatest guide is the Holy Spirit, and living a clean, holy life will enable me to hear

His voice and recognize conviction when I sin or even at the moment of temptation."

"And whatever you do, whether in word or deed, do it all in the name of the Lord Jesus, giving thanks to God the Father through him."—Colossians 3:17

Words from God

"Seek Me; seek My ways and turn from your wickedness, and then I will show you My kindness. This day is the day I will show you My blessings. Desire the true path, and do not turn from it. Do not seek the things of this world, but seek the things of My kingdom. My wrath will be poured out; however, you shall not be touched by the pain and suffering if you serve Me and walk after My ways.

"Be prepared for the future, and set your mind on My will. Put away your folly and foolishness. I have come to you with a plan and a purpose. That plan and purpose will be accomplished in My perfect timing."

"Today is a new day with new possibilities. I want to serve the Lord and be cleansed by Him today. Lord, wash over me and make me as white as snow. Create in me a clean heart this day, this hour, and this minute."

"Let those who love the LORD hate evil, for he guards the lives of his faithful ones and delivers them from the hand of the wicked. Light is shed upon the righteous and joy on the upright in heart. Rejoice in the LORD, you who are righteous, and praise his holy name."—Psalm 97:10–12

No More Pain from Words and Letters

Back in June I had received the nineteen-page letter from Lynn sharing the things that prompted her to leave nearly a year earlier. I had read the letter three times and agreed with Lynn's account of my past behaviors. I did not want to forget those things, but on the recommendation of a friend, I now decided to rip up the letter and throw it away.

Getting rid of the letter released me, because over the past year, I had already asked Lynn for forgiveness for most of the things written. Of course, ripping the letter up could never erase the pain and hurt that I had caused, but I could do no more than what I had already done to right the wrongs. I hoped and prayed that Lynn, too, would find release from the pain she had suffered over the twenty-six years of our marriage.

Clean Hands and a Pure Heart

"I want to be a new man with a new lease on life. I want to be a man loved, cherished, and respected by others. I will strive to be a better man, a better friend, and a better husband in the future.

"Most importantly, I want to be a better servant to the Lord. I know He will never leave me or forsake me. Others can and have, and others will do so in the future; but no matter what happens, Jesus will stick with me and make me better in all the areas where I have failed Him. He will forgive and forget, and He will give me a new lease on life and new relationships."

"I consider that our present sufferings are not worth comparing with the glory that will be revealed in us."—Romans 8:18

"What direction do You want me to go in life, Lord? I want to follow You with clean hands and a pure heart. Help me as I put on the armor You have provided."

Running to God's Camp

"Abram's camp or Lot's camp—which camp do I want to live in? Do I want God's camp and the promised land, or Satan's camp and the false view of perfection? Abram was right to let Lot make his own choice. Abram, however, was wise enough to rely on God and His direction.

"I need to stop looking at what I 'feel' is the best direction. The past few weeks I have waffled between God's ways and my ways. I want to turn completely to God and His kingdom. I need to release the world and grab hold of God and His kingdom! I need to be a role model to others, including Kayla."

"The grass withers and the flowers fall, because the breath of the LORD blows on them. Surely the people are grass. The grass withers and the flowers fall, but the word of our God stands forever."—Isaiah 40:7–8

One Year and Counting, but It Seems Like Only Yesterday

"One year ago, I was forced into a deep valley. Lynn's decision to leave threw me into a tailspin I did not think I could recover from. Over the year, however, I have recovered. With my feet set on a solid foundation in Christ, I have lived at peace with others as healing came into my life.

"One year ago today, I woke up after a very hard night and went to church. I asked Lynn to go with me, but she didn't want to put on a 'face.' I now realize that when Lynn left on the twenty-seventh of September, she was leaving for good and never coming back. I still do not understand why, and I might never know.

"Last night I felt happy and contented, knowing where I am headed in life. I am growing in the Lord, and I am seeking His face, His plan, and His ways. Lord, grant me the will to always move in Your plan for my life. Help me this day to figure out the next step I should take."

"Let us then approach the throne of grace with confidence, so that we may receive mercy and find grace to help us in our time of need."—Hebrews 4:16

"I know beyond a shadow of a doubt that God will give me what I need when I need it."

Thoughts Within a Candle's Light

As I observed a burning candle, I gained a parallel insight into human life. Like the candle's flame, our lives have their highs and lows. Sometimes they shine bright, and other times they dim; sometimes they burn fast, and other times they burn slow. But like the candle, our lives will burn until the day they are finally extinguished. The flame of life will sputter and dim and eventually go out, but even then, it leaves behind a wisp of smoke that fills the hearts and minds of others with the knowledge of what we stood for, the people we touched, and how we will spend our eternity.

Our lives on this earth are most fruitful when the energy to burn daily is found within Christ our Lord. When we burn bright, pure, and clean, we create an aroma that is pleasing to the Lord and draws the world to the Master and King. May we always stay close to the Bread of Life and blend our hopes and dreams with His in the fire of His burning flame.

> "However, as it is written: 'No eye has seen, no ear has heard, no mind has conceived what God has prepared for those who love him' — but God has revealed it to us by his Spirit. The Spirit searches all things; even the deep things of God. For who among men knows the thoughts of a man except the man's spirit within him? In the same way no one knows the thoughts of God except the Spirit of God. We have not received the spirit of the world but the Spirit who is from God, that we may understand what God has freely given us." — 1 Corinthians 2:9–12

> *"Tonight I feel great as I read the Word of God and stay pure in mind and body. The Word is a great place to find peace and enjoyment."*

> "Ah, Sovereign Lord, you have made the heavens and the earth by your great power and outstretched arm. Nothing is too hard for you." — Jeremiah 32:17

"Whatever God wants me to do, I will do it with all my heart, mind, soul, and body!"

Meeting with Joanne

Throughout this whole process of separation and divorce, I had seen the true Lynn and what she was about as a person. Going to the Waters church one last time, the church where Lynn and I had worshiped together, was also part of my closure. Joanne encouraged me not to feel bad about that. Also, we discussed my need to set boundaries in relationships and to go slow, slow, and even slower. "Do not rush into relationships," Joanne stressed.

"Last night Dave, Judy, and I met and talked about the Lord, a future Bible study, and our desire to follow the Lord at both work and home. We had a great conversation and decided to study the book of Romans together. Hopefully, other people at work will join us and we can make changes that will bring glory to the Lord, build up the company, and change lives, including our own. Better days are ahead if we stick close to the Lord our God.

"Dave and I also met that morning and talked about the Lord, our struggles, and the future. I know I am blessed with many wonderful people in my life, and I look forward to seeing Dave blessed as well."

All Things—Including Separation and Divorce— Work Together for God's Glory

"This morning I read in 1 Thessalonians 5:18, 'Give thanks in all circumstances, for this is God's will for you in Christ Jesus.' Should I really give thanks for what has happened to me? Should I give thanks for the pain and suffering Lynn's decision has cost me? I do not think so! This verse gives me hope that regardless of what has happened, God can take the pain and suffering and turn it for good in His long-term plan for my life. I do not believe Lynn wanted to cause me pain, but rather I think the hurtful thoughts she shared were an attempt to find healing for herself."

"I also read Romans 8:28: 'And I know that in all things God works for the good of those who love him, who have been called according to his purpose.' Since I know that God works all things for good, I can find great relief in knowing that He will somehow use this difficult time and work it for good in my life. By giving thanks, I can maintain a positive attitude towards Lynn, even though we are going through a most painful time together.

"Lord, thank You that You work for the good every trial, challenge, and difficulty I face. You are always behind the scenes, working things out for my good. Help me to see Your hand in everything."

Slow Fade No More

As I read about King Solomon, I absorbed the sober warning to stay close to God and not allow the things of the world to get in the way of my walk with Him. Like Solomon in his life, I could look back and see the slow fade that had taken me from God's presence. It had taken the shock of separation and divorce to force me to confront my sinful behaviors and cleanse my life of them. I had cried out to God so many times in the past about my lifestyle. But now I would tolerate it no more, but rather go on the offensive to take back the ground lost in the past several years.

More to Learn and Process

It had been weeks since I had heard anything from Lynn's lawyer. When I called her, she said she would get things moving. "I want this done as quickly as you do," she insisted, but since it had been so long since I had first submitted the paperwork to her lawyer, I knew they must not be happy with its terms. Five months ago, we had started mediation in an effort to resolve all matters fairly, and I sincerely hoped that when everything was finalized, we could both move forward without either of us feeling taken advantage of or filled with anger, pain, and unforgiveness.

"I may be dismayed at how long this divorce process is dragging on, but I know Jesus knows the path He has me on. He goes before

me, and He surrounds me on every side. As my shepherd, He will not lead me down an impassable path or one that is just too much for me to handle. He knows exactly how much I can bear. Since I know He knows, I can move forward with faith that He will provide what I need when I need it. He knows the way to the promised land, the land flowing with milk and honey. That is the place I want to be, and sooner rather than later. I know my future is bright because the Word tells me all things work together for my good!"

"There is no wisdom, no insight, no plan that can succeed against the LORD." — Proverbs 21:30

"It looks like the settlement package will arrive on Tuesday of next week. I hope and pray it is fair and something both Lynn and I can agree to quickly. While I didn't ask for this divorce, I want to move on in life. It seems unbelievable at times that Lynn's lawyer originally said it would all be over in thirty to sixty days, and that was five months ago. There must be a good reason it has taken this long; I hope I understand it going forward."

God Loves Me! The God of the Universe Really Loves Me!

"God is with me wherever I go in this world and the world to come. Wow! Think about that: the God of the universe is with me and cares for me! He is awesome, caring, loving, providing, and sharing all the time, even when I do not feel Him. God can use everything I go through for His glory. Every day I will use what God has given me for His goodness and will to be accomplished through my life."

"You are my hiding place; you will protect me from trouble and surround me with songs of deliverance." — Psalm 32:7

"Since, then, you have been raised with Christ, set your hearts on things above, where Christ is seated at the right hand of God. Set your minds on things above, not on earthly things." — Colossians 3:1–2

I Want to Be Jesus with Skin On

"Am I like Jesus? Do I show mercy, grace, and forgiveness? I want to follow Him, but at times my flesh is so weak it cannot stand up for Him. I struggle back and forth in the old ways, the ways that caused grief, pain, destruction, and heartache. But deep inside, I never want to go back to the old days. Lord, open up new ways for me to serve You, walk after You, and be guided by You. May Your glory fall on me this day, in Jesus' name."

"He who speaks on his own does so to gain honor for himself, but he who works for the honor of the one who sent him is a man of truth; there is nothing false about him."—John 7:18

Meetings with Pastor Doug and Accountability Partners

I met with Pastor Doug and also with Dave and Steve the following day. I was struggling and desperately needed not only their help but also the Lord's.

"I have to get through to the other side, Lord God. Free me of my pain, frustration, and hard feelings. Enough is enough—I cannot continue on like this. I need a breakthrough. Help, help, help!"

Words from God

"Trust in Me. Be prepared, and trust in Me and My ways. I have led you on a path you did not choose and do not want to walk in, but fear not, for I am the one guiding and directing you in this way. I have a plan and purpose, and you will fulfill My plan for your life. Trust in Me and in My ways this day as I unveil My plan for the future. Seek Me, walk after Me, and be guided by Me."

Kayla's Birthday! She Is a True Blessing from the Lord

When Kayla was born, she was truly one of the best things that ever happened to me. She burst into my world that day and had been a source of major blessing ever since. Now this gift from God sent to change the world was turning twenty.

"Lord, bless Kayla today with Your Spirit, love, and happiness. Give her every good thing she seeks from Your kingdom. May she follow Jesus all the days of her life. I pray that Kayla and I will always walk after You and share from Your throne room together. Let her love for others pour forth from her to change the world for the better."

Time to Sow in God's Garden

"I want to begin sowing the seeds of new actions and responses today. I know God will give the increase as I continue to do well and sow life into others. I want to be a seed-provider, and I want to sow seeds of righteousness. I know the kinds of seeds I sow today will determine the kinds of fruit I reap tomorrow. I want to reap good fruit, and that is to see God's righteousness instilled in others."

"Let us not become weary in doing good, for at the proper time we will reap a harvest if we do not give up."—Galatians 6:9

Creating Long-Lasting Friendships

I went out to eat with friends, Dave, Judy, and Colleen, and then we went to hear two Christian bands. It was a great evening together.

The next morning, Steve, Dave, and I had a great conversation about the Lord and the direction each of us was going in life. We prayed for each other and our families. I was learning just how critical it is to expand the circle of friendship to include other believers to share with and lean on in both good times and bad. We were enriched and challenged as we supported each other through the valleys of life, and we rejoiced together on the mountaintops we experienced.

"Make it your ambition to lead a quiet life, to mind your own business and to work with your hands, just as we told you, so that your daily life may win the respect of outsiders and so that you will not be dependent on anybody."
— 1 Thessalonians 4:11–12

"I need to slow down in life and let God lead the way. The Lord God knows what is right for my life and the lives of those around me. I must take heed to follow the path on which the light is shining and steer clear of the foolish path and ways of the world. I must be patient and walk according to the Word and the ways of the Lord. I must find my happiness and my future in God and His ways. I seek You this day, Lord, knowing full well You are there for me in my time of need and want.

"I want my longing to serve the Lord to be so intense that others can feel the heat of my desire for Jesus, my God and king. If people can see my longing, maybe they, too, will be inspired to seek out the only truth in life—Jesus Christ is Lord and Savior!"

Looking into the Mirror Called Marriage

After much soul-searching, I concluded my marriage had died a long time ago, although exactly when and how I did not know. Somewhere along the line, true love and intimate friendship fell by the wayside, and my relationship with Lynn became a marriage based solely on commitment and lacking in love and compassionate caring.

I still believed deeply in marriage, and I longed for a marriage with someone who would love me fully and that I would love fully in return. I desired a marriage where communication and open sharing led to resolution of problem areas, not one in which submerged feelings and desires one day burst forth into separation and divorce.

If you are reading this book and walking through the broken dreams and heartache of a struggling marriage, I urge you, before it is too late, get counseling, seek God and His grace, and recapture the love of your youth. It might be buried or hidden beneath the scars of past hurts, but it is not too late to salvage it. Do everything you can to recover it, and when you think you have done enough, push forward and do more. Separation and divorce are ugly and much more painful than anything you can imagine. It hurts the man and woman, it hurts their children, it hurts their family members, and it hurts their friends. No one is a winner when it rears its ugly head.

> "I lift up my eyes to the hills—where does my help come from? My help comes from the LORD, the Maker of heaven and earth. He will not let your foot slip—he who watches over you will not slumber."—Psalm 121:1–3

The Curtain Is Closing on My Marriage

The final days of my marriage were closing in on me. I had never wanted this, but now I had to walk through it in order to move on with life. Though I often felt like Job, deep inside I knew better, greater, more blessed days were ahead.

Much as we might not like it, God does sometimes allow bad things to happen to good people who are trying to live by His calling. Although pain and suffering can come at any moment, absolutely nothing has the ability to destroy us when our lives are hidden in Jesus Christ.

> "We are hard pressed on every side, but not crushed; perplexed, but not in despair; persecuted, but not abandoned; struck down, but not destroyed. We always carry around in our body the death of Jesus, so that the life of Jesus may also be revealed in our body."—2 Corinthians 4:8–10

"I must beware of enticements that seem to offer a shortcut to happiness. Though they may seem to cost little, I must test to see what is behind them. I have found that the past months spent in mediation was just that type of enticement. Everything was going smoothly towards a fair outcome for both Lynn and me until roadblocks arose and basically started the entire process all over again. Now months have gone by and more money is being spent to reach a fair outcome for both Lynn and me. I believe we were being fair with

each other, but then more enticements came into play. I must beware of the days ahead and what might be lurking."

Turning Towards the Future

While there was much sadness in looking back at my marriage, there was also the promise of joy in trusting God for the future. Even in a devastating loss such as the ripping apart of divorce, we have this hope: the Lord provides joy in the midst of grief.

I was slowly getting joy back into my life. I was making new friends, walking deeper with God, attending a new church, and helping out in the community. These were all good things, but I also had to continue to work on my attitudes and behaviors so I would be better prepared for a future relationship.

"I want to be on fire for the Lord, doing His will and being led by the Holy Spirit. I can see the light at the end of the long tunnel, and that light is the love of the Lord and new friendships."

"Commit to the LORD whatever you do, and your plans will succeed."—Proverbs 16:3

"In his heart a man plans his course, but the Lord determines his steps."—Proverbs 16:9

Seven Days and Counting

"In one week, my life will change from being a married man to being a divorced man. I am part of a failed marriage and never want to go through this fire again. I need help from God to succeed in a future relationship and to be a loving husband, best friend, and attentive lover. I want to live happy and on fire for God and His kingdom."

"This is love for God: to obey his commands. And his commands are not burdensome, for everyone born of God overcomes the world. This is the victory that has overcome the world, even our faith. Who is it that overcomes the world? Only he who believes that Jesus is the Son of God."—1 John 5:3–5

More Hurt and Pain Inflicted on My Soul

"Late yesterday I finally received the response from Lynn's lawyer, but it was very hurtful. I was a good husband in many ways, and I am a good person who is honoring his words. Why can't Lynn just leave without destroying every part of me? Why does she have to inflict pain on me before she goes on with her happiness? I am broken and poured out, dazed and confused, but I will serve the Lord with all my heart, mind, soul, and body. I will not turn back!"

These Are the Darkest Days

"Kayla called, upset with her boyfriend and with what is going on with Lynn and me. She told me she is now taking medication for depression. What is life dealing us? Why can't the days of enjoyment visit the household of Steve and Kayla Kirk?

"Darkness seems to be all around us as we try to walk in the light of Jesus. I do love Jesus, and I love Kayla, but I am sick of this drawn-out process with Lynn. What is the purpose, and what is the plan, Lord? Can You open the windows of heaven and rain down Your blessings? Can You send forth Your Word and Spirit this day? Can You please strengthen Kayla and her relationships, especially her relationship with You? I want to thank You in advance for all the help and care You are giving and will be giving us, Your children, and also for what You have done in the past.

"So this is life and the new normal? Well, despite the darkness, I am starting to enjoy my time alone and my freedom. Though my thoughts still wander and I know I must remain vigilant against the sins of the past, I feel the healing process is coming to completion. I worry and pray more about Kayla and her way in life than I do

my own. I want to start creating new memories to fill my mind with goodness and happiness. The old is passing away, and a wonderful new is coming in its place."

The Marriage Flatlines and Is Pronounced Dead on November 24

"Today is the day the divorce will be final. I never wanted this day to come, but it is here nonetheless, and I must go through it. I do not know what God's plans are; however, I want to be in the center of His will at all times."

Words from God

"Today is the day I will set you free of your burdens. I am with you, My son. The journey has been long and rough, but I have been with you. Know that the days ahead will be filled with pain and suffering, but they will bring about My glory in you. Blessings will also come, and My favor will be upon you as you seek and desire My will for your life.

"I am standing here today, and I send My angels this day to guard and protect you from all harm. Fear not what man can do to you; fear only what I can do. Seek Me and love Me this day, and see My mighty right hand move on your behalf."

    " 'Test me in this,' says the LORD Almighty, 'and see if I will not throw open the floodgates of heaven and pour out so much blessing that you will not have room enough for it.' "—Malachi 3:10

Chapter 15

The Smoke Clears and New Life Prevails

"Forget the former things; do not dwell on the past. See, I am doing a new thing! Now it springs up; do you not perceive it? I am making a way in the desert and streams in the wasteland."
Isaiah 43:18–19

A New Normal: I Am a divorced Man and a Statistic

"*Well, today is the first day of my new normal. It's hard to believe that twenty-six-plus years of marriage can be decided so quickly, but really it was decided even before that fateful September 27. I must now look forward to the future and my new life ahead.*

"*Kayla and I talked, and our relationship will always be strong. I have the Lord in my life and will never go back to the depression, pain, and hurt of the past few years. I must also remember I am a selfish person at heart. I need the Lord in my life to keep me unselfish. Lord, fill my life with Your Spirit, love, and beauty.*"

Thanksgiving Day and Looking Towards the Future

As Thanksgiving approached, I knew I had a lot to be thankful for. Newness and wholeness were set before me for the coming days. The past was the past, and the future was bright. I deeply loved the Lord, my family, and friends and was bolstered by the certainty that all things work together for good for those who love God and are called according to His purpose. But even in the midst of my gratitude, I still struggled somewhat.

"God, I complain when things do not go my way. I want abundance of everything rather than what is sufficient to sustain me. I would rather be elsewhere than where I am at this moment. I would rather have the gifts You give to others than what You provide for me. I would rather have You serve me than me serve You. Forgive me, Lord, for my lack of gratitude for what You give.

"Lynn often shared that I want what I cannot have, and I have found that to be sadly true. In the future, I will be happy with what I have and find enjoyment in it. I also need to do things for others and be happy for what other people have.

"What am I doing, Lord, and where do You have me going in life? I am trying my best to live a life that is pleasing to You. I am sorry, I am sorry, I am sorry for everything I have done against You, my family, and other people. I just want to enjoy a peaceful life and walk uprightly with You. Guide me and teach me Your ways this day."

Financial Mediation with Lawyers

At long last, the mediation day concerning the financial settlement of the divorce arrived. With God's help and perfect timing, it would mark the ending for Lynn and me and free us both to move on with life.

After several hours of the mediator going back and forth between us, Lynn and I reached an agreement. I wanted nothing more than to just move on with my life, and Lynn had shared the same thing several times in the past. Nonetheless, there were several items in the agreement I found hard to accept, but I had no fight left in me and just wanted to move on.

The birthing process was now complete. Never had I thought it would end in haggling over dollars, possessions, and payments, but sadly, it did come down to that. I totally regretted that, and I hoped Lynn would find whatever she was looking for in relationships and life as a whole.

Rooted in God's Word

My life was now rooted firmly in God's Word. Over the years, I would get into the Word and devour it for a while, and my life and marriage would improve. But then, ever so slowly, I would revert to other activities and find myself far from God. I vowed never again to allow such foolish behaviors to gain a foothold in my life.

Now I was focused on the unending and refreshing source of God's Word. This Word gave me the strength to endure all things — including divorce.

"Lord, may I drink from Your source, know You in a deeper way, and walk according to Your ways. I want to hear from You and know You more each moment of each day."

Financial Package Is Now Complete

"Another new normal took place today. I signed off on the financial portion of the divorce Lynn wanted. I want my conversations to be filled with love, joy, peace, kindness, goodness, and faithfulness."

"Remember this: Whoever sows sparingly will also reap sparingly, and whoever sows generously will also reap generously. Each man should give what he has decided in his heart to give, not reluctantly or under compulsion, for God loves a cheerful giver. And God is able to make all grace abound to you, so that in all things at all times, having all that you need, you will abound in every good work." — 2 Corinthians 9:6–8

"Do you not know? Have you not heard? The LORD is the everlasting God, the Creator of the ends of the earth. He will not grow tired or weary, and his understanding no one can fathom. He gives strength to the weary and increases the power of the weak." — Isaiah 40:28–29

"But those who hope in the LORD will renew their strength. They will soar on wings like eagles; they will run and not grow weary, they will walk and not be faint."—Isaiah 40:31

Last Words with Lynn

Lynn and I didn't talk for months, but then she called to inform me that Kayla had been injured at work. We talked briefly, and then I called Kayla to make sure she was all right. A few days later, Lynn called again. We again talked about Kayla, and I also asked Lynn if she was happy. She said she was. I was glad she was finding her place in the world and discovering joy in her decisions. I wished her nothing but the best and hoped she would live the life she wanted.

Completing the Journey

It had taken fifteen months to move from separation to divorce and into newness of life in God, but the process was now complete. Truthfully, most of what I learned through the process was painful, but eventually the journey came to completion and life moved forward in a positive way.

From start to finish, God was with me. I was blessed with Kayla, family, friends, and a church that walked with me through this time. I was determined to never forget what I had learned and how I had applied it with God, Lynn, and Kayla. I was a better person because of this period of my life. Out of the fire sprang newness of life for the coming days.

A New Relationship Begins with Judy

"I just had one of the best phone calls of my life. My friend Judy and I talked for over three hours, getting to know each other better. What a true woman of God she is! Her convictions and stand for the heavenly Father are amazing and a major draw to me. I look forward to talking more and getting to know this person who has such life to release and a ministry to the lost and dying of this world. Great days lie ahead, and I am starting to see the purpose of being

here in central Minnesota. I have new friends, new life, a new sense of God's calling, a new spirit, and new flesh. I am more in alignment with God than ever before."

Judy called again, and we talked about the Lord, life, and the future as we see it. I was discovering a wonderful person who was sensitive, caring, kind, and generous with her words. She had a clear perspective on God, family, church, and her fellowship in Christ, as well as a good outlook on friends, relationships, and finances.

Talking with Judy helped me in my personal walk with God. As I shared my past spiritual history and relationship with God, she encouraged me that I could live differently. Because of her strong beliefs and focus in life, I felt challenged and more compelled to live a godly life of my own. But I also wanted our budding relationship to be mutually beneficial. I hoped maybe she could learn from me more about God's love, kindness, and goodness. Iron does indeed sharpen iron, and godly friends can encourage and promote godly living in each other.

"My new friendship with Judy continues to develop. I see her as a major blessing in my life, right now and into the future. God has blessed me with not only a new relationship with Him, but also with a godly woman. Both Judy and I feel we want to share our lives right now and into the future.

"Judy reads the Word, prays, lives a relaxed life, and shares her thoughts and opinions openly. When we have disagreements, as all couples do from time to time, we talk about them. As do I, Judy values trust, honesty, and faithfulness at a very high level.

"We are also doing a study on holiness together over the phone. The book we are using is outstanding! We are building our relationship on the foundation of God and His perfect ways.

"Lord, birth a spirit within Judy and me to be holy and set apart for Your kingdom, together and separately. Let us both make a major impact on this world. Purify us, cleanse us, and wash us to become holy in You, this day and in the days ahead."

Third Day had a song out called "Born Again," and it captured the way God and Judy were making me feel. We talked for five hours one day, and we shared how we felt about each other. I also enjoyed seeing her at church and joining her in worshiping the Lord.

Blessing Prayed over Judy

I wanted this relationship to be different right from the start. Prayer had to be a big part of it. Here is one of the first prayers I prayed over Judy:

"Lord God, I pray over Judy right now, that You bless her when she is fully obedient to You. As she follows You each and every day of her life, may she be blessed beyond belief by the standards of Your kingdom and the standards on earth. May she be blessed in the city and blessed in the country. May she be blessed coming in and going out of her apartment, and may she be blessed at work. May anyone who fights against her be defeated by Your Spirit, and may those who come at her from one direction flee from her in seven. May each dollar Judy makes be blessed and multiply like the loaves and fishes and the widow's oil of old. May everything Judy puts her hand to prosper beyond that which is normal, and may she lift up Your name in glory as others see the blessings You have given her.

"Lord, may You grant Judy abundant prosperity in Your Spirit, and grant her wisdom, knowledge, and understanding in Your ways and the ways of man. Lord, open Your heavens, the storehouse of Your bounty, and send blessings to the work of Judy's hands. May she lend to many but borrow from none. Lord, make Judy the head and not the tail. May she always be on top and never on the bottom.

"Judy, may the Lord bless you and keep you; may the Lord make His face shine upon you and be gracious to you. May the Lord turn His face towards you and give you peace. As you seek more from the Lord and follow His ways, may He pour out His Spirit in ways that you cannot keep contained. May His Spirit burst forth from your spirit and fill the earth with love, joy, peace, patience, kindness, goodness, faithfulness, gentleness, and self-control. May He bestow His gifts of the Spirit into you, and may they then flow out of you. May each gift of wisdom, knowledge, faith, healing, miracles, prophecy, distinguishing between spirits, tongues, and interpretation of tongues be used mightily many times in your life to set the captives free and to heal the sick.

"May you have perfect health all the days of your life. As you seek the Lord, His kingdom, and His ways, may His glory shine through you in such a radiant way that people are drawn to you, asking questions about your source of strength and health. May you have eyes to see and ears to hear the Spirit's calling on your life and the ministry He has for you to reach the lost and dying world. May the Great Commission burn so intensely in your heart that you are compelled to accomplish that calling. May you do as Jesus commanded and make disciples of all nations, baptizing them in the name of the Father and of the Son and of the Holy Spirit, teaching them to obey everything Jesus has commanded you."

Kayla Meets Judy

As my relationship with Judy progressed, we made plans to have Kayla join us for dinner at the Olive Garden. I knew it would be difficult for Kayla to see her father with another woman; however, I also believed she sympathized with what I gone through and understood my need to find a person to share life with going forward.

It was a good meal, and Judy and Kayla enjoyed great conversation together. I continued to be amazed at the great young lady Kayla had become. After dinner, Kayla and I had a great conversation alone, and she said Judy seemed like a very nice person—in fact, Judy was a "beautiful person," in her words.

Giving Up the Past in Order to Move Forward

"After reading from the book Magnificent Obsession, *I finally realized what I had to do. I had to give God my past relationship with Lynn and our marriage. I had to do that before I could move on in life with Judy.*

"The past is the past, and the future is a bright future. My future is with God first and foremost! God, take my life and use it for Your

glory and power. I am nothing without You, and Your plan is better than any plan I could make on my own."

Judy and I celebrated Valentine's Day together. I did everything I could to make it a very special day for both of us. I hoped she would enjoy it as much as I enjoyed putting it together for us. Judy was such a special person. I looked up to her and cherished every moment we had together.

In my efforts to make the day extra special, I wrote the following poem for her and shared it with her:

Beautiful One

I say, "Oh, beautiful one, you make my life complete.
I see so clearly everything beneath my feet.
The things of old shall be no more, for the things of new are so
much more.
It is the time, it is the rhyme, it is no crime, to be with you and
dine.
You are so fine, I look forward to your being mine.
If you are mine and I am yours, we shall open up the door.
The door will be the core of what we both adore, which is the
Lord.
Oh, I say to the Lord, as I say to you, the one I adore, "We shall be
three beneath the tree,"
The tree of life that has no fright of the things of old and of the
night.
Our relationship is new, and God is the glue.
Neither of us will be blue or any of our parts come unglued.
The world is yours, beautiful one; all your dreams, all your hopes,
and all your cares will be fulfilled.
"Why?" you may ask. Because of your faith, your love, in the true
beginning and the ever last.
He is faithful and true, the one who rides on the horse to see you
through.
You have walked, you have stumbled, and have even crawled;

But now is the time, this is the place, that you will be filled with grace and hopes renewed.

Oh, beautiful one, God will see you through. So have your faith, take up the grace, and be ready to see us face-to-face.

May our relationship pick up the pace at the right time and place.

I look forward to seeing your face in that place where we shall fall under His grace.

Release yourself, open your heart, and be prepared to be blessed by His hand and my plan.

My plan is simple; it is to cause you to smile and show your dimples.

So open yourself up and be prepared to gain something special and something new.

Always remember, God loves you, and I do too!

Spending Easter with Judy's Family

Judy and I went to church on Easter and enjoyed worshiping the Lord together. That was followed by a visit to her mother's house, where I was introduced to her family. It was nice to meet her family for the first time. Her mother, sister, brothers, sister-in-law, nieces, and of course the dog were all great. We ate a nice lunch, had an Easter egg hunt for the kids, and later enjoyed dinner together.

Judy Meets My Family

The following weekend, Judy met my family at my father's eightieth birthday party. We had a great day playing games, eating, and talking with everyone. These meetings were necessary for us to get to know each other's family before moving on in our relationship. Fortunately, both families seemed to look forward to getting to know the new person in their loved one's life.

Dating Several Months and Everything Going Great

Judy and I had been dating for several months. While building our relationship with each other, we were also building our relationship with God. We went to church together, did Bible studies, prayed together, attended concerts, and read *The Love Dare*. I soon made plans for a special dinner at our favorite restaurant in St. Cloud, where I planned to ask her to marry me.

"Last night at the end of dinner, I asked Judy to marry me, and she said yes! The doors are open, the healing is complete, and newness of life has been birthed through this fire that began so long ago. I am so happy she said yes, and I can't wait to start our life together.

"Our plans are to get married on September 14 in New York at Niagara Falls. This will be breaking new ground for both Judy and me. We are joining our lives together, and the foundation is and always will be the Lord. Better days—the best days—are ahead for me, for Judy, and our days together in the Lord!"

The Lord Is the Foundation in My Life and Will Be Forever

"Through this journey that started in the fire on September 27, I have realized that nothing, no one, no material possession, and no relationship in the flesh or spirit can take the place that God wants to occupy in my life. The Lord is my source of nourishment, strength, guidance, and help in time of need. More importantly, Jesus Christ has given me something no one else could ever offer, and that is the promise of eternal life in heaven. I look forward to that great day ahead.

"However, as long as I am in this world, I will remember the words of Matthew 7:24–27: 'Therefore everyone who hears these words of mine and puts them into practice is like a wise man who built his house on the rock. The rain came down, the streams rose, and the winds blew and beat against that house; yet it did not fall, because it had its foundation on the rock. But everyone who hears these words of mine and does not put them into practice is like a foolish man who built his house on sand. The rain came down, the streams rose, and the winds blew and beat against that house, and it fell with a great crash.'"

Disciplines That Must Never Stop

Over the past couple of years, I had established certain practices in my life that had sustained me in even the darkest of times. I knew how important it was to maintain these disciplines and recorded my thoughts in my journal:

Daily Prayer

"I have prayed daily for the past two years. I believe it has changed me, though it has not changed everything I hoped for. I know God uses prayer, and it helps to center us in His perfect will each day."

Daily Reading of the Word

"I read God's Word each day for at least fifteen minutes in conjunction with a devotional called Daily Bread. *This time centers me in what God desires for my life."*

Weekly Church Attendance

"Worshiping with others and hearing God's Word from a knowledgeable, studied teacher benefits me and encourages me for the week."

Accountability Partners

"It is great to have brothers who can lift you up when you are down and whom you can lift up when they are down. We have been meeting for three years now and have become very close. We are now in the stage of sharing, caring, and challenging thoughts, behaviors, and attitudes in the light of God's Word."

Reading Godly Books

"I spend about three hours a week reading Christian books that magnify truths of God's Word and show me how to apply them to my life. Some of my favorite authors are Charles Stanley, Anne Graham Lotz, Stephen Arterburn and Fred Stoeker, Joel Osteen, Dr. Henry Cloud and Dr. John Townsend, and Stormie Omartian."

Life Groups

"I have been involved in several small groups in people's homes and have led many of them. These groups are fruitful to gain knowledge of the Word and to connect with and draw closer to people who want to walk after God in a deeper way."

Journaling

"I have found it very helpful to write down my thoughts and key feelings as well as relevant Scripture verses. I have been able to go back and identify trends in my life and pinpoint what I have learned. Journaling will become the basis for the book I plan to write."

When God Speaks, I Will Be Obedient

"It is great to connect in so many ways with God's Word and His people, but if I do not apply the learning and become obedient in every way, I will fail God, my family, my friends, and all other people. Going forward, I feel the most important action in life is to obey God and walk after His ways."

In Closing

I started this journey from separation and divorce to newness of life by merely going through the motions, well aware that I had not done the things I should have done prior to Lynn's leaving. But Lynn left, and my journey to God's fullness of life and better, healthier relationships with all people began. Sad to say, Lynn decided to leave for good, but I continued to move forward in God and new relationships.

"I pray nothing but the best takes place in Lynn's life, and I pray the same for my life and the life I will share with Judy. Because of God and this journey, I am a better person. Judy is getting a new man with a very good understanding of how a woman wants to be treated. I have also come to realize that I must communicate how I like to be treated and that we both must set clear boundaries if our love is to continue to expand.

"I so look forward to the days ahead, days filled with doing God's work and soaring in my love for Judy. Truly my life has gone from a flat line to a beating heart for the things of God!"

"Now all has been heard; here is the conclusion of the matter: Fear God and keep his commandments, for this is the whole duty of man. For God will bring every deed into judgment, including every hidden thing, whether it is good or evil."
—Ecclesiastes 12:13–14

The Last Words

"Only be careful, and watch yourselves closely so that you do not forget the things your eyes have seen or let them slip from your heart as long as you live." — Deuteronomy 4:9

Many books read through the journey

I read many books through my three year journey and placed some of their thoughts in my journals. I would like to recognize the great men and women who have put so much Godly wisdom in books for the greater help of all people hurting, seeking, and desiring a better walk and relationship for God and all mankind. I would highly recommend each one of the books and authors listed.

The Power of A Praying Husband
Stormie Omartian
Harvest House Publishers 2001

The Power of Prayer to Change Your Marriage
Stormie Omartian
Harvest House Publishers 2007

90 Minutes in Heaven
Don Piper with Cecil Murphey
Revell a division of Baker Publishing 2004

Holiness
Nancy Leigh DeMoss
Moody Publishers 2004

Boundaries
Dr. Henry Cloud & Dr. John Townsend
Zondervan Publishers 1992

Every Man's Battle
Stephen Arterburn, Fred Stoeker with Mike Yorkey
WaterBook Press a division of Random House, Inc 2000

Love & Respect
Dr. Emerson Eggerichs
Thomas Nelson 2004

The Secrets Men Keep
Stephen Arterburn
Thomas Nelson 2006

Praying Through the Deeper Issues of Marriage
Stormie Omartian
Harvest House Publishers 2007

The Upside of Adversity
Os Hillman
Regal Books 2006

Life's Challenges Your Opportunities
John Hagee
Charisma House 2009

The Magnificent Obsession
Anne Graham Lotz
Zondervan 2009

Success God's Way
Charles Stanley
Thomas Nelson 2000

Boundaries in Marriage
Dr. Henry Cloud & Dr. John Townsend
Zondervan 1999

Homilies for Active Christian
Fr. Arnold Weber, OSB
Cabin Six Books 2006

Every Man's Challenge
Stephen Arterburn, Fred Stoeker with Mike Yorkey
WaterBook Press a division of Random House, Inc 2004

Every Man's Marriage
Stephen Arterburn, Fred Stoeker with Mike Yorkey
WaterBook Press a division of Random House, Inc 2004

The Purpose Driven Life
Rick Warren
Zondervan 2002

Become a Better You
Joel Osteen
Free Press a division of Simon & Schuster, Inc. 2007

In Step with God
Charles F. Stanley
Thomas Nelson 2008

Believe That You Can
Jentezen Franklin
Charisma House 2008

Quiet Strength
Tony Dungy with Nathan Whitaker
Tyndale House Publishers, Inc. 2007

Wild at Heart
John Eldredge
Thomas Nelson 2001

Landmines in the path of the Believer
Charles F. Stanley
Thomas Nelson 2007

Shaken Not Shattered
Matthew Hagee
Charisma House 2009

The Owner's Manual for Christians
Charles R. Swindoll
Thomas Nelson 2009

How to Reach Your Full Potential for God
Charles F. Stanley
Thomas Nelson 2009

CPSIA information can be obtained at www.ICGtesting.com
Printed in the USA
BVOW041531300912

301697BV00002B/49/P